Dear Reader:

The book you are about to read is the latest bestseller from the St. Martin's True Crime Library, the imprint the *New York Times* calls "the leader in true crime!" Each month, we offer you a fascinating account of the latest, most sensational crime that has captured the national attention. St. Martin's is the publisher of bestselling true crime author and crime journalist Kieran Crowley, who explores the dark, deadly links between a prominent Manhattan surgeon and the disappearance of his wife fifteen years earlier in THE SURGEON'S WIFE. Suzy Spencer's BREAKING POINT guides readers through the tortuous twists and turns in the case of Andrea Yates, the Houston mother who drowned her five young children in the family's bathtub. In Edgar Award-nominated DARK DREAMS, legendary FBI profiler Roy Hazelwood and bestselling crime author Stephen G. Michaud shine light on the inner workings of America's most violent and depraved murderers. In the book you now hold, A FAMILY CURSED, acclaimed author Kevin F. McMurray follows the path of two brothers toward the same tragic end.

St. Martin's True Crime Library gives you the stories behind the headlines. Our authors take you right to the scene of the crime and into the minds of the most notorious murderers to show you what really makes them tick. St. Martin's True Crime Library paperbacks are better than the most terrifying thriller, because it's all true! The next time you want a crackling good read, make sure it's got the St. Martin's True Crime Library logo on the spine—you'll be up all night!

Charles E. Spicer, Jr.
Executive Editor, St. Martin's True Crime Library

ST. MARTIN'S PAPERBACKS TRUE CRIME LIBRARY
TITLES BY KEVIN F. McMURRAY

If You Really Loved Me

A FAMILY CURSED

*The Kissel Dynasty, a Gilded Fortune,
and Two Brutal Murders*

KEVIN F. McMURRAY

St. Martin's Paperbacks

ISBN: 0-312-94201-X
EAN: 978-0-312-94201-4

Printed in the United States of America

St. Martin's Paperbacks edition / December 2007

St. Martin's Paperbacks are published by St. Martin's Press, 175 Fifth Avenue, New York, NY 10010.

10 9 8 7 6 5 4 3 2 1

A FAMILY
CURSED

PART ONE

DISTRESSED DEATH

CHAPTER ONE

Some people just look right for their job. Frank Shea is one of them. If central casting asked for a streetwise New York City cop, a double for Frank Shea would answer the call. In his late fifties, with a wavy pompadour of reddish brown hair, the map of Ireland on his face, Shea was hardwired by genetics to be a cop. Socially, and perhaps even environmentally, he was destined to don New York City blue.

Hailing from the Rockaways in the borough of Queens, Shea had plenty of company from his home turf joining the force. For years this sandy peninsula that juts out into the Atlantic has provided many of the rank and file for the New York City Police Department (NYPD). No doubt, the disproportionate numbers of Irish-Americans who flocked to the Rockaways in the early 1900s had something to do with that. The century-old Irish lock on the NYPD and the fire department is easily proven simply by noting the preponderance of Irish surnames on the two departments' rosters.

After high school, Shea joined the Marine Corps in 1965 and served his three-year stint with a thirteen-month tour of duty in Vietnam, coming home to New York in 1968. Discharged honorably in December of '69, Shea took the NYPD entrance exam on a whim, because a buddy was taking it.

Shea scored high on the test, but because the city had a freeze on hiring, he took a job with Anheuser-Busch selling beer products. Three years later he received a call from the NYPD notifying him that they were hiring. At 22 years of age, Shea wasn't sure he wanted the job, thinking he might want to take advantage of the GI Bill and go to college, but with a wife expecting, he had to consider the job. He had an uncle, Bill Shea, who was a gung-ho detective with the department and he encouraged his nephew to give it a try, advising him that Frank was young and could always change his career if he didn't like it.

After the academy, Shea was assigned to the 26th Precinct in Manhattan's Harlem section. After six months in uniform he was put into plain clothes in an anti-crime unit for three years. Following his detachment to anti-crime, he went undercover with the Street Crime Unit based on Randall's Island in the middle of New York's East River. The most elite squad in the department, limited to just 200 members, it was arguably the best crime-fighting force in the world. Its purpose was to stamp out violent street crime by spotting it before it happened, which meant most of its work was done at night in the most crime-ridden neighborhoods of the city. Frank Shea never went back to selling beer.

A new unit called the Career Criminal Unit was formed in 1978 and Shea was only one of five picked for this hazardous duty. The purpose of the unit was to tail hardened inmates recently released from prison who had a repeat history of violent crime.

Transferred to Brooklyn's 75th Precinct as a whiteshield detective in 1980, Shea was assigned to homicide. In 1982 he was involved in a shooting where his partner was hit, and in the return fire, Frank shot the assailant. For his heroism, Mayor Edward Koch promoted Shea to goldshield detective by proclamation. Brooklyn's street gangs were not so generous. A contract on his life was issued, which prompted another transfer.

Shea's luck ran out in 1985 when he was involved in a

car accident on his way to interview victims of a shooting at a Brooklyn hospital. Shea had to be cut out of the vehicle. After six months of rehabilitation the department doctors "surveyed" him out because he had suffered extensive nerve damage to his right arm and serious head injuries. Shea had given NYPD fourteen years of his life. He left with no regrets. He'd had a great career, made great friends and was content with the knowledge he had done his best.

After taking two years off for more rehabilitation, Shea became a salesman for a boat dealership in Farmingdale, Long Island, and did divorce and personal injury investigation work for some local attorneys on the side. With more work than he could handle, he formed Alpha Group Investigations in 1997. He now employs five full-time investigators and a handful of per diem operatives out of his Farmingdale office suite.

Alpha Group handles private cases, such as divorce, child custody and personal injury, as well as corporate work. The corporate investigation mostly involves due diligence, electronic counter measures (sweeping for bugs) and a lot of overseas travel. In his divorce work Shea found that most of his clients "just wanted to know" to dispel or confirm their suspicions about the infidelities of a spouse. "Usually," Shea would relate, "all they want is proof." Often child custody and a large amount of assets were at stake.

All of that came into play when Robert Kissel contacted the Alpha Group.

CHAPTER TWO

Prime Focus Communication is an audio/video company specializing in whole house electronics—security, telephone, structured wire and computer systems, plus media rooms, home theaters and whole house audio-visual distribution networks. The product is decidedly upscale and most of the work done averages in the tens of thousands of dollars. Lance DelPriore started the business twenty years ago in the quaint, picturesque town of Brattleboro in the southeast corner of Vermont on the banks of the swift-running Connecticut River.

Twenty-seven years ago Lance and his four siblings migrated up from rural northeast Connecticut. They were escaping from an unhappy home life. The children's father had deserted the family when Lance was just 4 years old. Lance remembers how his father had promised to return soon. His older brother Mike sat diligently every day in their home's living room, which afforded a view of the street, waiting for his dad to make good on his promise. One day two months later, young Mike, just 6, stormed out of the room and angrily announced that their wayward father was never coming back. He was right.

Young Lance couldn't exactly blame his father for his abrupt departure. Mrs. DelPriore was a terrible wife and a disaster of a mom. The five kids were routinely beaten, or having their heads stuffed down a flushing toilet for the lamest of transgressions. It still rankles the short but powerfully built Lance, a man with a penchant for muscle cars and Harley-Davidson motorcycles, who sports the obligatory tattoos.

When Lance was 16, his mother tried "whomping" on him as she had done so many times in the past. Lance grabbed her by the neck and threatened that if she ever laid a hand on him again, he would kill her. And not with a gun, Lance warned, but with a knife. Thus ended the relationship with his mom. As far as Lance was concerned, his parents were "two assholes who had children together."

In and out of children's shelters, Lance, while still a teenager, began to work for an uncle who had a satellite dish installation business in Brattleboro. With a state population of only 600,000, satellite dishes were popular with the mostly rural and small-town folk of Vermont, where cable TV was not a viable economic option. A hard worker, strong and smart, Lance struck out on his own in 1986 and started his own satellite dish business, knowing he could be more successful than his uncle.

Word spread slowly but surely, and Prime Focus became swamped with work. Starting with the big dishes, the company got an exclusive from DirecTV™ for installation of the smaller dishes that were springing up all over the Green Mountain State like wild mushrooms. Lance DelPriore, seeing other opportunities in the burgeoning electronics field, jumped into the audio-visual field as well as computer networking, which was followed quickly by security systems. Security systems were particularly popular among the wealthy who owned vacation ski homes in the numerous ski resorts in Vermont and nearby New Hampshire. Still, the paltry demographics of the small state could not sustain the growing Prime Focus Communications. Lance DelPriore found himself taking on clients as far away as South Carolina and in the wealthy enclaves of Manhattan, Boston, Westchester County, New York, and

Greenwich, Connecticut. Business was good and, always a family-oriented man, Lance generously brought in his sister and two brothers. He knew his older brother Mike might prove to be difficult, but hired him anyway. Today, 42-year-old Lance rues that decision, made against his better judgment.

In 1999 Andrew Kissel, a wealthy real estate investor from New York, had heard about Prime Focus from his drywall installer and called Lance about some work he wanted done on his six-room house at the base of Stratton Mountain, one of the largest and most popular ski resorts in the northeast United States.

Andrew and Lance hit it off immediately. "He was a really nice guy," Lance recalled, ". . . he never treated me like a laborer, no pretenses, and I liked him a lot."

Lance wired his house and did all Kissel's audio-visual installations, security and computer networking in the palatial Stratton escape home on Brookwood Drive.

Hayley Kissel took a little longer to warm to the hardworking, friendly and outgoing Lance. But she eventually came around, and Lance considered her, like Andrew, not only a good client, but a friend. The Kissels, good friends as they were, spent over $100,000 on the work Prime Focus provided. Money was never an issue with Andrew Kissel, who always paid promptly and without complaint—not always the case with the wealthy, who, Lance had learned from experience, had a curious penchant for whining about how much money the work was costing them.

When Andrew's brother Rob bought his vacation home in Stratton, Lance did all his audio-visual work as well. Rob, like his brother, was a "great guy" and Lance developed a good rapport with the successful, A-personality Wall Street trader. As he was apt to do, Lance brought in his older brother to put in much of the work on Rob's house.

Lance would be the first to say that as a kid he got into a "boatload of trouble." Knowing that a lot of his problems stemmed from his dysfunctional childhood, Lance, in his early twenties, turned to God for support and became a born-again Christian, making a pact with his wife, Mary, to be a good, supportive and understanding person. Mike, being the oldest, had taken his father's desertion the worst. He developed into a brooding, selfish introvert who kept his family at arm's length. Lance, nonetheless, loved him as the brother he was, and tried to help.

Mike, like his younger brother, had worked for their uncle out of Brattleboro. When Lance struck out on his own with his nascent business, Mike stayed on with their uncle. At about that time Mike had married his first wife, Sherry, "a beautiful, wonderful woman," Lance recalls.

Mike had always said throughout his adolescence that he would never be like their dad and desert his family. "But history repeated itself," said Lance. Four years later Mike left his wife and two small children a note, took everything and ran off with a pretty 18-year-old, and relocated to Alabama to be near his dad. Mike soon left his pregnant girlfriend and at the age of 30 began pursuing Melissa, a vivacious girl of 15. According to Lance, his brother "left that girl at the altar for a stripper."

Mike DelPriore reconciled with the 15-year-old and married her when she turned 18. He began to communicate again with Lance, who by this time had three children of his own with his wife, Mary. Lance became convinced that Mike finally had come to terms with his past and was ready to settle down. It was Lance's self-described "ignorance and lack of discernment" that made him believe what he wanted to, that is, that his brother Mike was a "changed man." Lance offered his brother a job, and Mike eagerly said yes and moved back north with Melissa and a newborn daughter.

At first the brother/boss relationship went well for Mike, although within a few months, he insisted on being a partner in Prime Focus. Lance was willing to accede to the demand, but only after cautioning his brother that he would have to share in the losses as well. Mike didn't want that financial burden, so Lance put him on as a salaried employee.

Prime Focus paid Mike well by Vermont standards, and at Christmas the first year he was paid a $10,000 bonus and given a company van. After putting up Mike and family in his home for nine months, Lance also loaned him a down payment on an attractive trailer home across the river in Hinsdale, New Hampshire.

Lance began to hear complaints about Mike from his customers. They didn't want him in their homes because he was rude and had "an attitude." Lance would confront his brother about the complaints and Mike's usual retort was "For all the customers who complain about me, just as many complain about you."

Lance could get nowhere with his brother. Mary couldn't stand him and didn't want him in her home. She wouldn't put up with his rudeness or the constant frown on his face. Mike, however, was one of Prime Focus's best workers. He was smart, diligent and very talented at the detail-demanding job.

Mike's forte was the security end of the business, something he'd picked up while working in Alabama. Lance was happy to let his difficult brother take charge of the security installations. That way Mike worked mostly alone and out of Lance's busy but content life. Mike did all of Andrew Kissel's security work and later Rob's.

In Lance DelPriore's opinion, Rob, like his brother Andrew, was a "fantastic guy," generous, friendly and down-to-earth. His wife, Nancy, on the other hand, had an aggressive personality and a certain "callousness" about her. Nancy was sharp with her domestic help and was apt to bark out orders to them. On a couple of occasions Lance heard her "rip into" building contractors. Lance believed it was her spoiled moneyed lifestyle that made her that way. Intent on making clients happy with his work, he showed an accommodating attitude, and developed a good rapport with the demanding Nancy. She never complained about Prime Focus' work.

Lance admired her good looks, with her expensively coiffed short blonde hair, shapely figure and stylish outfits.

When she wanted, she could turn on a "bubbly personality" and charm the pants off of you.

The work on Rob Kissel's house extended for over two years, for reasons Lance really couldn't discern. At Andrew's house they'd completed all the work in just two weeks. Lance wrote it off to decision-making processes and the second-home mentality, which reasoned that everything could wait.

Mike began to relate stories to his brother that spoke volumes about a friendship with Nancy that extended beyond a working relationship. He said that Nancy and Rob had invited him and his oldest daughter to dinner on numerous occasions. Once Lance received a call from Mike asking him if it was okay to pick Nancy up while her car was being fixed. Lance was uneasy with the favor. "Number one," Lance said, "I don't know why you are telling me this, and number two—no!"

He reminded his brother that Nancy was another man's wife and, for appearances' sake, he should keep everything above board. The Kissels, after all, were rich and could afford a hired car. It was all kinds of weird to Lance.

Stratton was one of the largest and most popular ski resorts in a state that counted winter tourism as its largest industry. With all the money the Kissel brothers were making, it was inevitable that they would both buy luxury homes near the beloved ski slopes they had visited as boys.

While the SARS epidemic was reaching its peak in Southeast Asia, Nancy Kissel returned to the States with her two children from Hong Kong, where her husband was employed. Severe Acute Respiratory Syndrome (SARS) was an atypical pneumonia that first appeared in November 2002 in Guangdong Province, in the city of Foshan, of the People's Republic of China.

After the Chinese government suppressed news of the deadly disease, it reached Hong Kong in late February 2003. With panic at a fever pitch, many Westerners fled Hong Kong. Rob stayed behind, tirelessly working for Merrill Lynch in the distressed debt division of the company.

In the spring of 2003 Lance had Mike return to Rob's house to do some finishing work. Mike was familiar with the Kissel job, having spent a good amount of time there over the past two years, though usually in two-man teams. Now he was working alone. As far as Lance knew, the work was getting done, they were getting paid and that was it.

While Michael labored on getting the sound system installed in the Kissel home, he and Nancy had developed a friendship. Even after his work was done, Michael had a habit of dropping by, sometimes with his small daughter in tow. A single parent, Michael found a sympathetic ear in Nancy, who was, herself, temporarily single. Over the summer of 2003, the friendship developed into something deeper.

CHAPTER THREE

One September evening Lance DelPriore was having a Bible study session with some buddies at his home in Brattleboro when he got an unexpected visit from Mike. Clearly upset, Mike asked Lance and a friend, Russell George, to step outside. Mike immediately began to break down in tears. Lance asked him what was going on. Mike blurted out, "I've done what I never thought I'd do." Lance started to panic, he later remembered, thinking, "Oh my God, what is this!"

Lance thought it might be another installment on the seemingly endless saga of Mike's marital troubles. His second wife was divorcing him, and Mike could see his daughter only in court-supervised visits. There were other things that had also surfaced about Lance's troublesome brother. One day, Mary saw him in Brattleboro when Mike was supposed to have been on a job over in Stratton. Looking further into the situation, Mary and Lance soon discovered that Mike was charging customers for his time on the job when he was elsewhere, and billing Prime Focus for the hours. He was also caught using the company credit card to purchase personal items.

Stepping out on the porch off the kitchen, Mike, between sobs, explained to Lance and Russell that he was having an affair with Nancy Kissel and that Rob probably knew about it, having intercepted some compromising e-mails between the two. He said Rob might be calling Lance and that Nancy didn't want him to say anything about them to her suspicious husband.

"You idiot!" Lance screamed. "Mike, did you ever think of the impact that this would have? Our family, our business? As usual you are thinking only about yourself. What a moron! She's married! You don't have an affair with a married man's wife!"

Mike offered no defense. Lance asked if the relationship with Nancy was over. Mike quickly replied, "It's over!"

Lance noticed that Mike was sporting an expensive watch. Lance told Mike that the watch must be burning a hole on his wrist. The watch had been paid for with Rob's money. Lance, in effect, was accusing his brother of stealing from Rob. Trying to gauge his brother's sincerity, he demanded that Mike turn over the watch to him. If indeed he was remorseful, he would want "to shed himself of anything dealing with the regrettable situation." Mike refused to hand it over. Lance told him he had a choice, either give him the watch or he was fired. Mike turned away from his brother and strode off into the night.

Lance mulled over his brother's revelation with Russell and wondered aloud what he should do. If it was his wife who was having an affair, Lance said to Craig, he would want to know. Should he tell Rob? He was at a loss as to what action to take. Left alone, maybe Nancy would see the error of her ways and have a better relationship with her husband. Lance continued to agonize over the course of the evening about what he should do. He came to the conclusion that he should do nothing.

Over the next few days Mike approached Lance's pastor and mutual friends to try to get them to side with him about giving up the watch, but to no avail. Mike eventually relented and turned over the watch to his brother. Lance didn't want the "stupid watch," he just wanted to see where his brother's heart was. It was a test that Mike finally passed.

Two weeks later Lance learned from one of his employees that Nancy Kissel had bought Mike another watch. That made Lance's decision what to do next easy. Lance was on a job in Connecticut when he placed a call to Mike and told him he was fired. He realized he himself was not perfect, but he had tolerated "a lot of crap" from Mike. As a born-again Christian, Lance could not tolerate Mike's behavior. What statement would he be making if he kept Mike on the staff when and if Rob, Andrew and the rest of his work force found out?

Mike "screamed and yelled" at his younger brother and threatened to ruin him and his business. Mike hung up the phone.

The next day a contrite Mike called Lance. Plaintively he asked his little brother "why things could not be like it used to be" between the two. Lance patiently explained to him that he, Mike, was not the victim here. The victims were himself, Rob Kissel and the business. Frustrated with his lack of success to win his brother over by appealing to Lance's sense of family loyalty, Mike resorted to more threats and then demanded a generous severance package. Lance replied that Mike should consider himself lucky he didn't get "a pounding" from him. Mike then told Lance he wanted the first watch back. Lance told him he could have it, since he needed to cleanse himself of the whole sordid affair.

That evening at 10 PM, Mary and their oldest son Lance Jr. drove over to the business storefront to change the locks on the door. Mary had young Lance wait at the store while she went home to retrieve the keys, which she'd forgotten. In her absence, Mike showed up. Lance immediately called the police. Mary arrived back on a scene that was bathed in the flashing lights of squad cars. Mike dismissed the whole hubbub. Mary asked him why he was there at 10 o'clock in the evening. Mike answered that he was just there to pick up his last paycheck. Mary turned to the cops and explained that "this man" had just threatened her husband and this business. She demanded that he leave the property and she wanted a restraining order.

One week later Mike called his brother to apologize once again, admitting that he had overreacted. But in the interim, Lance had discovered other details about his brother's relationship with Nancy Kissel. He had learned of overnight trysts in New York and secret meetings at local bars in Vermont, and how they had planned a trip together to San Francisco. It was readily apparent to Lance that the illicit affair was still continuing. But, as far as Lance was concerned, his relationship with his brother, both professionally and personally, was over. Not wanting to leave his brother high and dry financially, Lance turned over the security end of the business to Mike and washed his hands of him.

CHAPTER FOUR

It was pretty clear to Rob Kissel—Frank Shea called it a "gut feeling"—that Mike DelPriore was interested in Nancy, and that she was encouraging him. In early June, Rob telephoned the Alpha Group out on Long Island and had a consultation with former NYPD detective Frank Shea. He had gotten Shea's name and a glowing recommendation from a colleague at Merrill Lynch. Kissel wanted to know for sure if his wife was unfaithful to him. He told Shea that if there was anything going on between Nancy and Michael, it was happening at Kissel's ski vacation home in Vermont, or in Michael's trailer home in nearby Hinsdale. Shea dutifully noted the names and addresses that Kissel gave him. Kissel told Shea that the house in Vermont was now their primary home in the United States since he had transferred over to Hong Kong and sold his apartment in New York.

Rob confronted his wife in August in Vermont when he arrived back in the States to have some minor back surgery done at Lennox Hill Hospital in Manhattan. Nancy admitted to the obvious, but promised to end the affair with Michael. As Rob later learned, while he was in the hospital,

Nancy and DelPriore had met out on Long Island for a tryst.

In August the Kissel family was back in Hong Kong for the beginning of the children's school year. Rob had hoped that the summer fling would wither on the vine, and that he would have the undivided attention of his wife. But Nancy had changed. She was distant and not at all the loving wife she had been in the past.

Wanting desperately to believe the affair was over, but not obtuse to the obvious, Rob carefully began to go over his phone bills and installed spyware on his home computer to track Nancy's e-mails. Rob discovered that his wife was lying to him. She had made numerous calls on a secret cell phone to DelPriore's New Hampshire number when Rob was at work, and the computer spyware picked up a daily correspondence with her distant lover. There was another disturbing development that Rob confessed to his now friend and private investigator Frank Shea: Rob believed he was being drugged by his wife.

After a long stressful day at his office, Rob was in the habit of unwinding with "two fingers" of a single malt scotch while stretched out on his easy chair in the living room of his luxurious Hong Kong apartment. The expensive liquor was kept in a crystal decanter on a dry bar in the apartment. Rob told Shea that as of late the drink made him feel "strange and woozy," not at all like the normal mellowing effect that it had on him. Frank Shea advised him that he should immediately have the scotch chemically tested, as well as his urine and blood. Rob said he would take a sample to a lab. Shea offered to bring it to one of the labs he used in New York, but Rob insisted on taking care of it locally.

Shea also strongly suggested that Rob speak with his attorney in Hong Kong. Certain that Kissel was either being drugged or slowly poisoned, he wanted Rob to know what ramifications there would be if his marital problems became known. A scandal of this nature could jeopardize his important position with Merrill Lynch. Kissel assured Shea he would see his attorney.

Rob Kissel and Frank Shea had several conversations over the next few weeks, all of them about how he was feeling. Rob was careful not to drink any suspect liquor, but he still did not "feel right." Frank kept on him to get a physical because, in Frank's words, Nancy was "trying to kill him." Rob refused to believe it. The mother of his children, the woman he had married and loved dearly, could not possibly do such a terrible thing. He kept telling Shea he would undergo a physical, but never said when. On September 3, 2003, Frank Shea flew over to Hong Kong from New York.

Shea had some business to attend to in the former crown colony of Great Britain, so he pushed up his travel schedule so that he could meet with Rob Kissel. Shea and Kissel had dinner at the swank China Club, which overlooks, from a lofty high-rise, downtown Hong Kong and the harbor.

Shea told Rob again that he was sure that Nancy was trying to kill him. The private investigator says that Kissel, who was once skeptical of the shocking conclusion his friend had come to, was now convinced of it himself. Sitting across from him at the dinner table, Kissel confessed that he knew "something wasn't right." Rob told Shea that he had a sample of the suspect scotch in his office and he was definitely going to have it tested. Shea urged him to do so, but sensed Rob was just giving him lip service and that he really needed to be pushed. So he pushed. Rob waved him off and said he would get it done, but Shea doubted it.

Shea knew that Rob still loved his wife and he told his friend he was willing to forget everything if she were willing to reconcile. Rob said that there still were some highs amongst the lows in their troubled marriage. Those highs had given him hope. But Rob was also realistic. He told Shea that he had even offered to move out of the apartment and fly her lover to Hong Kong so that they could be together. That way, he reasoned, he could still see his children, knowing full well the courts would surely award her custody of them in the event of a divorce. Rob had no intention of putting his children and Nancy through an ugly divorce. He was prepared to give her anything she wanted.

Frank Shea concluded his business in Hong Kong and flew back to New York, but he kept in frequent contact with Rob with a steady flow of e-mails. Shea felt terrible about Rob's situation. Rob was a warm, outgoing guy who made everyone feel comfortable in his presence. Shea said that "if a building janitor sat on one side of Rob and a head of state on the other, Rob would be equally attentive to both." A family man himself, Shea admired Rob for the attention he showered on his kids, even after the long hours he spent at his work desk. He was a genuine good guy and a loyal friend.

CHAPTER FIVE

William "Bill" Kissel appeared to be the very embodiment of the American dream. Rising from a humble background in Whitestone, Queens, he went on to study chemistry at the prestigious Case Western Reserve University in Cleveland, Ohio, where he later taught. Entering the private sector, the brilliant and ambitious chemist quickly rose to become plant manager for the Sun Chemical Company in Fort Lee, New Jersey. As his fortunes improved, the five-member Kissel family—Bill, his wife Elaine, sons Andrew and Robert and daughter Jane—moved from a small apartment in Manhattan across the Hudson River to a modest home in suburban Woodcliff, New Jersey.

In 1972 Bill Kissel struck out on his own and founded Synfax Manufacturing in Belleville, New Jersey, which makes toner for copier machines. The company prospered. In 1980 the Kissel family moved once again, but this time to an elegant, spacious home in ultra-chic Saddle River, New Jersey, where one of their neighbors was former U.S. President Richard Nixon. Saddle River, with a population hovering around 3,000, is the thirteenth richest community in the nation—the average home now costs $940,500, which beats out even Beverly Hills, California, ranked at twenty-fourth.

The sprawling ranch-style home was built on two acres in the dream-like community. It sported an in-ground pool, a semi-circular driveway and a three-car garage where Bill parked his Cadillac Seville and wife Elaine's Mercedes-Benz convertible.

Bill Kissel was an adamant believer that the family who plays together stays together. The sport of choice was skiing. Bill had always skied himself as a young man and encouraged his daughter and two sons to excel at it. Skiing was a sport you enjoyed together as a family, Bill would say. As far as he was concerned, besides family love, skiing was the glue that bound them together.

According to Rob's high school sweetheart, Carol Horton, Rob was a terrific skier. "Skiing was basically everything to him," Horton said. "It seemed that whatever Rob did, he did well."

Horton also recalled how the two brothers were always competing trying to see who could go faster and jump the highest moguls. She added that "Rob never had trouble keeping up with his older brother."

Horton said the Kissel brothers "had to answer to their demanding father," who expected his two sons to turn their "smarts and hard work" into successful careers as he had done.

Colorado and Utah, the Swiss Alps and Whistler ski resort in British Columbia, Canada, were just some of the places the moneyed family enjoyed. But it was the Green Mountains of Vermont that held a special place in the collective Kissel heart. On most year's-end holidays, Stratton, Vermont, was the place they would congregate. Years later Bill would remember those days as the best of times for the Kissels, a family whose name would become synonymous with tragedy.

• • •

Daniel Williams has fond memories of his childhood buddies, the Kissel brothers in Woodcliff. His best friend was
Andrew Kissel.

Andrew was an avid collector of model cars, literally
owning hundreds of them, which he would lovingly detail.
Good with his hands, Andrew was always building things.
When a neighborhood street hockey team, the Avon Super-
sonics, was started, it was Andrew who dreamed up and im-
plemented a statistical system that he had printed up on
bubble gum–type cards. Andrew even built the goals himself from scratch.

Andrew, said Williams, was more "aloof" than his down-
to-earth brother, Rob, who was more athletic, better looking, more competitive and more popular at school. Andrew
was shy and avoided eye contact, yet he was sharp and quick
to please.

"But I always thought he thought he was better than
anyone else," Williams recalled. "He was kinda stuck up in
that way."

Williams remembers a Yankee baseball game that he
and the Kissel brothers attended. Robert had gotten a
scorecard and meticulously entered every detail of the
game into the boxes. Andrew followed suit, almost as if
compelled to mimic his brother, who was everything to
everybody.

When the two boys each turned 16, their father, William
Kissel, with Solomon-like wisdom, gave each of his sons a
credit card and told them they could buy anything they
wanted. Andrew, four years older than Robert, strutted
home adorned in a flashy fur coat. When given his chance
at a dream purchase, Robert came home with a very practical pair of plastic-tipped shoes from Sears, Roebuck.

Bill Kissel could look back at the boys' childhoods and
recall that Robert had always been the all-American boy, a

"great sportsman" who had "an intuitive facility with numbers." He was also what his dad would call a "man's man."

Andrew, according to his dad, was "very different" from his brother. He had a good sense of design and "incredibly good taste," yet Andrew also liked to take "shortcuts." When reminiscing about his oldest son, a far-off look would come across Bill Kissel's face, as if he were pondering the imponderable. Andrew had everything going for him, yet appeared to be so lacking. His oldest son was an enigma.

As Andrew put away the toys of his childhood, he acquired new ones befitting his age—muscle cars. People in the neighborhood remember Andrew always being under the hood of one of his cars, tinkering with the engine or waxing and polishing the sleek curvy lines of his latest acquisition.

Andrew did well in school, but did not thrive in the educational atmosphere. He wasn't interested in college, so he opted to work for his dad's company. After a year, at age 19, he opened his own business and, not surprisingly, it was automotive-related. The shop, located on busy Route 17 in Mahwah, New Jersey, sold accessories for 4×4 trucks and vehicles.

"I think," said long-time friend Danny Williams with a touch of melancholy in his voice, "he wanted it so bad. But the customers weren't coming in." The store stayed open for less than two years.

Andrew eventually pleased his parents by enrolling at Fairleigh Dickinson University in nearby Teaneck, New Jersey. His attendance as a commuter student was uneventful and unfulfilling. After two years at FDU, Andrew thought it was time for him to go away to school, so he convinced his father to subsidize his studies at Boston University, one of the most expensive schools in the nation.

It was in Boston where Andrew began to exhibit one of his more troubling habits—not communicating with his family. Never hearing from him, the family back in New Jersey worried about Andrew's well-being. He wouldn't call for months on end. Exasperated by his son's lack of response to his messages pleading with him to call home, Mr. Kissel had to hire a private investigator to track him down.

Bill Kissel is not even sure if his oldest son ever graduated from BU, despite the fact that Andrew listed on his résumé that he was awarded a bachelor's degree in communications. What Andrew did after his education ended, like much of his life, is unsubstantiated. On his website Andrew would claim he was once a group vice president at Shearson Lehman Brothers from 1989 to 1991, and that one of his responsibilities had been "management, acquisitions and disposal of $350 million real estate portfolio." Shearson Lehman would later claim to have no record of an Andrew Kissel ever working for them. William Kissel could neither confirm nor deny the website's accuracy. Andrew's professional life was a complete mystery to his father.

It is not surprising that Bill Kissel knew so little about Andrew. Andrew told friends that he kept his dad at arm's length due to the fact that the man had treated him as "a second-place finisher in a two-brother race." The continual feeling of belittlement and humiliation that was heaped on him by the senior Kissel, Andrew claimed, had driven him to go it alone.

Robert Kissel loved school. Excelling in high school, he was admitted into the highly regarded University of Rochester and elected to toil in the field of science like his father. Robert didn't distinguish himself in optical engineering, due mainly no doubt to his propensity to party with the fun-loving fraternity crowd at school. But he did well enough.

Michael Paradise, a college buddy of Rob's, was impressed with his outgoing friend's approach to everything. Rob always plowed ahead with a purpose.

"He was attractive; he was athletic; he was funny; he was smart," said Paradise. "He had a great future ahead of him."

After getting his degree in 1986, Robert, as his brother had done before him, went to work for his dad at his toner business. It was also the year he met the slim and pretty Nancy Keeshin, a part-time student and New York City waitress, at the Club Med in the Caribbean islands of the Turks and Caicos.

It was apparent to all of Rob's friends that he had fallen head over heels for Nancy Keeshin. Even father Bill could tell his youngest son was in love. Mr. Kissel was impressed too. He found Nancy to be attractive, vivacious and sexy. His son could have done a lot worse for himself.

Nancy had led a gypsy-like existence up to the time she met Rob Kissel. She and her older sister, Lauren, had been born in Adrian, a small town in southern Michigan in 1964. They moved often, living in Ohio, Minnesota and Illinois. Their mother, Jean, was 17 at the time of Lauren's birth. Their father, Ira, worked in the restaurant business.

When her father and mother divorced in the 1970s, Nancy moved out to Oakland, California, to be with her mother, who would later carve out an alternative hippie-like career as a metalsmith.

CHAPTER SIX

Bryna O'Shea was Nancy Kissel's best friend. Nancy, or "Nan" as Bryna called her, came to know the Bryna the career bartender at Caliente Cab Company in New York's trendy Greenwich Village in 1986 when she started to work there as a hostess. Nancy was also attending Parsons school of design at the time. Both women left Caliente and started working together at El Rio Grande at the corner of 38th Street and 3rd Avenue. Nancy eventually became general manager and, according to Bryna, over the course of three years they cemented their friendship.

Bryna was thirteen years Nancy's senior, but Bryna liked to think that they both connected. Bryna was settled and living with a boyfriend at the time, while Nancy was still testing the waters and dating. It was after Nancy's trip to the Club Med in the Turks and Caicos Islands that Bryna had first heard about Rob Kissel. Nancy was gushing about this great guy she'd met there and what a great time they'd had together—plus, he lived in New York! It wasn't long before the two were dating. Bryna, when she finally met this guy she had heard so much about, thought he was a "sweetheart."

After only a year and a half of seeing Rob, Nancy and he got engaged. The deepening of the friendship between the women, however, was the result of a tragedy.

Nancy's best friend was Ali Gertz. Ali had accompanied Nancy on the fateful Club Med vacation where Nancy had met Rob. Not long after their return to New York, Ali was diagnosed with AIDS. Nancy was devastated by the news. Nancy had asked Ali to be maid of honor at her wedding. But Ali was dying and couldn't share in Nancy's big day as close friends normally would have. It certainly was understandable, but to fill the void, Nancy drifted closer to Bryna. And Bryna was there for her.

Ali would later die from complications of AIDS in 1992 at the age of 26, but not before she had become a high-profile advocate for AIDS awareness. *Esquire* magazine named her "Woman of the Year" in 1989 for her work, and a TV movie made about her life, *Something to Live For: The Alison Gertz Story* (1992), starring Molly Ringwald, aired to national acclaim for its important message.

Nancy and Bryna shopped together for a dress, and Bryna, being artistically inclined, made Nancy's headpiece for her gown. Nancy had relied on Bryna as her "second-in-command," as Bryna put it, for the fast-approaching wedding. Both Ali and Bryna were there in the hotel with Nancy before the wedding at the posh Water Club on Manhattan's East River.

Bryna called the affair a "big old blast of a wedding." It was obvious to her that the pair "were really, really in love." She had no doubt that the two were destined for a wonderful life together.

Rob's college buddy Mike Paradise was impressed by Nancy, saying, "She was friendly, she was outgoing. And she seemed to love Rob incredibly." Like Bryna O'Shea, Paradise thought the couple was destined for marital bliss.

But the groom's father got a peek at another side of his daughter-in-law to-be and he was a little disappointed.

Elaine Kissel had been diagnosed with inoperable cancer in early 1989, and was desperately hoping that she would live to see her son's wedding, a first for the Kissel family. Bill had quietly lobbied for the couple to move their wedding date up a month or two from May so it would be more likely the dying Elaine would be there. But Nancy was firm on the date; May was to be the wedding month.

Bill Kissel understood despite the fact that he had given the couple $100,000 for the wedding. It was, after all, her day, and he sadly accepted her decision.

Elaine passed away in April.

Because of Rob's lack of focus in his chosen major of optical engineering at the University of Rochester, and his "facility with numbers," Bill Kissel was not surprised when Robert told him, after working for him for two years, that he wanted to return to school for an advanced degree in finance. His father encouraged him to pursue his dreams.

Rob entered New York University's highly respected Leonard N. Stern School of Business in 1990. To the surprise of no one, Rob did extremely well at his studies.

Rob was noticed by Professor Edward Altman in one of the classes he taught at NYU. Altman, like most graduate school professors, selects students he would like to have as graduate assistants. Approaching Kissel, who in Altman's words "excelled in my class," Altman asked if he would be interested in a part-time job as a research assistant in the second-year graduate program. Having a chance to work with an internationally acclaimed expert in Rob's chosen field was quite a coup for the young ambitious student. It also meant a little money, or a reduction in tuition. According to Altman it was a "plum job" that got his students direct entrée into the markets that Altman did research in and in which he had a wide following of admirers. Rob Kissel accepted the offer on the spot.

Professor of Finance Edward Altman, PhD, had built an impressive reputation as the cerebral academic guru in the field of restructuring and bankruptcies. Altman had international stock not only as an expert in corporate bankruptcy and distressed debt, but also in high yield bonds and credit risk analysis. He was named Laureate 1984 by the

Hautes Etudes Commerciales Foundation in Paris for his accumulated works on corporate distress prediction. Altman was an advisor to the central bank of Italy and several other foreign central banks, and is one of the founders and the executive editor of the international publication *Journal of Banking & Finance*.

Rob worked anywhere from ten to twenty hours a week for Professor Altman. Altman remembers a "very focused, intense student," and Altman prized intensity and focus.

In the spring of 1992 Robert Siegler got a phone call from his friend well-known distressed debt expert Edward Altman over at the NYU business school, about a prize student of his who was about to emerge from school and enter into the fray on Wall Street. Altman told his friend that the student, Robert Kissel, was going places. Considering the source, Robert Siegler was immediately interested. Within a few days Siegler contacted Kissel and arranged a job interview. Kissel had all the right skills and attributes Siegler was looking for in a "young, hungry, intelligent professional."

"Rob," according to Siegler, "was very energetic, friendly, bright, outgoing and a personable guy." Years later, he could not think of anything bad to say about his former protégé.

Robert Siegler had started working right out of college on Wall Street in 1981 as an analyst. Smart and ambitious he quickly climbed the corporate ladder to where he was running and managing the sales and trading departments and private investment portfolios at a succession of trading houses. Like young bulls in the world's financial capital, Siegler left one job after another for more responsibilities, more power and more money. After stints at financial giants Merrill Lynch and Bear Stearns in 1992, Siegler found himself at Ladenburg Thalmann & Co. Ladenburg was an old merchant bank/brokerage firm which had been doing business in New York for over a hundred years. Siegler was in charge of the general orientation and concentration of the restructuring of bankrupt and turn-around companies—distressed debt. At Ladenburg Kissel was doing a significant amount of the analytical work for the distressed debt department. His efforts helped evaluate, discover and identify, and process the opportunities.

Distressed debt is an obscure, almost mysterious realm of finance unknown to most and understood by few. The online *Encyclopedia of Private Equity and Venture Capital* (vcexperts.com) describes it as:

> Corporate bonds of companies that have either filed for bankruptcy or appear likely to do so in the near future. The strategy of distressed debt firms involves first becoming a major creditor of the target company by snapping up the company's bonds at pennies on the dollar. This gives them the leverage they need to call most of the shots during either the reorganization, or the liquidation, of the company. In the event of a liquidation, distressed debt firms, by standing ahead of the equity holders in the line to be repaid, often recover all of their money, if not a healthy return on their investment. Usually, however, the more desirable outcome is a reorganization, which allows the company to emerge from bankruptcy protection. As part of these reorganizations, distressed debt firms often forgive the debt obligations of the company, in return for enough equity in the company to compensate them. (This strategy explains why distressed debt firms are considered to be private equity firms.)

Being a teaching professional Edward Altman is able to put the little-known field of distressed debt in layman's terms. This is the way he explained it to the author:

> *Distressed debt used to be a small esoteric field in global financial world. Today it is the fastest growing field of hedge funds. In 2002 the economic climate led to a huge opportunity for investors in this area, culminating in very high returns. This motivated an increasing number of financial institutions to invest in distressed debt companies. Although not as big as the equity or corporate bonds market, but*

larger than the junk bond market, that year reached the staggering dollar figure of $940 billion in the USA alone! Even though it has shrunken to $700 billion in 2006 it is still a market that can't be ignored.

Recently, distressed debt has become a very attractive method for buying into, and actually taking control of companies by the private equity market.

According to Altman distressed debt is "a robust and important market" despite its moniker in the financial press as "vulture investing." Altman takes issue with the pejorative connotation of the term describing the distressed debt market.

Think of that term. What does a vulture do? It eats carrion; it waits for the animal to die and then comes down to have its dinner! But a "vulture investor" does not want the company to die. What it wants to do is buy the bonds of the loan at a deeply discounted price when it is in distress or default and then work with the company so that it gets rehabilitated so that its value of those securities increases in value. It is more like the mythical phoenix rising from its ashes than the bottom feeder vulture.

A poster child example is Kmart, the retail giant. The company came out of bankruptcy at about $17 a share and within a year was trading at ten times that.

In the Kmart example is a clear insinuation by Professor Altman that the distressed debt holders nurtured the company to economic viability and ensured the continuance of a vital entity in the retail business, albeit one that some savvy investors made a ton of money on. Today it is being done in steel, coal and textiles. Says Altman, the "vultures" actually add value to the firms they invest in.

Frank Murphy had just finished at Iona College in New Rochelle, New York, when he landed his first job on Wall

Street. Murphy finally could quit bartending in Greenwich, Connecticut, and sink his teeth into his first "real job."

Murphy started as an equity trading clerk on the floor of the exchange, trading stock for the "upstairs traders" in 1991. In 1992 he became aware of Robert Kissel. Scuttlebutt around the office had it that Kissel was a wunderkind, brilliant and focused, who had been snapped up out of graduate school, where he'd shined. The trading floor of the midtown office was a huge room with hundreds of desks. Kissel worked at a desk some fifty feet away from Murphy, in the distressed debt area—a new endeavor for the brokerage unit of the bank, considered to be an exotic, mysterious field to the equity traders.

Murphy, a new employee like Kissel, had occasional interaction with him, where he would execute a trade for him and follow up on the operational side. "Pretty benign stuff," Murphy remembered.

It was apparent to Murphy that Robert Kissel was very cerebral. Both men were about the same age, but to Murphy, Kissel seemed a lot older. Kissel was extraordinarily focused, seemingly oblivious to the manic pace of business around him. What particularly struck the young Murphy about Robert Kissel was his being an "unremarkable dresser." On Wall Street you had all types, but flashy, expensively tailored suits were the norm. Kissel favored white open-collar shirts, loosened tie, rolled-up sleeves and grey pants. He never seemed to deviate from the look. There seemed to be nothing social about the man. He never met his fellow workers at the bar across the street for BS sessions and drinks, as equity traders were apt to do. On the floor, when things were slow, the traders never went to the desk of the man of few words to "shoot the shit." Rob Kissel was all work, and all the traders gave him his space.

Robert Siegler, however, had a different relationship with the bank's prodigy.

Siegler and Kissel spent a lot of time together on the job, often sixty-five to eighty hours a week. Siegler found Rob "driven and motivated to succeed," and had no doubt he would. But Rob had a lighter side as well. Sometimes for an hour or so after work, the two men would play a video golf game—just a break from the minutiae of work. Rob was a nice guy, personable and social, and was fun to be around, said Siegler.

In 1992 Kissel left Ladenburg to forge ahead from a narrow sector of the market to a broader transactional role, assuming the post of vice president in the high-yield group at Lazard Frères & Co.

Rob Kissel was universally liked and respected by friends and colleagues. All would describe him, though obviously smart and successful at what he did, as "down to earth" and easily approachable. As he moved up the corporate ladder, Rob was compensated well for his hard work. Certainly Rob liked the finer things in life that a big salary and year-end bonuses bought—but those who knew him said he was not the flamboyant type. Nancy, however, was into the money.

Nancy was supportive of Robert in his NYU days, but she paid little attention to their finances. Robert and Nancy moved into an apartment on West 85th Street in Manhattan. It was a rental apartment, and the rent was relatively reasonable for a desirable neighborhood in New York. The apartment, however, was in poor shape. There wasn't even a kitchen, other than a hot plate and a very old refrigerator. Robert spent $40,000 to put in a modern kitchen that Nancy wanted. It was an untoward expense to dump into a shabby apartment. Even her sister-in-law, Hayley, had, in an offhand remark, mentioned that it was a stupid thing to add to that apartment.

According to the couple's friends, Robert was a pussycat for anything that Nancy wanted. Bill Kissel had given Robert $100,000 when he graduated from college, and this is where the money for the kitchen renovation came from.

Roz Lichter had an apartment in the same building where the Kissels had theirs. She had befriended the couple and would often drop by their apartment to socialize and chat. Roz, on one occasion, got to see what a material girl Nancy actually was.

Lichter had remarked in passing about what a "great" fur coat Nancy was wearing. "It is a great coat," Nancy replied, "but you'll never be able to afford it."

The neighbor was shocked and stung by the catty remark. But she did take something away from the encounter: she realized that Nancy Kissel was a spoiled, rich bitch.

Hillary Richard was another Manhattan friend of Nancy. She liked Nancy a lot and found her to be generous with her friends, but she did have one unnerving quality that Richard found hard to square with the woman she knew.

"She was one of those people who had the ability to basically cut someone from their lives completely, entirely, absolutely . . . as if they no longer existed, without what appeared to me to be much of a reason whatsoever."

In 1997 Rob Kissel was offered the job of his dreams with one of the biggest, most respected companies in the world of capitalism, Goldman Sachs Group, Inc. The position was managing director in its Asian Special Situations Group, a demanding job that put him in the very vortex of distressed debt in the late 1990s—Southeast Asia.

Rob and Nancy had two children by this time Elaine, 3, and June, 6 months. Despite the prospect of leaving a comfortable lifestyle, many friends and a great apartment behind in New York, Rob couldn't refuse the terrific opportunity. The job would pay $175,000 a year, with promises of multi-million-dollar year-end bonuses. The job also came with a spacious apartment in a wealthy enclave in Hong Kong. The $20,000-a-month rent was picked up by the company. Made up of eighteen high-rise apartment buildings, the Parkview was a self-contained elite expatriate development that included its own supermarket, three pools, three restaurants and numerous shops. Life would be very comfortable there, even though it was in a foreign corner of the world where non–Chinese-speaking residents could feel isolated and alone.

Kissel and his competitors at other firms were buying portfolios of non-performing loans from Asian banks. Most of these loans had real estate as collateral, but the banks did not have the know-how for collecting on defaulted loans. The banks generally were happy to rid themselves of the non-producing loans at 20–40 cents on the dollar, and they were snapped up by the distressed debt firms.

Rob had engineered one mega-deal with General Electric Capital Corp. where they paid $560 million, or 21 percent of face value, for the assets of bankrupt automobile finance companies. Reportedly they recouped their investment and made a hefty profit by turning around and selling the cars to the owners for 50 cents on the dollar.

Rob Kissel quickly began making a name for himself in the closed-door world of distressed debt. Merrill Lynch, an arch-competitor of Goldman Sachs, took notice and made an offer to the 37-year-old wiz. They wanted Rob to head their entire Asian distress debt business. Rob would stay in Hong Kong, where he would be better compensated both in salary and bonuses, and would have a freer hand to run the business than he'd ever had at Goldman.

Rob agonized over the decision. Working at Goldman, the pre-eminent investment firm, had been a dream job, and he was reluctant to leave. Merrill was the largest brokerage house in the world, but didn't nearly match up to Goldman in experience and prestige. Merrill was the new kid on the block, but was aggressive and determined, hence their offer to such a gifted manager as Robert Kissel.

As one old Wall Street hand told the author, "Nobody leaves Goldman for Merrill unless it's for beaucoup bucks. Goldman is the best, most successful, most prestigious house on the Street [Wall Street], hands down, and they don't stoop to raiding other houses since they always promote from within (in 2006 the average salary at Goldman, with bonuses, was $660,000 a year and the company gave a $53.4 million bonus to its chief executive, Lloyd Blankfein)."

Rob would spend many an hour on the phone with his father, Bill, back in Florida. Rob valued his dad's business acumen and wisdom and he obviously wanted to be talked into making the leap. Bill Kissel encouraged his son to accept Merrill's offer. Bottom line, he told his son, was that it was advancement. Rob took the job and, to the surprise of no one, did exceedingly well at it.

Rob had not kept in touch with his mentor Professor Edward Altman in the years that followed after graduate school. That was a bit unusual, says Altman, since former research assistants generally kept their mentors apprised of their careers.

It wasn't until August 2002 when Rob was in Hong Kong that Altman became aware of how high Rob Kissel had risen in the financial world of distressed debt. Altman was on a lecture tour in the Far East. One of his planned stops was on the island nation of Taiwan. The Taiwanese government was in the process of considering granting the banks and other financial institutions permission to sell non-performing loans to investment firms—the "vulture investors." A meeting was arranged for Altman to meet the president of the republic, Chen Shui-bian. There would also be a group of foreign investors in attendance, and local Chinese bankers who worked with them. Rob Kissel, representing Merrill Lynch, was among those invited.

It was the first time in ten years that the mentor and student had spoken to each other. Kissel was self-effacing, but it was obvious he had arrived.

The southeastern Asian situation had to do with the 1997 economic meltdown of the economies of Thailand, South Korea, Taiwan, Japan and China. From 1997 through

2002 it was a thriving market where the savvy could make astronomical sums of money.

As Rob Kissel's career continued on its meteoric rise, his personal life took a decidedly opposite path, and the new century would hold no promise to his once fairy-tale marriage.

CHAPTER SEVEN

Bill and Elaine Kissel first brought daughter, Jane, and sons, Rob and Andrew, to Stratton in 1962. Initially, they rented, and then in 1963 bought a house. Jane Kissel got to know Hayley Wolff through a ski program conducted by a Stevek Kenney. He was a part-time instructor who sold insurance in New York during the week and used the weekends to sell insurance in Vermont. Jane, Robert and, to a lesser extent, Andrew became good friends with Stevek. (It is ironic that Stevek was killed a few months after Robert Kissel's death. Jane cried hysterically when she heard of Stevek's death. In New York, he had stepped out of a taxi, and was killed by a doctor's car. It seemed as if Jane's whole world had collapsed around her.) Hayley was a highly motivated skier. Jane too was very good, but not on a level with Hayley.

Hayley's mother and father divorced when she was nine. The divorce between Eileen and Derish Wolff was acrimonious.

Elaine, the Kissel family matriarch, tried to be very kind to Hayley. She would sometimes come crying to the Kissel house that her stepmother had taken her ski gloves or poles.

Hayley attended the Stratton Mountain School, which was at the base of the mountain, and convenient for the young student to pursue her passion, studying during the morning and skiing in the afternoon.

As a teenager, Hayley could be snippy and sarcastic in her demeanor and had a reputation for being fiercely competitive on the slopes with no patience for the less talented who got in her way.

One year Jane and Hayley competed in the winter freestyle meet at Winter Park, Colorado. Hayley took to the ski runs like a tiger out of a cage. The slope was very steep, so steep that spectators had trouble walking down the sidelines.

The judges were in a big tower at the bottom. When Hayley completed her run, she waited at the bottom for the judges to announce her score. She was not pleased with their subjective analysis of her run; she protested it a little too loudly to make the desired impression. She was thrown out of the competition.

It was at a party after the meet that Hayley met Andrew. She said to Jane, "I didn't know you had such a good-looking brother."

Andrew was immediately smitten with the tall, leggy blonde with the impressive pedigree. She would go on to become a graduate of the University of Pennsylvania and then attend New York City's Columbia Business School, getting a master's degree in finance. It didn't hurt, Andrew must have thought, that she was rich too. Hayley's father was CEO of Louis Berger, an engineering firm in New Jersey, a company whose net worth was listed on Wall Street for $500 million. Peter Wolff, an uncle, was a senior executive at Time Warner Inc. Thirty-two-year-old Andrew married Hayley in 1992. The wedding by anyone's standards was lavish, with the reception at New York's posh and very pricey St. Regis Hotel on Fifth Avenue. Between 300 and 400 people attended, putting the cost of the wedding into the stratosphere, easily costing the father of the bride a six-figure sum. Hayley's father, Derish, was heard complaining about how much Hayley had spent on her dress, estimated to cost over four thousand dollars.

• • •

In 1997 Andrew, along with partner David Parisier, founded Hanrock Group LLC and opened an office in downtown Stamford, Connecticut. The company bought and sold and managed residential and commercial real estate. The Hanrock name was a concocted word made in part from the four initials of the two brothers' and their wives' first names. Brother Robert invested $500,000 of his money in the company.

Hayley had carved out a career of her own on Wall Street, starting as a stock analyst at Merrill Lynch, where she specialized in the leisure and toy industry. She would go on to work at Smith Barney, another prestigious brokerage house, and at Integrated Corporate Relations (ICR) as managing director. In just a few years Hayley's achievements were impressive indeed. She was named to the *Wall Street Journal* All-Star Analysts team and ranked #1 in the Reuters research poll. She made numerous appearances on CNBC, CNN and *Moneyline News Hour* and was quoted frequently in *The Wall Street Journal*, *Barron's*, the *Los Angeles Times* and dozens of trade publications. Hayley and Andrew Kissel were the epitome of the New York power couple. They seemed to have it all.

Michael Assael is a nervous ball of energy and has a boyish look that belies his 57 years. At 5'6" tall, grey-haired, wearing wire-rim glasses that frame inquisitive eyes and with the trim athletic body of a runner, Assael was the first person to discover Andrew Kissel's criminal real estate dealings. In late 2002, he grew curious about certain items on the monthly statement of his cooperative apartment building on East 74th Street. Andrew Kissel was the treasurer of the co-op owners' board of directors.

Assael had been living in the building since 1972, when he was a second-year graduate student at Columbia University's business school. Back then, the twenty-story white-brick modern luxury high-rise was rent-stabilized. Like many upscale apartment buildings in New York City, his residence became part of the wave of rental-to-ownership transfers that was undergoing a boom back in the late 1970s and 1980s. Today there are over 300,000 co-ops and condominiums in New York City. Assael's home went co-op in 1981 and he was a member of the original board of directors.

Being a real estate lawyer and a CPA (Certified Public Accountant) made his election to the board a no-brainer by his peer residents. In five years Michael Assael rose from board member to treasurer to vice president and stepped down as president at the precocious age of 36. During his tenure the building's apartments (and president of the block association) soared in value and prestige, in the process winning a management achievement award from *Habitant* magazine. His home on the swank and desirable Upper East Side, in Assael's eyes, was a "wonderful building," well maintained, fiscally sound and a very desirable address.

Andrew and Hayley Kissel moved into the East 74th Street high-rise, taking an apartment on the tenth floor in 1992. They paid $295,000. At that time Kissel had a relatively low-level job at the commercial real estate firm of W&M Properties in Manhattan.

Assael became acquainted with Kissel after the annual shareholders' meeting in May of '95 when Johnny-come-lately Andrew was the board of directors' treasurer. After that Assael had little contact with Kissel, occasionally running into him in the lobby, elevator or garage.

In 1998 Kissel approached Assael through one of the uniformed doormen to see if he would be willing to sublet his car space in the garage under the building to him. Assael declined and was offended by the approach. Building protocol called for getting on a waiting list for a coveted space off the crowded side streets of the Upper East Side, where parking spots were notorious for being few and far between. The attempt to subvert the system was a hint to Assael about Kissel's integrity and style.

Little things started to bother the long-time building resident about how the building was being run—the standards were clearly dropping. Doormen were snacking in the lobby, trash was being improperly cleared and repairs were slow in being performed. Assael had noticed on Kissel's board of directors' bio that he claimed to have a master's degree from the prestigious business school at New York University and that he managed over 4,000 apartment units in the tri-state area. Assael also heard from other co-op board members that Kissel often bragged that he was worth $20 million. If that were true, Assael remembers thinking, how could Kissel preside over such a precipitous decline in his own domicile?

With Hayley expecting a baby in 1996, Kissel bought an adjoining apartment for $160,000. In 1999, just before his second daughter was born, he bought the unit below him on the ninth floor for $350,000 and commenced an extensive renovation on his enlarged living space. Jack Haber, the president of the board, called the Kissel co-op the showpiece of the building, saying, "He had the nicest everything in the building, the nicest floors, the nicest doorknobs. He lived big."

All Michael Assael remembers was that the construction noise at all hours was upsetting many of the building's residents, including him. That wasn't the way things were done on 200 East 74th Street. With all his money, the grumbling went, why didn't the Kissels just move to a more expensive building on Fifth or Park Avenue with bigger apartments. Kissel dropped another peg in Assael's estimation.

One of Andrew's lavish purchases found its way into a motor sports magazine. In July 2000 his customized, top-of-the line Mercedes E329 4matic station wagon, whose sticker price was $60,000, underwent a make-over by Al Design. The Tuckahoe, New York, automobile customizer catered to clients such as King Hassan II of Morocco and

NBA superstar Charles Barkley. When the technicians were finished gutting Andrew's car and refitting it with a plush interior upgrade that included a digital video disc player for his kids, a six-disc CD-changer and a computer navigation system, Andrew had another $25,000 sunk into the vehicle.

In 2002 Michael Assael, along with five other reformers, ran for the board of directors again to see to it that the building became "great again." He was quickly voted to the post of secretary. Assael had something he wanted to look into: why a line item on yearly improvements to the common area—hallways, lobby and elevators—had jumped from $47,000 in 1998 to $1.4 million by 2001—over a thirty-fold increase—under Kissel's watch. How could painting, wallpapering and carpeting dramatically increase by so much? he wondered. Assael claimed that it was plainly visible that such costly renovations had simply not been made. Assael walked into, according to him, "a hall of mirrors" once he immersed himself into Kissel's accounting procedures. An experienced CPA, Assael called it a "bizarre experience."

Michael Assael and a fellow board member—they jokingly referred to themselves as "Woodward & Bernstein"—pestered Kissel on reserve fund statements at board meetings, often following up with e-mails to him. He still had the 2002 statement listed on the header as 2001, then, on page 8, listed as 2002. Kissel was also listing the money market accounts in the statement, interchanging "reserve accounts" in terminology, instead of supplying the bank statement as had always been done in the past. The little "ridiculous mistakes" were adding up to something suspicious to Assael.

The real estate tax escrow of $67,000 was also listed in the statement. According to the retired CPA, that just was not done, since the Charles H. Greenthal Management Corp. maintained a tax escrow account and paid the taxes, and issued statements to the fact. Assael wondered where the $67,000 was going. Mysteriously the finance committee of the board was abolished during Assael's sabbatical. That committee would have approved and overseen disbursement of monies. Michael Assael proceeded to "bug Kissel" with e-mails querying him about these inconsistencies.

Assael and his cohort called the managing agent to get the list of the capital improvements done under Kissel's watch. The list they got was not complete, and when queried about it, the agent told Assael that Kissel had the complete list and that he'd paid the vendors. The agent also told them something strange: Kissel had paid them by wire transfers. Assael knew as a CPA that that was not standard procedure in these situations, since there had to be an easy-to-follow paper trail in the form of canceled checks. Assael also discovered that Kissel was spending money from the building's reserve fund. Assael circulated an e-mail to the board on December 6, 2002, saying that the building's financial statement "did not paint a pretty picture" and that "when in a hole you stop digging."

Assael got an e-mail response from Kissel not to copy the board on finance issues, saying it was "unproductive" and they should discuss these issues at a meeting of the finance committee, which had been re-formed in September. Then, Kissel suggested, they could present it to the board. Assael knew then that their treasurer was hiding something. Assael pressed him for the invoices.

Finally the finance committee sent a letter to the board in the second week of February 2003 demanding to see the invoices, to determine how the payments were made—basically all the things they would need for an audit.

Kissel said he did not have the invoices—that they were archived in a warehouse in New Jersey. Assael believed Kissel was making up excuses as he went along. Kissel also began to complain how he was "getting fried after five fucking years!" When the meeting adjourned, Kissel was overheard saying, "I think I need some Valium."

Michael Assael was now certain that Kissel knew "the

jig was up." Kissel, however, had a few more cards up his sleeve.

The finance committee wrote a letter to the whole board demanding Kissel respond to questions on the improvements, claiming they were being stonewalled. They also insisted they hire an outside accountant to do "sources and uses of funds analysis" and the board agreed. The accounting firm Jacobs & Schwartz, reported that something was wrong and that the numbers made no sense. Jacobs & Schwartz and the building's accountant were asked by the board to work together on it and come up with some answers.

Kissel gave the board a paper, purportedly from the building's accountant, which stated a $400,000 lower figure for improvements. Assael knew an accountant would never produce such a document. Kissel had obviously concocted it, cutting and copying the accountant's logo and inserting it into his document.

Still, the board insisted on a breakdown of capital improvements. Kissel produced another 3-page document "reclassifying" the $590,000 improvements that he claimed had been done. The documents didn't make any sense to Assael. Kissel was obviously trying to confuse matters to a point he hoped would have everyone throwing up their hands and dropping the matter out of frustration. They didn't.

Now desperate to salvage his supposed good name, Kissel dropped off a sheaf of papers to the finance committee documenting the capital improvements on the building. They were such out-and-out fakes that Assael described them as "laughable."

Aaron Shmulewitz, a real estate lawyer who'd helped the co-op board find out what happened to their reserves, placed a call to Kissel up at his ski chalet in Stratton to confront him with the evidence of his financial misdeeds.

On March 11, 2003, the finance committee sent out a letter to all co-op owners listing the financial irregularities of Treasurer Andrew Kissel. Kissel resigned from the board the next day. A few days later, he wired the board $1 million in restitution.

Andrew Kissel was not seen in the building again, having quietly relocated to his vacation home in Stratton. Hayley and their two children stayed behind to finish out the school year.

After more digging into Kissel's handling of funds, the board determined the $1 million restitution was not enough. They wanted to get back all the money he had siphoned from the communal funds. They hired prominent defense attorney Paul Grand, who, not coincidentally, was the son-in-law of Robert Morgenthau, the long-sitting district attorney for New York County (Manhattan). Andrew Kissel hired a criminal justice attorney, Charles Clayman, and it was at Clayman's Midtown office that they met with Paul Grand.

On October 23, 2003, they hammered out a deal. Kissel was to pay all monies misappropriated, including fees and interest. The sum agreed upon came to a staggering $4.7 million, which averaged out to $31,000 per apartment at 200 East 74th Street. But for shelling out all that money, Kissel got something in return: a written release from civil liability. It was thought to be an important piece of paper. Without a filed complaint by the aggrieved party, prosecutors rarely pursued criminal fraud. It was if it had never happened.

Paul Grand said the concession the co-op made to Kissel was important. He explained the logic of it to the board this way: "If I want to collect what you took from me, I'm better off settling it than going to the authorities."

If they went to the authorities, Grand said, Kissel might end up spending all his money on lawyers rather than paying back the co-op in full.

But there was a difference between civil and criminal law. Even though Kissel was released from civil liability, that didn't mean he was released from any criminal action against him, something that was explained to him by attorney Clayman.

Apparently there were some in the building privy to the agreement who weren't satisfied simply with restitution. The district attorney's office launched an investigation upon receiving the leaked information on the financial misdeeds of Andrew Kissel. This is exactly what the co-op board did not want. The board didn't want the authorities involved. It would be detrimental to the building's prestige, surely lowering the value of the apartment units. Getting the money back was only part of Grand's job—keeping scandal out of the papers was another.

The scandal and the fact that Andrew Kissel had gotten caught with his hand in the till didn't seem to slow him down much. He was still living large. His collection of exotic cars grew in number to seventeen, he bought a $3 million boat that he berthed in Florida and also acquired a time share in a private jet. But Andrew Kissel covered his bets.

Apart from his acquisition of toys, Andrew showed a practical side. He contributed generously and frequently to campaign committees of local, state and national politicians—on both sides of the aisle, in tried and true method. According to the Federal Election Commission, during the years 2000–2005, Andrew legally contributed $42,500. He was particularly generous to various Republican election committees, to the tune of $19,500. Andrew may have thought that he might one day be in a position where he needed a favor.

CHAPTER EIGHT

After getting married in 1989 Bryna O'Shea moved to San Francisco, and for the next five years only saw Nancy and Rob when she was back East visiting family. Apart from occasional phone calls and e-mails, the two friends had pretty much drifted apart. It wasn't by design—just that the physical distance had conspired against them.

After Nancy and Rob had moved to Hong Kong in 2002, Bryna noticed that Rob's name came up less and less in phone conversations and e-mails. Nancy never said how Rob was or what he was doing. Bryna, knowing Rob as well as she did, admitted being curious about the omissions and specifically asked how he was. Nancy would reply that she "didn't feel like talking about it." Bryna knew that something was wrong, but she did not know to what extent things had soured between the couple.

It was Bryna's opinion that Nancy had been suffering from postpartum depression since the birth of her son Reis in 2001. Bryna was certainly no expert on the affliction, but it was the only thing that could explain Nancy's behavior, especially since Nancy appeared to be having difficulty juggling her duties as a wife and mother of three small children. Bryna now believes the syndrome was the beginning of the end of the marriage and that Nancy had spiraled into a chronic depression.

When the SARS epidemic struck Hong Kong, Bryna received a frantic call from Nancy in April of 2002, saying that she and her kids had to leave in a hurry. Bryna told Nancy to call her and let her know what was happening when she got to New York. It had been very stressful, but Nancy had arranged the hurried departure from the Far East all on her own. Bryna sensed from the phone calls that Nancy had "been pushed over the limit" handling all those details. Bryna backed off of the questioning, sensing Nancy's exhaustion.

After Nancy and the kids had left, Bryna got a call from Rob. He confessed that things were not going well between him and his wife. Bryna, although already aware of their troubles, was "shocked" about how bad things really were between them.

Rob asked Bryna if he could continue to talk to her about his marriage. Bryna told Rob that she was not sure, since Nancy was her friend and she didn't want to betray her confidence. But Bryna sensed that Rob was really "hurting," so she relented and agreed to keep up their conversations. Rob seemed genuinely concerned about Nancy's well-being. In retrospect, Bryna rued the day when she involved herself. She got calls from Rob in Hong Kong every day, sometimes a dozen a day.

In the phone conversations that followed over the next few months, Rob said he suspected Nancy was seeing someone else. That was news to Bryna, since Nancy had said nothing about a paramour to her. Bryna had told Nancy that she was talking to Rob, and promised not to betray their confidence. But, at the same time, she would not betray Rob's confidence either. Later Bryna would admit she had stuck herself in a "stupid position."

Bryna felt she could ask Nancy, without fear of being exposed to her husband, if she indeed was having a "fling" with another man. Nancy replied, "Oh God, no!" Bryna believed her and thought that it was Rob's imagination and paranoia running wild.

Rob called late one evening and told Bryna that he had proof of Nancy's infidelity. Bryna replied, "What do you mean you have proof?" Rob said that even as they were speaking, he had an investigator outside the house in Stratton. "Mike the stereo guy" had gone into Rob's vacation home at 10 PM and Nancy and Mike were "hanging out together." He abruptly said the investigator was calling him, and hung up. Bryna was convinced that Rob was making himself nuts.

Rob called back the next day and told Bryna he was willing to erase all of Nancy's cheating just so he could have his family back. It was all so sad to Bryna to see two people she loved come apart at the seams. She had thought they were so stable and in love with each other. By her own admission, Bryna and her husband could at times be "volatile." In exasperation, her husband had once said after an argument that there was no such thing as a perfect relationship. Bryna's retort was, yes there was—Rob and Nancy Kissel had one. She felt the Kissels had pulled the wool over her eyes. Bryna started to wonder if she really had a strong relationship with Nancy. Hadn't she told Nancy everything about her life and always been a hundred percent truthful?

Later Rob would tell Bryna in one of their many conversations that he thought Nancy was trying to kill him. There was a long pause in the conversation. She finally said, "Rob, you've got to be kidding me!" She then added, "But if that is the case, put me in your will." They both had a good laugh at that. She told him, in all seriousness, that his imagination was getting the best of him. Rob dropped the subject and would not say anything more about it in later conversations.

Bryna now believed that Nancy had been lying to her. Bryna wanted to know what was going on in her friend's head that had been closed to her. It was not how best friends treated each other. Bryna was from "the Woodstock Generation," and wouldn't have cared if Nancy "had screwed around." But the fact that she had not told her about Mike had bothered Bryna. Apparently Nancy wanted to keep some things to herself.

In retrospect Bryna believes that Mike was a guy who showed Nancy attention and was vulnerable because of the divorce he had been going through. Nancy was the powerful one and she "just ate it up."

In the waning days of October 2003 Robert Kissel was ever so near to closing a deal of a lifetime. He had been working diligently on the biggest buyout of bad debt in Asian history. The non-performing loans were held by the Bank of China and totaled in at the astronomical sum of $14 billion. The fourteen-hour days were about to pay off big time: The buyout would not only net a sizeable profit for Merrill Lynch, but also millions in bonuses for the 40-year-old investment banker. Still, as always, there was plenty of competition. The Asian financial collapse of 1997–1998 had made Hong Kong a mecca that had drawn distressed debt traders like Rob Kissel to Hong Kong in the first place.

"It was historic," said Joseph Draper, head of Asia Principal Investors for the New York–based banking behemoth Citigroup, "and we all wanted to be there."

On one Sunday in late October, Robert Kissel was standing outside the United Jewish Congregation synagogue waiting for his children to finish their religious study class. As he so often did, he fell into a conversation with fellow expats who also worked the lucrative distressed debt market for profit in the Asian epicenter of the field.

Jonathan Ross from the Bank of China fielded questions from Rob Kissel, as Clifford Chance and Jonathan Zonis of Merrill Lynch and Ian Johnson from competitor Allen & Overy listened carefully.

"Rob was saying," recalled Zonis, "the field of distressed debt was more competitive than it had ever been and at the same time, he was perhaps more open about the transaction than I thought he would have been."

All the men present were in awe of Rob Kissel's savvy and skill in the field of distressed debt, so they were surprised he was discussing the deal with them and revealing some details that might have been considered proprietary information. Zonis remained quiet while Rob gave Ross a "hard time" about the documentation on the deal that the bank had provided him.

Friends of Rob recalled that the months of September and October had not been kind to him. Although the Bank of China deal was looming, Rob was clearly troubled by events at home. He complained that his marriage had broken down and that divorce was inevitable, but custody of the children was an issue that he and Nancy would have to work out.

He told some of his friends that Nancy couldn't be trusted to raise the children properly, since she was prone to violent rages. Her attitude to the youngest, Reis, was particularly troubling to Rob. Rob claimed that the boy was "out of control" and that Nancy was "ambivalent" toward the problem. It troubled Rob that his children were being described by teachers as being "undisciplined" at school. A friend of Rob's recalled that he had said Nancy was "an angry, angry person" and he didn't want his kids to grow up like that.

About the only thing Nancy did well, according to Rob, was spend his hard-earned money. On one of many visits to the beauty salon at the Parkview complex, she reportedly spent $5,000. Despite the fact that she was a good customer there, she was not well-liked. The *South China Morning Post* found a patron of the salon who knew Nancy Kissel and described her as being an "asshole."

During that last week in October, Kissel's colleagues from Merrill Lynch and the fierce competition from Morgan Stanley, Goldman Sachs, Standard Chartered and Citigroup adjoined to the Stormy Weather, a watering hole in downtown Hong Kong popular with the traders. It was there Rob revealed to his friends that his marriage was over.

He told the men over beers that his wife was having an

affair and he was planning to divorce her. Rob said that he would not challenge his wife's demand for custody of their three kids as long as he had access, and that he would be generous in any financial settlement with her. One of the men there described the revelation as "uttered quietly by a man without color in his face," a man who appeared to be resigned to the fact that his marriage of fourteen years had failed.

They were all stunned by the impending divorce, since they thought the Kissels were as happy as Rob was successful. Despite the shock of the news from their friend, it was quietly put aside in the traders' minds; there was the Bank of China deal to worry and mull over.

On Sunday evening, November 2, the tight circle of distressed debt experts called one another to wish good luck in the coming week. Rob Kissel did not answer his phone or return calls. His friends and colleagues understood. He was in the midst of a family crisis that would have no happy ending.

On the evening of October 30, Bryna spoke with Nancy in Hong Kong. Nancy had told her friend that she was planning a birthday/Halloween party for Reis. Rob was going to attend as Batman and she would dress as sidekick Robin. The following week was also the time for her visit to San Francisco to have a breast lift done by a plastic surgeon there. The two old friends would once again be able to hang out together just like in the old days when they'd both lived and worked in New York. They had both been excited about the prospect and eagerly started making plans for her stay in San Francisco.

The next day Rob called Bryna and told her that Nancy had not cut ties with Mike as she had promised to do. He had found a secret cell phone belonging to his wife. Also, his lawyer had mistakenly faxed divorce papers to Rob's home instead of to his office at Merrill Lynch. Nancy had seen them. Rob said he intended to sit down with his wife and tell her he wanted a divorce. He said he was willing to give her the house and she could have custody of the kids as long as they could stay with him on the weekends. He even was willing to rent another apartment at the Parkview to make living arrangements easy for her and the kids. Rob didn't sound furious, just exhausted and resigned.

CHAPTER NINE

In late October Rob Kissel called Frank Shea and told him that he had come to the conclusion that his marriage was over and he was resigned to it. He was planning to see a divorce lawyer. Frank Shea was relieved to hear Rob say that, thinking that maybe the worst was over. He offered to help Rob in any way he could.

The World Series between the New York Yankees and the Florida Marlins was under way at that time and Rob, being a rabid Yankees fan, craved e-mails recapping each inning, since the night games in the States were being played while Rob was stuck at his desk. At the conclusion of the sixth game, Shea sent Rob the disappointing news: the Yankees had lost the game and the series in a 2–0 shutout. Rob replied simply, "Go, Knicks!" It was to be the last communication the two men would ever have.

For the next couple of days Frank Shea was giving testimony in a trial. When the trial concluded, he tried contacting Rob with no success. Two more weeks went by without a call or e-mail from Hong Kong. He knew Rob had several trips planned throughout Southeast Asia, so Shea figured Rob was just too busy. But then Shea's e-mails to Rob's Merrill Lynch address started getting bounced back as undeliverable.

• • •

Nancy called Bryna at 5 AM San Francisco time on November 6 and got her answering machine. When Bryna arose that morning she played the message at 8:30. She listened as the voice of Nancy said in a monotone:

"We had a big fight. He [Rob] beat the shit out of me and chased me around the bed trying to have sex with me."

Bryna remembers thinking that this didn't sound "kosher."

Bryna tried calling Nancy several times during the course of the day, to no avail. She finally got through to her the next morning, Hong Kong time. Bryna first asked if Rob was with her, and Nancy replied, "No, he left."

She then asked Nancy how she was doing.

Nancy said she had a couple of broken ribs and had had to go to the hospital. She didn't elaborate. Bryna tried to coax more out of her, but she wouldn't go into it.

Nancy then made a strange comment, something to the effect of "Fucking Merrill Lynch tying my kids' tuition up in a trust fund and I got to write a check!"

Irritably, she told Bryna she had to take care of the kids and hung up the phone.

Bryna got her on the phone the next day and Nancy said she was still hurting. She cried as she told Bryna that she had called Bryna first. Bryna told her she was sorry that she couldn't be there for her. Nancy said her dad was flying in from Chicago and would be arriving soon. Bryna said she would call back later.

When she got Nancy on the phone later, Bryna reminded her of the upcoming trip to San Francisco and how she couldn't have her breast lift if she had broken ribs. Nancy told her she would be there and not to cancel the reservations they had made. Bryna assured her she wouldn't.

Something wasn't right; thinking out loud, Bryna asked, "Where the hell is Rob?"

Bryna had left several messages on his voice mail and

had sent dozens of e-mails, all of which went unanswered. That wasn't like him.

Connie, one of the Kissels' two housekeepers, called and told Bryna that something was very strange in the Kissel apartment, but she didn't know what. She said she was very scared. Connie mentioned that a rolled-up carpet had been removed from the apartment and that there was a strange smell about it.

Bryna told Connie that she would have to go down to the storage room and investigate. Connie replied that there was no way she would do that. Bryna couldn't believe what was going on there. She tried the Merrill Lynch telephone number several times before she finally got a person on the phone. It was David Noh, whom Bryna had heard Rob speak of. David knew who Bryna was, as well, from his conversations with Rob.

David said they were trying to locate Rob too, but had so far had no success. He said he had checked just about every hotel in Hong Kong and Rob wasn't registered at any of them. Bryna told him that Nancy had said Rob had left on foot and hadn't taken his car keys, which was odd. She also claimed that he wasn't wearing shoes or a jacket. Bryna told him about her conversation with Connie and how she wouldn't check the storage room. Bryna told Noh that since she was in San Francisco that he had to call Connie and get the facts straight. David said he would. After speaking with the housekeeper he called HKPD and filed a missing persons report.

Bryna got Nancy on the phone one more time. She didn't let on that she was suspicious, and simply told her long-time friend that she was concerned about her. Nancy replied that it was "all about trying to stay calm right now."

Nancy would be all right, Bryna assured her, but added that she was also concerned about Rob.

Nancy answered, "Bryna, I have always been concerned about Rob's well-being." Nancy quietly returned the handset to the receiver.

Hours later Connie called Bryna. She was sobbing audibly over the phone. Between sobs, Connie was able to tell her that the police had come and found Rob's battered and bloodied body in the storage room in the basement of the apartment.

Mary and Lance DelPriore were at home on Thursday night, November 6, relaxing and watching TV when they received a phone call. It was Andrew Kissel. The first words out of his mouth were, "Your brother killed my brother." Lance remembered that he could have been knocked over with a feather. Stunned, he could only say, "What?"

Lance could hear a third party's voice in the background. "I have been encouraged by counsel," Andrew went on, "to get off the phone."

"Andrew, what are you talking about? What's going on?" Lance screamed into the phone. Lance didn't know if Andrew was speaking metaphorically or literally. He'd believed that the affair between his brother and Andrew's sister-in-law was finally over. He asked Andrew again what was going on and whether Rob was dead or alive.

"Rob is dead!" Andrew said. "Nancy killed him."

Lance told Andrew he had fired Mike two months ago. Andrew simply repeated, "I have been encouraged by counsel to get off the phone." With that, the phone line went to a dial tone.

On the evening of November 6, Bill Kissel had taken a nap prior to hosting a party at the Florida home that he and his companion Gail shared. A disturbing dream woke him from his slumber. In the dream he saw his second son Robert lying prone and lifeless on the floor of a bedroom. The patriarch of the Kissel family shook off the unsettling vision, rose from bed and proceeded to get ready for the party.

In the midst of the festivities that evening he was summoned to the telephone. His son Andrew was calling. He rarely heard from Andrew, so he thought it must be important. Andrew said he had some very bad news: Rob had been found murdered. Bill Kissel collapsed.

The next thing he knew, he was being loaded into the ambulance and driven, siren blaring, to the local hospital. Once admitted, the elder Kissel was checked out by a physician. All his vital signs seemed to be normal for a robust 75-year-old man. He was kept overnight for observation and released the following morning. He and Gail left for Hong Kong the very same day.

The thirteen-hour flight from New York, and their arrival in Hong Kong, where they were driven to their hotel by the Hong Kong police, was a blur. Bill has very little memory of those first twenty-four hours. It was as if he were living through a very bad dream, a dream no parent expects to experience. The police were very solicitous and had even arranged for them to be checked into the hotel under assumed names, so they wouldn't be bothered by the media, who were all over the sensational murder.

After they were settled, and briefly rested, Mr. Kissel insisted on being taken to his son. Senior Inspector See Kwong-tak escorted him into the Hong Kong morgue where Robert's shrouded body awaited him. The inspector advised the victim's father not to turn back the rubber sheet that covered his son's body. See explained that the body had decomposed in the storage room and the skull was severely damaged. Bill was told by the experienced policeman, who had seen more than his share of grieving parents, just to "remember Robert as he was."

Funeral services for Robert Kissel were held at the United Jewish Congregation in Hong Kong on November 16. Rob's neighbors at the Parkview, colleagues from work and his friendly competition paid their last respects at the somber affair. Upon the services' conclusion, his body was delivered to the airport and was sent home to New York on the first available flight. Another service was held at Temple

Sholom in Greenwich, Connecticut, on November 18 for the friends and family of Rob at home in the States. The Greenwich synagogue was Andrew's house of worship. Graveside ceremonies and interment were at the Riverside Cemetery in Saddle Brook, New Jersey, later that day. The services were private and were attended by Rob's immediate family and a close circle of old friends. Press photographers and TV news crews filmed from a discreet distance while Rob's body was laid to rest next to his mother. The *New York Times* noted in Robert's obituary a few brief words from Bill Kissel that said, "May Robert's memory eternally be for blessing, and may comfort, strength and consolation be granted to his family."

Several weeks later Lance DelPriore got another call at home in Vermont from Andrew Kissel, a man he'd never expected to hear from again. Andrew wanted to wish Lance and his family a merry Christmas. Lance thanked him and took the opportunity to tell Andrew how terribly sorry he was about Rob, that he had known about Nancy's affair, but hadn't known what to do. So he'd done nothing.

Andrew said he wished Lance had informed him—that way, maybe Rob might still be alive today. Lance ended the conversation by saying, "I guess you're right."

PART TWO

THE "MILKSHAKE MURDER" TRIAL

CHAPTER TEN

In 1847 the British established a trading post on the Kowloon Peninsula archipelago much to the chagrin of the ruling Mandarins in distant Peking. The archipelago lay on the underbelly of mainland China on the South China Sea. Blessed with deep harbors, the peninsula and surrounding islands were also of strategic value, both militarily and commercially. The trading post was christened Victoria City after the beloved English monarch, Queen Victoria. Hong Kong, a name given to the colony and taken from the largest island of the archipelago, grew and prospered rapidly.

The peninsula was ceded to the "blue-eyed devils" under the Convention of Peking in 1860 as a prize of war upon the conclusion of the infamous Second Opium War. The British wrote themselves a generous lease of the islands for 99 years in July 1889 and continued to dominate trade in that area of the world into modern times. It bolstered the claim by the Brits that "the sun never set on the British Empire." After 150 profitable years of rule, the British handed back the Crown Colony of Hong Kong to China on July 1, 1997.

Under Chinese rule some things didn't change. In 1984 the People's Republic of China and the United Kingdom signed a Sino-British Joint Declaration establishing that Hong Kong territories would maintain their capitalistic economy and society for at least fifty years, or until 2047. The policy is euphemistically known as "One Country, Two Systems." Hong Kong still enjoys a high degree of autonomy, except in the area of diplomacy and national defense. In 2047 the capitalist stronghold, supposedly, will integrate into the socialistic system of mainland China.

In the meantime a strong municipal police force maintains order in the former colony. A nearby 4,000-strong contingent of the Chinese Red Army keeps an understandably low profile.

One of the British holdovers of the Sino-British Joint Declaration is Hong Kong's legal system. According to the U.S. Department of State's Bureau of Democracy, Human Rights, and Labor, Hong Kong's legal system has, more or less, maintained its British character.

The judiciary has remained independent since the handover, underpinned by the Basic Law's provision that Hong Kong's common law tradition be maintained. According to the Basic Law, the courts may rule on matters that are the "responsibility of the Central People's Government or concern the relationship between the central authorities and the (Special Administrative) Region," but before making their final judgments (which are not appealable), the courts must seek an interpretation of the relevant provisions from the Standing Committee of the National People's Congress. When the Standing Committee makes an interpretation of the provisions concerned, the courts, in applying those provisions, "shall follow the interpretation of the Standing Committee." The National People's Congress vehicle for interpretation is its Committee for the Basic Law, composed of six mainland and six Hong Kong members. The Hong Kong members are nominated by the Chief Executive, the President of the Legislative Council, and the Chief Justice. Human rights and lawyers' organizations have expressed concern for some time that, if broadly applied and loosely interpreted, these exceptions to the Court of Final Appeal's power of final jurisdiction could be used to limit the independence of the judiciary. In May the Government decided to seek interpretation of the Basic Law in the "right of abode" case from the Chinese National People's Congress (NPC). The NPC's interpretation of the law in this case effectively overturned a ruling by the Court of Final Appeal, Hong Kong's highest court, and raised questions about the continued independence of Hong Kong's judiciary.

The Court of Final Appeal is Hong Kong's supreme judicial body. An independent commission nominates judges; the Chief Executive is required to appoint those nominated, subject to endorsement by the legislature. Nomination procedures ensure that commission members nominated by the private bar have a virtual veto on the nominations. The Basic Law provides that, with the exception of the Chief Justice and the Chief Judge of the High Court, who are prohibited from residing outside of Hong Kong, foreigners may serve on Hong Kong's courts. More than 35 percent of Hong Kong's judges come from Commonwealth countries. Judges have security of tenure until retirement age (either 60 or 65, depending on date of appointment).

Beneath the Court of Final Appeal is the High Court, composed of the Court of Appeal and the Court of First Instance. Lower judicial bodies include the District Court (which has limited jurisdiction in civil and criminal matters), the Magistracy (exercising jurisdiction over a wide range of criminal offenses), the Coroner's Court, the Juvenile Court, the Lands Tribunal, the Labor Tribunal, the Small Claims Tribunal, and the Obscene Articles Tribunal.

The law provides for the right to a fair public trial, and this is respected in practice. Trials are by jury, and the

*judiciary provides citizens with a fair and efficient judicial
process.*

Nancy Kissel was about to test that system.

The Court of First Instance of the High Court is in Admiralty, a business and commercial area near to the Central District of Hong Kong. The courthouse is a 14-floor building next to one of the main government office buildings and adjacent to a popular expatriate shopping center called Pacific Place. Inside the courtrooms it is "very Ikea," according to veteran reporter Albert Wong of the Hong Kong newspaper *The Standard*. Red seats, with light-colored wooden boards on the walls, and "benches"—a bench being the long table which accommodates lawyers from both parties, sitting on opposite ends—make up the practical furnishings of the courtrooms.

Justice Michael Lunn was the presiding judge for the Kissel murder case. Lunn, a former government prosecutor, had a judicial reputation for being pro-prosecution. Defense lawyers who wanted to argue before the trial started that some of the evidence should be inadmissible either as being hearsay, prejudicial or unlawfully obtained, were usually resigned to the fact that Lunn would admit all the evidence anyway. According to court watchers, that is generally the way the Hong Kong courts work. Justices like to see all the evidence, but will warn the jurors to bear in mind certain aspects. The book on Judge Lunn is that he is a very professional judge. He takes detailed notes and tries his best to explain to the jurors and the public what's going on.

The seven-person jury was composed of five men and two women. All were ethnically Chinese and were bilingual. They ranged in age from approximately 30 to 60 years and all were college-educated.

According to the tradition of English jurisprudence, every citizen has a right to be tried by a jury of his peers. The city of Hong Kong takes its legal responsibilities seriously. Nancy Kissel could not have gotten a better jury in America.

"Juries here are stoic, stone-faced, pragmatic and with their feet on the ground," barrister Kevin Egan told *The Standard* prior to the start of Nancy Kissel's trial.

When prosecution witness Frank Shea saw the accused for the first time in court, he was shocked. He had known Nancy Kissel as the wealthy and glamorous wife of a successful international financier. Nancy was the shining example of what money and prestige bought. The woman who sat at the defense table bore no resemblance to the Nancy Kissel he knew.

Nancy's hair was no longer fashionably blonde, but a dull and inconspicuous dark brown. Shea could swear her makeup made her appear to be Chinese; it was subtle but very obvious. She wore a plain black dress and no jewelry. To Shea it was an apparent attempt to make herself look sympathetic to the jury, a tried and true defense tactic in the States. He wondered if this Hong Kong jury would buy into it. He would have to wait till the trial's conclusion to find out.

In front of a hushed room of the Court of First Instance of the High Court, the government's Senior Assistant Director of Public Prosecutions Peter Chapman outlined the case against Nancy Kissel.

Chapman said that Nancy Kissel had drugged her husband by "lacing a milkshake with a cocktail of sedative drugs while he drank it on that fateful Sunday afternoon." While Rob was on the bed in their master bedroom, passed out from the drugs, Mrs. Kissel had wielded a heavy ornament and struck her husband on the right side of his head in "a series of powerful and fatal blows."

Chapman went on to accuse Nancy Kissel of embarking

on an ill-conceived cover-up in an attempt to conceal a premeditated act. The prosecutor cited proof of the cover-up by revealing that Mrs. Kissel had written an e-mail to a friend canceling a pre-arranged date, giving the reason that her husband was not well and "I need to take care of something." Nancy had tapped out the e-mail on November 4, a day after Robert Kissel was already dead.

Chapman put forward the prosecution's claim that the murder had been committed to rid herself of a husband who stood in the way of a torrid affair between her and a "TV repairman," Michael DelPriore, whom she had met in early 2003 when she and her children and nanny fled Hong Kong for the United States in the wave of the SARS epidemic that year. Chapman claimed that DelPriore had "become the man in her life in place of her husband."

The prosecutor related the story of how Robert Kissel had hired the private investigator, New York–based Frank Shea, and how the PI had discovered that Nancy was carrying on an affair with DelPriore, reporting his findings to the suspicious husband. Mr. Kissel had also confided in Shea that he thought Nancy had been poisoning him. Frank Shea had advised his client to get his blood and urine tested for poisons and then to notify the police. The prosecutor opined that Robert Kissel had not gone for testing because "he felt guilty about his suspicion."

The senior prosecutor told the rapt jury that Robert had installed an eBlaster spyware program in the family's home computer and his wife's Sony VAIO laptop in early 2003 with the intention of monitoring her e-mail activity. Copies of e-mails from Nancy's lover in Vermont were found in the deceased's office desk drawers. Chapman said one read, "I love you when you call my name. It makes me melt."

Prosecutor Chapman related that the marriage was "apparently a stable one" until 2002 when Robert's sister, Jane Clayton, noticed that Nancy had become distant while they had vacationed together in Vermont. The prosecution also cited a claim by Bryna O'Shea that Nancy rarely mentioned Rob in conversation or e-mails anymore.

The prosecution also contended there was a financial reason for the murder of Robert Kissel. Nancy was the primary beneficiary to three life insurance policies worth over $5 million taken out by her husband. But Robert Kissel had been in consultations with lawyers over the "deteriorating state of their marriage" and was considering divorce three months before his demise. Robert Kissel had asked his lawyers about custody of the couple's three children, jurisdiction and "financial matters." Even though he was advised to make up a new will, he never got the chance.

To buttress the prosecution's claim of a monetary motive for the murder, Chapman cited an e-mail from Robert to his brother Andrew indicating that he'd intended to bring up the prospect of divorce on November 2, the same day authorities say he was killed.

One day later, the prosecutor said, Nancy e-mailed a friend to say that she would have to break their date since "My husband's not well, I need to take care of things." Chapman claimed Mr. Kissel "was far from unwell" and that, in fact, he was dead.

On the second day of the trial Chapman continued with his opening remarks to the jury. Nancy Kissel's face showed no emotion as Chapman reiterated a lot of the information he'd spoken of the previous day. Chapman was obviously pounding the main motive for the murder of Robert Kissel: Nancy Kissel wanting to eliminate her husband so she could be with another man, reap the economic benefits of Robert's hard work and collect on the life insurance he had taken out on himself.

The prosecutor described how, on the day after the killing, Nancy had told her maid not to disturb the master bedroom, and then proceeded to go out on a shopping spree where she bought a bed, pillows and sheets. Nancy then had asked about the availability of a storage room and was told she already had one in the basement of the building.

On November 5, two days after the murder, Nancy had asked maintenance workers in their apartment building to remove a carpet she had rolled up for storage. The Kissel maid commented to Nancy that the carpet seemed unusually bulky, which her employer explained away by saying she had rolled some pillows and bedding in it. The building maintenance men had complained that it smelled like rotting fish.

On November 6, a colleague and friend of Mr. Kissel at Merrill Lynch had contacted Nancy and inquired as to the whereabouts of her husband, who was missed at work. Nancy told him that the couple had had a fight and that he'd stormed out of the apartment. She claimed she had no idea where he was. That same day Nancy, accompanied by her father, went to the police station and reported how she was physically abused by her husband after she had refused him sex. Later that day Robert's colleague at Merrill Lynch filed a missing persons report with the police.

That evening at 10:50 the police arrived at the Parkview apartment where the Kissels resided. The police told Nancy that they would have to search the premises. That completed, they asked if she had a storage area, which Nancy denied. She then asked to speak with her father in private. The officers told of how they heard her father cry out from behind closed doors, "Oh my God, I don't believe it."

Returning to the area where the police impatiently waited, Nancy gave them the key and told them it opened the door of their basement storage room.

The police officers left the apartment to search the storage room and quickly located #15112 in block 15. When they opened the door, there was "a strong smell of a decomposing body."

When police unwrapped the rug and sleeping bag from

around it, the body was found to be dressed in white T-shirt and underpants—Robert's usual bedtime attire, the Kissel maid had said.

Chapman related that the post-mortem confirmed that the victim was drugged and most likely unconscious and defenseless when he was bludgeoned to death by a heavy object. The prosecutor employed graphic photos of the wounds to the victim's head. The pathologist reported that there were several lacerations found on the right side of Robert Kissel's head which had resulted in "massive spillage of brain substance."

The court also learned that lab tests revealed that five types of "hypnotics and anti-depressants" were found in his stomach and liver. Chapman claimed that the drugs would have rendered Robert unconscious and defenseless during the bludgeoning that killed him.

When Hong Kong detectives searched the apartment, they found blood spatter in the master bedroom where Nancy Kissel was accused of carrying out the murder. Police discovered in one of the sealed boxes a metal ornament that consisted of two figurines that had become detached from the base "as a result of the force required" to bludgeon the victim. Chapman contended that the broken ornament was the murder weapon.

The court learned that Nancy's fingerprints were found to match those on the sticky surface of the tape that was used to bind the four boxes used to hide the murder weapon, bloody clothing and bedding found in the storage room. DNA would later confirm that it was Robert Kissel's blood.

On November 7, Nancy Kissel had checked into the Ruttonjee Hospital, where she had been diagnosed to be suffering from emotional distress. She had been trembling, crying and unable to talk. Abrasions on her lip, chest and knees were found by doctors examining her. She was also discovered to be suffering from muscle injuries, something Chapman stated was a result of "vigorous exercise." The "exercise," claimed the prosecutor, was a result of "the

considerable effort in wrapping the body with the carpet—
and placing the body in the rug."

Jane Clayton, Rob's sister, who lived in Seattle, Washington, was the first witness to give testimony. Distraught in
the witness box, Clayton confirmed that the woman in the
accused docket was Nancy Kissel. Clayton went on to tell
the court that Nancy had been the sole beneficiary of her
brother's will. She estimated that the estate, made up of
stocks, cash, real estate and insurance, was worth some
US$18 million.

Clayton claimed that she had been aware of the marital
difficulties the couple were having, but, "Robbie thought if
he tried harder, he could fix things up and make everything
better."

Senior counsel to Nancy Kissel, Gary Plowman, took
the floor.

Plowman was a New Zealander, about 5'10" tall and
quite stocky. He had a reputation of having a dry, under-
stated sense of humor, and most court watchers found him
entertaining to watch.

In his cross-examination Plowman challenged Clayton's assertion that she was aware of the bad state of her
brother's marriage and that Robert had lied to her when he
said his wife was prone to disrupting family vacations by
leaving early without explanation.

Plowman asked her if it was unusual for Robert not to
spend Christmas with his family. Clayton replied, "Yes, but
we're Jewish [and Christmas] is not a big deal."

He asked if Robert had ever spoken to her about his
wife being depressed or acting distant.

She replied that, "Robbie didn't talk about people behind
their backs." Plowman answered by suggesting that her relationship with her sister-in-law was only "superficial."

Justice Michael Lunn interrupted the proceedings and
reminded the seven jurors that Jane Clayton's perspective

of her brother Robert's marriage was only a reflection of her brother's view and his state of mind. Judge Lunn said, "It is not evidence that those assertions were true."

Jane Clayton was followed by testimony from her brother Andrew, which was read in court, as he was not in attendance. Andrew had related that his dead brother had told him of Nancy's affair with Michael DelPriore and that Robert had been looking into initiating divorce proceedings against his wife as early as October 2003.

Scott Ligertwood was the next witness to take the stand. Ligertwood was a popular children's entertainer in Hong Kong and a friend of Nancy Kissel. He told the court that Nancy had missed an appointment with him at an outdoor café, which was very unusual for her. They had agreed to meet to discuss a planned children's show. She had not called to cancel. He'd tried to reach her on her cell phone, but was unsuccessful. Later he had received an e-mail from Nancy in which she wrote that "my husband's not well, I need to take care of things." He got this e-mail a day after Robert Kissel was murdered.

When cross-examined by the defense, Ligertwood admitted that he respected Nancy for her efficiency and care and how "she got things done." He added that she was a "very caring parent, very easy to deal with."

The court day ended with Yuen Tse-on, the property officer at the Parkview, who testified that Nancy Kissel had called him and inquired about renting an additional storeroom, but he'd told her that there were no more available.

On Friday, June 10, the prosecution seated Dr. Daniel Wu, an orthopedic surgeon who'd treated Robert Kissel and had prescribed drugs to alleviate some of his chronic back pain. Dr. Wu testified that none of the drugs that Kissel had in his body in the post-mortem had been prescribed by him.

In cross, Plowman asked the doctor about the other injury he had treated Kissel for in September 1999. Robert

Kissel had twice broken a knuckle on his right hand, suggesting the damage was done as a result of punching a hard object. On the admittance sheet at Adventist Hospital, the wealthy expatriate claimed he had "punched the wall." An operation on the hand followed and Dr. Wu discovered an older fracture that indicated that the same kind of injury had happened before.

The defense's clear intent was to insinuate that Robert Kissel was a violent, volatile man and quick with his fists.

Private detective Rocco Gatta was the next witness called by the prosecution. Gatta was employed by Frank Shea's Alpha Group. Shea had assigned Gatta to observe the Kissel family vacation home in Stratton, Vermont, while Nancy Kissel was there, ostensibly to be safe from the SARS epidemic that had been raging in Hong Kong.

According to PI Gatta, he'd conducted two surveillances of the Kissels' "multi-million-dollar home" in June and July 2003. Gatta said that he noted that on four occasions a blue van with New Hampshire plates had been parked "discreetly" in a ditch or down the road some distance from the Kissel house so "it was not visible to the roadway." Two videotapes of the parked van on the Kissels' street were shown to the jury. Gatta told the entranced courtroom that the van would drive away with its headlights off late the same night it had arrived. The driver of the van was never identified by the private investigator, but it was later learned by the Alpha Group that the blue van was registered to Michael DelPriore, the alleged lover of the accused.

The written testimony of an investigative officer who worked for New York Life Insurance was read to the court. He confirmed that Nancy Kissel was the sole beneficiary of her husband's insurance policies, which were valued at $5 million.

The defense countered by noting that the victim's sister, Jane Clayton, and brother, Andrew, had refused to answer investigators' questions about Robert's sports injuries, and his driving record, and "How often does he drink?" The defense claimed the insurance investigators are required to ask such questions. It left the jury wondering why such routine questions remain unanswered by his family. Were they hiding something?

The first week of testimony was proving to be the trial of the decade for the money-obsessed Far East city just as the O. J. Simpson case had been to Americans a decade before. The British paper the *Daily Telegraph* reported that Hong Kong was "enthralled by the saga of 'White Mischief' in the expatriate compounds where wealthy foreigners are pampered by Filipina maids and Chinese staff."

A Chinese reporter who was covering the trial for a local newspaper was quoted in the *Telegraph* as saying, "For us, this case is a throwback to the colonial era. It has all the ingredients our readers are most interested in. Sex, murder, *gweilos* [Cantonese slang for white foreigners]—and lots and lots of money."

Another reporter, Polly Hui, declared that, as theater, the trial was "better than a Hollywood movie."

The *Guardian* newspaper opined that the trial revealed "the decadent lifestyle of some of Hong Kong's wealthiest expatriates." It, of course, failed to mention that Robert Kissel was extremely successful in his chosen field and often worked sixteen-hour days. The size of the estate Kissel left behind seemed to grow by the day.

The wire services were well-represented. *Pravda*, the Russian service, took delight in reporting on the case and it, too, often referred to the "decadent lifestyle" of the American expatriates in Hong Kong.

Local newspaper copy never failed to point out how the accused had dyed her blonde hair brown and wore simple dark dresses.

On Monday, June 13, private investigator and friend of Robert Kissel Frank Shea took the stand.

Shea related how on September 1, 2003, Robert Kissel

had confessed to him over dinner at the China Club that he feared his wife was trying to poison him. He said he was sure she was spiking the scotch that he kept in a decanter on the bar in his apartment. Nancy, of course, knew that one of his rituals when he came home after a long day at work was to kick off his shoes and sit back in his favorite chair with a tumbler of single malt scotch and watch a little TV.

According to Frank Shea, Rob Kissel had said the drink tasted strange, not like what he was accustomed to. He said the effects "were quite remarkable," adding that the expensive scotch made him feel "woozy and disoriented."

This testimony confirmed what prosecutor Chapman had said in his opening statements to the jury, that Shea had advised Rob Kissel to get his hair, blood and urine tested for poisons. Rob had never gotten tested because he'd "felt guilty about his suspicions," Shea added.

In his cross-examination of Shea, defense attorney Plowman asked if Shea had warned Robert Kissel that the samples he'd provided for testing would reveal the presence of dangerous drugs in his system. "By dangerous drugs," Plowman explained, "I mean drugs such as cocaine." Shea denied that the subject of cocaine was ever raised by him or Robert Kissel.

Plowman pressed on the subject of drugs and asked if the second opinion on hair samples was discussed, just in case cocaine turned up in the first testing. Plowman was alluding to a September 17 e-mail exchange between the two men. Shea explained that a second opinion was brought up because Rob was bald and could not provide enough hair for the samples. Plowman suggested that Shea was warning Kissel "that the hair will test for illegal drugs and arsenic."

Asked about Nancy Kissel's purported lover, Shea said that Michael DelPriore was a TV repairman who lived in a trailer park close to the Kissels' vacation home in Stratton, Vermont. Plowman pointed out that in the surveillances conducted by his investigator, Rocco Gatta, Michael DelPriore was never physically identified as the man who'd appeared at the Kissel home. Shea conceded the point.

Plowman asked Shea if he knew where Kissel had gotten the information that possible activities would be occurring at his house when he was not there. Shea simply answered no.

Shea was asked about the spyware that Robert Kissel had installed in the computers. Had the two men discussed issues of admissibility in a court trial?

The private investigator said they had discussed possible legal proceedings, but added that he was only aware of the spyware after the surveillances were completed in Vermont.

Asked what he had been paid for his services, Shea replied "a little under twenty-five thousand dollars."

Why had he met Robert Kissel in Hong Kong in September, long after his work was done for the suspicious husband? Shea was asked. Shea told the court that Kissel had wanted to introduce him to two general counsels of Merrill Lynch to discuss the possibility of availing his services to the company. Shea added it was not the sole reason for his being in Hong Kong, since he'd had other business there to attend to.

The prosecution next called Moris Chan to the witness box. Chan was Kissel's secretary at Merrill Lynch. Chan testified that she had been approached by Kissel's colleague David Noh, who'd asked him to request CSL—the Hong Kong telephone service—to provide phone records with a billing address of the Hong Kong International School where Nancy Kissel had volunteered her time. Robert Kissel had been sure that was how his wife kept in touch with Michael DelPriore back in the States.

Plowman elicited from witness Chan that after Nancy

got the information, she was told by Noh to fax it to police.

On June 14, Andrew Tanzer took the stand. Tanzer was another expatriate and also a Parkview resident. Tanzer and his wife had first met the Kissels on November 2 when he and his 7-year-old daughter were about to get a taxi. A Mercedes with Nancy Kissel behind the wheel pulled alongside. Nancy had noticed the United Jewish Congregation (UJC) badge on the little girl's bag and offered them a ride. Tanzer's daughter recognized Nancy's oldest daughter June from the apartment complex and quickly arranged a play date. Invited up to the Kissel apartment, Tanzer had a pleasant hour chatting with Robert Kissel while Nancy disappeared into the kitchen. The children played together in another part of the apartment. Tanzer thought it was "odd" that Nancy never came out of the kitchen to join in the conversation.

At about 4 PM Tanzer was getting up to leave when his daughter approached him with two tall glasses of pink liquid.

Tanzer described the concoction as "a kind of a strange milkshake, fairly heavy, sweet, thickened, tasting of bananas and crushed cookies and reddish in color, probably from the strawberry flavoring." Tanzer said he wanted to leave so he "drained it quickly" as did Rob. He added that he thought it tasted "strange" and unlike anything he'd ever had before.

Nancy popped her head out of the kitchen as he and his daughter were leaving. He asked her what was in the milkshake and Nancy had replied jokingly that it was a "secret recipe."

Tanzer's wife, Kazuko Ouchi, testified that when her husband had returned to their apartment, she'd thought something was wrong with him. "His face," she told the court, "was very red."

According to his wife, Andrew had stretched out on the living room sofa and appeared to fall asleep. When she'd tried to rouse him, he was in a stupor and couldn't manage to get up from the couch. Kazuko kept shouting at him and slapped him on his face.

Her husband had fallen into a deep sleep. At 7 PM Tanzer awoke and joined his family at the dinner table. Kazuko related that he had been quiet during the main courses until he'd started on dessert. As she watched in amazement her husband "devoured" three containers of ice cream. She was afraid to stop him, believing that he would be angry. She was dumbfounded by the display. Afterwards, he made a mess over the furniture like a baby, Ouchi said.

Returning to the sofa, Tanzer fell asleep again. Kazuko thought about calling an ambulance, but when he was woken by a telephone call in the morning he seemed to be fine. She wrote it off to her husband being overtired.

Tanzer claimed that, outside of the telephone call and drinking the milkshake, he had no memory of his behavior that night.

In August, almost three months before the murder, family lawyer Robin Egerton testified, Robert Kissel had wanted advice about separation proceedings. Kissel told his lawyer that his wife was "committing adultery." When he had confronted her with evidence of her betrayal, he'd said, she appeared to be "unfazed." Egerton testified that just two days before his murder, Rob had told him at a second meeting that he planned to discuss the separation arrangements with his wife on the afternoon of November 2.

After Egerton stepped down, another written statement was read to the court. This one was from Fung Yuet-seung, a pharmacist, stating that Nancy Kissel had been prescribed Stilnox, Lorivan and amitriptyline on October 30, 2003. The prosecution noted that, according to the government laboratory, those same drugs had been found in the stomach contents of the deceased.

On June 15, the first witness presented by the prosecution was a friend of Nancy Kissel from the United Jewish Congregation, who had known her for over a year. Samantha Kriegel prompted by prosecutor Chapman, told the court that Nancy was a devoted mother whose life revolved around her three children. Kriegel also said that Nancy was creative, intelligent and an accomplished photographer, who was dedicated to volunteering at the children's school.

The day before the murder, November 1, 2003, Kriegel had hired Nancy to take pictures of her family in the garden area of the Parkview apartments. Kriegel said Nancy had talked to the children and kept them entertained, and showed great patience. The witness spoke to the jury about how much her children liked Nancy.

Early on the morning of Thursday, November 6, Kriegel had received a phone call from Nancy, who'd seemed upset. Nancy told her friend she was having "issues about Rob's health." Later that same morning Kriegel went to the Kissel apartment to pick up the invitations for a black-tie gala for the UJC scheduled for December. Nancy answered the door wearing dark glasses and Kriegel noticed relocation boxes on the floor of the apartment. She told the court that Nancy had "looked terrible."

While there, Kriegel met Nancy Kissel's father, Ira Keeshin. Kriegel was under the impression that he had just arrived in Hong Kong.

Kriegel had asked Nancy if she was planning to return to the United States because of Rob's health issues. At that, Nancy had broken down in tears.

Kriegel did not press for an answer, realizing that there was a crisis in the Kissel household. Kriegel added that, despite Nancy's obvious distress, she'd rattled on about the gala and worried about the invitations, since the RSVPs were still addressed to the Kissel apartment.

Under cross, Plowman asked Kriegel if her work for the Hong Kong International School was important to Nancy. Kriegel answered in the affirmative.

"Did she ever mention to you," Plowman asked, "that her husband had forbidden her to be further involved at HKIS?" No, came the answer.

Upon stepping down from the witness stand, Samantha Kriegel mouthed some words of encouragement to Nancy Kissel. Nancy began to weep.

The prosecution called another Kissel neighbor to the stand, David Friedland. He testified that he had seen Rob Kissel playing with his son at the Parkview clubhouse between 4:30 and 5:00 PM, a half hour before he'd allegedly drunk the poisoned milkshake. The two men had chatted briefly. Friedland said that when they parted company, Rob had signaled an "Okay" as a farewell gesture.

The court day ended with the testimony of Maximina Macaraeg, one of the Filipina housekeepers for the Kissels. Macaraeg spoke in a Philippines dialect, Ilocano, and her responses were translated into English by an interpreter.

She told the court that Mrs. Kissel had instructed her not to clean the master bedroom on November 3. The door to the room had been closed.

The last time Macaraeg had seen Mr. Kissel was at around 5 PM in the apartment's parking lot.

An hour later, she saw that the master bedroom door was slightly ajar. Mrs. Kissel had instructed her to tell the children to keep quiet because their father "was sleeping in the room."

Upon returning to the Kissel residence on Tuesday, Macaraeg said she had noticed a wound on Mrs. Kissel's right hand between her thumb and forefinger. She'd asked about it, and Mrs. Kissel said she had hurt it on the kitchen stove. Mrs. Kissel also volunteered that she and Mr. Kissel had actually had an argument and he was presently staying at a hotel.

On Wednesday morning, while looking after the Kissel children, Macaraeg said that "all of a sudden" Mrs. Kissel had ordered her to remove some boxes from their storeroom and place them outside the room in the corridor. Once that was completed, Mrs. Kissel, complaining that her ribs were sore, sent Macaraeg to the Adventist Hospital to purchase a Velcro belt brace. The accused had also told her maid to stop by a hardware store and buy her some rope. Macaraeg said she'd bought some red-and-white nylon cord.

Chapman showed Macaraeg some photos taken from the Parkview's security cameras and asked her whose image was in the pictures. She identified Mrs. Kissel. Chapman noted that the photos had been taken in the apartment complex's parking lot at 2 AM, and they showed the accused on two occasions, fifteen minutes apart, carrying a rug and then a suitcase into the apartment building.

Macaraeg was asked by the prosecution to comment, from her perspective, on the state of the Kissels' marriage. She said when she'd first come to work for the Kissels in 2000, they'd seemed "happy," but by late 2003 "there was no sweetness anymore."

"I could see that they didn't talk together front to front, and when Mr. Kissel moved, say took a trip, Mrs. Kissel would never go, say goodbye or ever kiss."

Macaraeg said Mr. Kissel was "good, calm, loving and kind," adding that Mrs. Kissel was also a "good woman," but that she had a "hot temper."

"She was a person who could not forgive. If you made a mistake, she would hate you," Macaraeg said.

The domestic was also asked about Mr. Kissel's drinking habits. She claimed she had no knowledge of that. Asked if she'd ever noticed any violence or injury to Nancy Kissel, she answered no.

Macaraeg recounted that on Wednesday, November 5, three days after Robert Kissel's demise, she'd noticed two new carpets in the living room. Admiring them, she'd then seen the old carpet rolled up behind the living room sofa. "When I saw it," she said, "I felt uncomfortable."

Asking why it was so big, the witness said Mrs. Kissel had replied that it was stuffed with old pillows and bedding. Macaraeg said she did not believe that explanation, and that for the rest of the day she was "not at ease." She said she had phoned the Kissels' other maid and told her that Mrs. Kissel might have "done something wrong to Mr. Kissel." The voice on the other end of the line had expressed disbelief.

Macaraeg told of how she'd heard Mrs. Kissel using the packing tape to wrap the bulky carpet before the four workmen arrived with a dolly to remove it. When the Kissel's 4-year-old son opened the door for the workmen, he'd groaned and said how bad it smelled as the bundle was pushed passed him. When Macaraeg went to pull the boy away, she noticed the foul odor too.

Prosecutor Chapman showed Macaraeg a picture of the rolled-up carpet. She said she recognized it because of the red-and-white cord binding it. When asked how she recognized the rope, she replied through the interpreter that it was the same she had bought at a hardware store on Mrs. Kissel's instructions.

Defense attorney Plowman, in his cross-examination of Macaraeg, asked about her relationship with Mrs. Kissel. She replied that it was strictly an employer-employee relationship.

"Would you have counted her as a close friend?" Plowman asked.

"No," she said.

Pressed, Macaraeg also revealed that things had not been good between her and Mrs. Kissel, starting in 2002.

"I was not happy, because her attitude was bad," she said.

In April she had decided to quit her job, but Mrs. Kissel would not permit her to leave, so she stayed in her room for five days and did nothing until Mr. Kissel finally talked her out of resigning.

For the first time the prosecution produced a key piece of evidence to their case. It was placed on the clerk's desk and the jury was invited to file past and examine it. The metal ornament consisted of two figures of girls kneeling that would normally be attached to a base to form one piece. On display it was in two pieces. The base was about twelve inches in diameter.

Judge Lunn asked if the defense wanted to inspect it. Plowman declined.

"Very well," Lunn said, "I'm going down to look at it myself."

Upon the judge's return to the bench, Macaraeg's testimony continued.

She commented that although the ornament was small, each figure was not much larger than a clenched fist; it was "very heavy."

Asked to examine some of the items in the photos he was about to project, Chapman said some of the close-ups might be disturbing. Macaraeg agreed to look at them, but added, "I don't want to see the face of Mr. Kissel."

Judge Lunn selected which photos would be shown to the nervous woman. Macaraeg sat sideways with her face turned away from Nancy Kissel and the jury. She looked at each picture just long enough to identify it. The process visibly upset her.

She confirmed that the T-shirt in the photo was typical of what Mr. Kissel had worn to bed and around the apartment. Chapman asked if she had seen the bloodstains on the bedcover as depicted in the photo. "I didn't see that before when I was fixing the bed."

"How is it different?" Chapman asked.

"It was covered by a brown cover . . ."

"Which now seems to be cut off or removed," Chapman completed the witness's response.

The domestic would not face the defense counsel nor look in Nancy Kissel's direction. When this was pointed out by Chapman, Judge Lunn replied that the witness could look in any direction she pleased.

Next she identified the sleeping bag that Robert Kissel's body had been stuffed in as belonging to the Kissel children. Macaraeg also confirmed that there was some strawberry ice cream in the kitchen freezer on November 2.

On the ninth day of the trial, and for a second full day, Maximina Macaraeg was back on the witness stand. Defense attorney Gary Plowman asked the former Kissel maid if Mr. Kissel had kept a baseball bat in the master bedroom. When she replied in the affirmative, Plowman produced a photo of the room and asked her where he'd kept it. She pointed to an empty spot between some furniture, saying, "That's where he kept the baseball bat."

The prosecution took the floor again. When asked about what happened on Monday, the day after the alleged murder, Macaraeg said that Mrs. Kissel had told her she'd had an argument with her husband and that the master bedroom was not to be cleaned.

Chapman asked why she had signed a statement prepared by the HKPD on November 7 and another on November 18 that read, ". . . in the morning, Nancy told me she was hit and assaulted by Robert."

"That is my mistake, sir." She explained, "I did not read them because the police hurried us."

Macaraeg also testified that when she'd returned to the Kissel apartment on November 8 to get some clothes for the Kissel children, who were now staying at a hotel, she had found a bag full of bloody clothes in their room. She confessed to being surprised that it had somehow been missed by police. Macaraeg told the court that after the body had been found, the apartment had become a busy place, what with family members, staff and police coming and going.

On November 19, in preparation for returning the Kissel children to the United States, and on instructions from friends of the Kissels, Macaraeg had returned to the apartment to pack up any useable but unwanted items for donation to the Salvation Army. All the remaining contents of the medicine cabinets were thrown out.

Chapman showed photographs of the Kissel bar and in a close-up, pointed out a scotch bottle. "Did Mr. Kissel like to drink scotch whiskey?"

"I have no idea," Macaraeg replied.

Prosecutor Peter Chapman asked the witness if any of the visitors to the apartment had taken anything. The maid replied that a friend of Mrs. Kissel's had taken a camera.

Chapman also asked Macaraeg whether she remembered if Mrs. Kissel had had a black eye and was wearing dark glasses anytime in September or October of the past year. Her response was no.

Macaraeg also denied knowing that the accused had suffered broken ribs as she was recorded saying earlier in a statement. She explained that she had been sent out to the hospital for the Velcro rib support because her employer had said she had a "sore back."

Plowman asked if Mr. Kissel "was a man who liked to be in control of the family."

"That is what I feel, he wants to discipline the family."

"Including his wife?" Chapman asked.

"Possibly," Macaraeg replied.

At the start of the third week of testimony, another of the Kissel domestic workers took the witness stand. Conchita "Connie" Pee Macaraeg was the sister-in-law of Maximina Macaraeg, and had been at the Kissel apartment on Tuesday, November 4, 2003. She spoke through another Filipino translator, but this time in another dialect, Tagalog.

Connie said she'd been told by Mrs. Kissel that the couple had quarreled on Sunday night. Mrs. Kissel had said that her husband was drunk and under the influence of cocaine. She told the court that Mrs. Kissel had said, "Mr. Kissel kicked her ribs and then left."

"Why is he doing this to you?" she had asked her employer.

Mrs. Kissel replied that it was because of his work, and that he was under a lot of stress "because of power and money."

Connie said Mrs. Kissel had shown her the injuries on her left knee and right hand, then a "self-inflicted" wound on her finger, which she said had been made with a fork.

Connie Macaraeg, who had worked for the Kissels since 1998, then described the comings and goings of Michael DelPriore to the Kissel vacation home in Stratton, Vermont, in June and July of 2003.

According to her, DelPriore came to the home frequently to "fix cable and telephone wires." Many of the visits were at night, she said, when Mr. Kissel was in Hong Kong. Mrs. Kissel had attributed the evening calls to Mr. DelPriore not being available during the day, and said that he was doing them a "huge favor" by coming by at all.

At Chapman's prodding, Connie told of the time she'd gone to bed with the youngest Kissel child. Michael DelPriore had still been in the house. At about 11 PM that evening, Connie was awoken by one of the Kissel daughters, who had been sleeping with her mom. She asked the housekeeper where her mother was.

"Is she not in the room?" Connie had asked.

The little girl shook her head, so Connie took her by the hand and went to look for Mrs. Kissel in the living room. They then heard voices that seemed to come from the front door. Connie told the child to go look for her mother. "She's in there," she replied. Satisfied that she had found her mother, the daughter returned to her bed.

The witness told the court that she had known "Mike" since 2002, when he'd started to work at the Kissel home installing sound, telephone and alarm systems for his brother Lance's company Prime Focus. At the time Nancy Kissel was in Vermont because of the SARS epidemic in Hong Kong.

Connie related how, on a day in June 2003, Mrs. Kissel had told her that Mike was bringing his daughter over to their house so she could play with her eldest daughter. Asked by Chapman what had happened that day, Connie said DelPriore had come over for lunch with his daughter and wound up staying all day.

"Michael and Mrs. Kissel would be somewhere. When they are together, she would tell me to go down and watch the children play."

Connie claimed not to know when he was there, or what time he would leave for the day. She did know that he was usually still in the house when she went to bed at 10 PM.

When asked by Chapman what kind of man Mr. Kissel was, she told the court he had been a "thoughtful and loving [father] who never shouts and was never hot-tempered at all."

Queried about his drinking habits, she described him as a social drinker, adding "over the five years I worked there, I never saw him really drunk."

Connie had some good things to say about Nancy Kissel as well. Nancy had treated her "like a sister" and was a very good mother, but Connie did notice a change in her after the birth of the Kissels' last child. She said Mrs. Kissel used to have a "bubbly personality," but had become subject to mood swings with a "hot temper."

"Before," Connie explained, "whenever she got angry, we would talk about it afterwards and reconcile and say 'Sorry' to each other. But after the change," she continued, "whenever she got angry, there was no reconciliation, she would continue to be angry, we wouldn't talk anymore."

Connie also said that Mrs. Kissel had become so busy after that, with her work at the school and her photography, that she didn't spend as much time with her children.

Moving on to the events of Wednesday, November 5, 2003, Connie Macaraeg said she had noticed the rolled-up carpet behind the sofa. She'd asked Mrs. Kissel how she'd managed to roll the carpet up by herself when she'd said the night before that her ribs were hurting. Mrs. Kissel said that she'd had help.

When Mr. Kissel's colleague and friend at Merrill Lynch, David Noh, had called asking about Rob's whereabouts, she told him of the "strange events" of late at the Kissel apartment, and that he'd better call the police.

Afterwards Mrs. Kissel had told Connie to go out and buy a new bed cover, because the old one reminded her of Rob and it "made her very lonely."

Next Edwin Chow, a Parkview worker, told the work about helping to move the carpet from the Kissel apartment to the basement storage room. He described the rug as being about eight feet in length and sealed at both ends with packing tape. He said it was so heavy that two dollies were needed to move it, with men supporting both ends.

"Also," he continued, "I smelled something like the salted fish Chinese people eat."

Asked by Chapman where the offensive odor had come from, Chow replied, "the roll of carpet."

Once the carpet had been delivered to the storage room, Chow returned the keys to the Kissel apartment. He also told the court that he'd collected the fee from "a thin, blonde, medium-built foreign lady."

She'd asked if everything was okay and he'd replied yes, except for the smell. Chow said she'd ignored the remark, said goodbye and closed the door.

Back on the stand, Connie Macaraeg was asked by counsel for the defense Plowman, in cross-examination, if it was true that Robert Kissel had injured the elbow of his daughter June by manhandling her while on vacation in Phuget,

Thailand, during the Christmas holiday in 1999. Plowman contended that Robert had told his wife to keep the children quiet while he made a long distance phone call. June, then 3 years old, and her sister Elaine, 6, were jumping on a bed and laughing loudly while he was trying to talk on his cellular phone. He went into the bedroom and roughly pulled June off the bed and told her to behave herself. The child ran off crying to her mother, at which time he grabbed her and pulled her by the arm again. Plowman claimed that an ambulance had had to be called to treat the little girl, and Mr. and Mrs. Kissel had gotten into a loud argument about his rough treatment of the children.

Connie denied that it had happened that way, and absolved Mr. Kissel of all blame, saying that the injury had happened while the children were playing and watching TV, and the couple had not even been there at the time. Connie told the court that Elaine had jumped on June, landing on her elbow and injuring it.

On the subject of disciplining the kids, Connie did agree that the couple often argued about how the children should be disciplined.

Plowman asked her if Mr. Kissel had had a "strong personality."

"Yes," she said.

"And he was a man who liked to be in control of his family?"

Connie Macaraeg said she didn't notice that.

Plowman continued with the cross-examination, obviously looking for the housekeeper to agree that Robert Kissel was a rough man with his family.

The attorney reminded Connie that she had said in an interview with lawyers for Mrs. Kissel on December 14, 2003, that twice a week she would find a whiskey glass left in the kitchen sink when she awoke in the morning.

Connie replied that she had no memory of saying that. What she did say was that she did find a cracked whiskey glass in the sink one time. Again she reiterated that she never saw Mr. Kissel drink whiskey.

After that exchange, Plowman showed the domestic an e-mail from Mrs. Kissel that had been sent to Mr. Kissel at his office at Merrill Lynch. It read:

> $$$$ [in the subject box].
> As I owe Connie HK$5,000 [US $645], can you please bring that back home tonight? I can't take that out.

Chapman asked the witness if that meant he had been withholding money from his wife. Connie doubted it, adding that Mrs. Kissel would often give her her ATM card, which had a daily HK$7,000 limit, and that often she was unable to take any money out because the limit was exceeded.

Connie affirmed Mrs. Kissel's generosity towards her. Besides being trusted with the ATM card, Mrs. Kissel had given her a club credit card and HK$30,000 [US$3,900] to renovate her house in the Philippines.

At the end of the day the prosecution presented evidence that Nancy Kissel had purchased ten tablets of Rohypnol (commonly called "the date-rape drug") on October 29, 2003.

On Wednesday, June 22, the twelfth day of trial, the prosecution presented Suzara Serquina, a salesperson who worked at the furniture outlet store Tequila Kola in Hong Kong. She testified that a Caucasian woman, dressed casually and wearing dark sunglasses, had come into the store on Monday, November 3, 2003, to shop. Despite her effort to not be noticed, Ms. Serquina said the woman was "noticeably loud."

Serquina had helped the mysterious shopper in picking out carpets, bed covers, cushions and a chaise longue. She spent over HK$15,000 (US$1,933). She returned the next day and bought two carpets and spent an additional HK$27,120 (US$3,500). She paid with a credit card.

Chapman asked the witness, "Whose signature was at the foot of the slip?"

"Nancy Kissel's," Serquina replied.

David Noh, Robert Kissel's friend and colleague at Merrill Lynch, took the stand next for the prosecution. Noh related how he and Rob had conversed on the phone at about 5 PM on Sunday, November 2, 2003. The two men had planned the call in preparation for a conference call scheduled later that day at 7:30 PM.

"He was on a different tangent. . . . he sounded very sleepy and tired," Noh testified. "He started talking about export growth instead of real estate prices. It was bizarre."

Noh also described Rob's voice as slow, "slurred . . . and very mellow." Noh found it "strange." He also told the court that since they were good friends, he'd even made fun of Rob's condition.

Continuing with his testimony, Noh told how Rob had confided that he was consulting with a lawyer about divorcing his wife and how he would attempt to get custody of his kids. He also gave Noh a daily update on his marital problems and told him that he was prepared to give Nancy as much money as she needed in a settlement.

"He was prepared to let Nancy bring her boyfriend [Michael DelPriore] to Hong Kong if that meant he could see his kids," Noh elaborated.

Noh said Rob believed that a dramatic and ugly event between him and his wife was the catalyst for the downward spiral of their marriage. Noh couldn't recall the exact date of the argument, but it was sometime in May of 2003.

He related that during the shouting match, Rob had shoved Nancy because she wouldn't stop the yelling. "He told me that she then said, 'You'll pay for that,' or 'You won't live that down,' or something to that effect," Noh testified.

Several weeks later, Rob told Noh that in Vermont, Nancy had been carrying on an affair behind his back. Rob said Nancy had had a secret cell phone and all the calls were made to Vermont or New Hampshire. He'd also had spyware installed on her laptop and home computer which revealed e-mail communications with her lover. Rob told him he had even hired a private investigator. Noh said Rob was "heartbroken" about his wife's infidelity.

When Rob and Nancy had returned to Hong Kong in August after Rob had back surgery in New York, the couple sought out a marriage counselor. Noh said their relationship had improved "at first." But the two had soon had another bad argument and Nancy demanded a divorce.

In cross-examination, attorney Plowman pointed out that Noh had made no mention of Robert Kissel's sleepiness in his written statement on the missing persons report for HKPD. Noh explained that he'd mentioned it verbally when he spoke with them later that day.

Plowman revealed to the court that David Noh had kept in contact with the HKPD inspector involved in the case and that Noh had filed another written statement mentioning the "tiredness" of his friend Robert Kissel. Plowman's tack was obvious.

"When you made the second statement, it was made with the knowledge of the post-mortem report?" Plowman asked.

"It could be," Noh replied.

Plowman then asked Noh if he'd discussed with the police that Robert was planning on divorcing his wife. Noh said he had. Digesting that answer, Plowman then asked Noh if he'd told police that Rob was concerned about the issue of custody of his kids. Once again, Noh confirmed that he had. Plowman sat down.

In the hands of the prosecution, David Noh spoke of the history he shared with Robert Kissel. They had met when they worked together at the investment bank Goldman Sachs. Both men left Goldman together to form a team at rival Merrill Lynch in 2000. Rob was made Asia-Pacific managing director of global principal products and Noh became his vice president.

Noh said Rob's annual salary was US$175,000, but that in three years, he had amassed $5.9 million in bonuses. The HK$152,000 (US$19,500) rent on his apartment was paid by Merrill Lynch.

Noh told the court that he and Kissel had worked closely together in the distressed debt of the investment bank giant. They'd both put in long hours, often not getting home until midnight. Noh said Rob was "extremely professional and thoughtful, and he got along with everyone."

Prompted by the prosecutor, Noh related to the court that his friend Rob was devoted to his kids and that there was little doubt they were the most important thing in his life.

Chapman asked Noh what Rob Kissel would do after work. Noh replied that he would go home, and on the weekend he would spend his time with his kids.

In talking about their social life together, Noh said that Merrill Lynch had its "fair share of company functions," but it was a rare occasion when both men would attend any of them. Noh opined that Rob didn't appear to have a drinking habit "other than a social beer or two."

About their conversations on his divorce, Rob had told Noh that he'd received legal advice to tie up as many lawyers as possible to make it difficult for Nancy to find one. Rob also spoke of the "dark websites involving drugs and death" that his wife had been visiting. Rob claimed he had learned of it through the spyware he'd had installed on the computers she had used. He claimed to have knowledge of Rob's plan to discuss the divorce with his wife that Sunday.

When Rob had failed to take part in the conference call the evening of November 2, and didn't show up at work for the next few days, Noh had made several calls to his home and cell phone in an attempt to reach him. Finally, when he got Nancy on the phone, she first claimed he couldn't come to the phone because they were having "family issues." In a subsequent call to the apartment, Noh was told by Nancy that Rob had "health issues."

In cross-examination, Gary Plowman suggested that Robert Kissel's move to Merrill Lynch from Goldman Sachs had brought undue stress on him because of the added responsibility of running the department.

Noh replied that it was just the opposite. At Goldman Sachs, he claimed, there was more stress, since Robert and others were competing for promotions, describing it as "trying to figure out who was the last man standing." But at Merrill, Noh explained, Rob was secure in the knowledge that he was in charge.

Plowman concluded the questioning of Noh by adding, "Your career path was very much in his hands."

The implication was clear to all present, including the jury, that David Noh may have felt he owed his benefactor Rob Kissel the testimony he'd just given.

On Thursday, there was a big shake-up in Nancy Kissel's defense team. Gary Plowman resigned his position as senior defense counsel and was replaced by flamboyant criminal defense attorney Alexander King.

The scuttlebut among trial pundits was that Plowman was doing a good job defending his client. Courtroom chatter had it that Nancy Kissel was becoming increasingly difficult to work with, and it was also apparent to many trial watchers that Nancy Kissel was in charge of the defense.

Alexander King was well-known to the Hong Kong legal community. Reporter Albert Wong of the *Standard* newspaper said that King was much more "American in trial presence" than most lawyers who appeared in front of the bench in Hong Kong courtrooms. An eloquent speaker with a flair for the dramatic, King was expected to inject some spark into a trial that had so far become a staid recollection of events.

On Friday, June 24, HKPD police Sergeant Mok Kwok-chuen took the stand. When Nancy Kissel had come into the Aberdeen police station on Hong Kong Island on Thursday, November 6, 2003, to report that she had been beaten and that her husband was missing, Mok testified that he'd seen the bruises on her face and arms. He said she'd also submitted a medical report from her private doctor which detailed the injuries.

"She told me she was pushed against the wall and beaten up by her husband. Then he left their flat and she didn't know his whereabouts after that," the policeman said.

Prosecutor Chapman then proceeded to read the medical report to the court. Besides detailing the bruises to her face and arms, the report also stated that Nancy Kissel had suffered fractures to her lower right rib and left hand.

Chief Inspector Yuen Shing-kit, formerly the chief inspector of crime at the Western District police station, followed his subordinate officer. Yuen testified that he'd interviewed Nancy Kissel at her apartment on the night of Thursday, November 6, into the early hours of November 7. He said Mrs. Kissel had described the fight and shown him where it had taken place. Yuen also claimed that at first she had denied any knowledge of a storeroom. She then asked the policeman if she could speak to her father privately.

Yuen said that after speaking with his daughter a few moments, Ira Keeshin had jumped up from the sofa, cupping his hands to the sides of his head, and exclaimed several times, "Oh my God, I don't believe it."

"At that time, I looked at Mrs. Kissel," said Yuen, "and saw her sobbing . . . shuddering more severely than the first time [when they entered the apartment]. I sensed something unusual."

After the private talk with her father, Mrs. Kissel admitted the existence of a storage area and turned over the keys to the inspector.

Yuen testified that he'd seen the large roll of carpet covered with a plastic sheet in the Kissel storage room. There was also some furniture and a bag of golf clubs.

"I smelt a strong smell [which], according to my experience, was [from] a dead body," Officer Yuen said.

He continued by saying that a pathologist had cut open the wrappings and inserted his gloved hand into the carpet.

He confirmed that he could feel a human head. It was 2:15 AM on Friday, November 7, 2003.

King said that police had already been granted search warrants when they entered the Kissel apartment on the night of November 6. The warrants were based on the presumption that a murder had taken place. King wondered aloud why a team of twelve police conducting a preliminary investigation had failed to take notes of Mrs. Kissel's claims of being beaten.

At the interview King asked if it wasn't true that the police had already spoken to David Noh at Merrill Lynch and been informed by Parkview management of the "stinking" carpet in the storage area of the building.

"With your long experience, you must have already had a real suspicion a body was in the carpet?" King asked.

The chief inspector said it could have been something else. The smell, he claimed, might have come from a dead animal.

"But you weren't investigating any missing animals, were you?"

"No," Yuen replied.

King asked the policeman what superintendent Nichols was doing when they looked around in the storage room area before going up to the Kissel apartment for the interview with Mrs. Kissel. Yuen replied that Nichols was "around" and "in the vicinity."

Earlier in the day, before any search warrant had been presented, two police officers had already been in the storeroom area looking around. The defense attorney was able to elicit from Yuen that the chief inspector would be "failing his duty" if he "allowed a crime scene to be contaminated in any way."

King then pointed out that the Kissel storage room could have been opened by police without asking Mrs. Kissel for the keys.

"Whose decision was it to go up and speak to Mrs. Kissel?"

Yuen claimed it was Superintendent Nichols' call.

Without a pause King asked, "You didn't tell her that you were investigating a murder, did you?"

Yuen replied simply, "No."

When questioned further by King, Yuen admitted that when he and other officers had arrived at the Kissel apartment, they'd told Mrs. Kissel that they were investigating a missing persons report and her claim of assault before they were admitted inside.

King asked Yuen if the reason for not taking notes on the fight and the missing persons report was that they were only interested in the alleged murder.

Before he could answer, King continued, "At no time while in the apartment did you caution her, tell her you suspected she had been involved in the death of her husband and had a right to remain silent. Nor had you informed her that you had search warrants on the basis that she had killed her husband." King stared at Yuen and waited for his answer.

"Yes," Yuen said.

King then asked about the exclamation—"Oh my God, I don't believe it"—that Ira Keeshin had supposedly uttered. King suggested that maybe he'd said, "Oh my God, it can't be."

Yuen said that no, there was no mistaking what Mr. Keeshin had said.

"Did you make a note of it?" King asked.

"No," Yuen answered.

The lead defense attorney spoke about the "substantial amount of information" taken from the computers in the Kissel residence. The information was gathered by the spyware Mr. Kissel had had installed in them and then e-mailed to his office computer.

"Are you aware that the police at no stage seized the hard drive of Mr. Kissel's work computer in his Merrill Lynch office?"

Yuen said he was not, and agreed with King that, just because it was at his office was no impediment to seizing Mr. Kissel's computer.

* * *

On Monday, June 27, the defense continued attacking HKPD's investigation, specifically their intent when they'd arrived at the Kissel residence at the Parkview on Thursday evening, November 6, 2003.

After recounting the events of that evening, Senior Investigator See Kwong-tak, officer in charge of the investigation, also told how he had returned to the apartment on November 7 to search for evidence, and again on the 8th. It was on the 8th that he'd found the "foul-smelling" black plastic bags that contained blood-soaked items. He said the search of the apartment had been concluded at that time, but that he'd returned to seize the Kissel computers on November 12. Finished with the time line, See awaited cross-examination by Alexander King.

See, like his subordinate Yuen the day before, had stated that the intention of the police was to investigate the alleged assault of Nancy Kissel and the disappearance of her husband, Robert.

King asked the senior investigator about his suspicion that the missing husband had been killed. See replied, "I had a little suspicion that the deceased had been killed. But I did not have a deep suspicion that the defendant had killed her husband."

"Why was that?" King asked.

See explained that upon entering the master bedroom, he'd suspected something was wrong when he surveyed the space and noticed the "disarray." He hadn't been listening to Nancy Kissel describing her husband's physical abuse of her to Chief Inspector Yuen.

King suggested that at that point, See must have suspected murder. See said no, he still hadn't been sure. Pressing, King said that the police had obtained the search warrant on the suspicion that Robert Kissel was dead. See wouldn't concede the point.

King pointed out that, in obtaining the search warrants, See had written a statement to the magistrate that, "It is very suspicious that Mr. Kissel had been killed by his wife and was concealed by the carpet inside the storeroom which was rented by Mrs. Kissel."

"So are you telling the magistrate," King said, "that Mr. Kissel is dead, that you suspect his wife is responsible and you suspect a body is inside the carpet?"

See confirmed that what King said he'd written was correct.

"Are you still saying that, when you rang the doorbell at twenty-two fifty [the Kissels' apartment number], your suspicion of murder was still only a very little suspicion?"

"If we had a real suspicion, I would not apply for a search warrant, I would apply for an arrest warrant," See replied.

King accused See of avoiding giving him a straight answer, telling the senior police inspector, "You are just playing around with me, like a cat playing with a mouse."

King asked the witness if he would have been compelled to inform Mrs. Kissel of her right to remain silent before he questioned her about a possible murder. See confirmed that that would be the case.

The defense attorney stated that if the police were just investigating an assault and missing persons claim, then they wouldn't have needed a search warrant based on the assumption that a murder had taken place. King also said that the police could have easily opened the door to the storage room without first asking Mrs. Kissel for the keys.

On Tuesday, June 28, defense counsel King continued to hammer police witnesses with evidence that they had not shown up at the Kissel residence on November 6 to investigate an assault as they'd led the accused to think. In fact, they were actually looking into a potential murder. The major concession the police made on the stand was their failure to take ample notes of their interviews with Mrs. Kissel.

On Wednesday the jury had to endure, as one Hong Kong newspaper reported, "a stomach-churning day." The prosecution was now in the hands of assistant prosecutor Polly Wan.

The prosecution presented bloodstained evidence taken from the Kissel master bedroom, consisting of bloody bedding, towels, a T-shirt and nine pieces of tissue paper. The evidence had been kept in a storeroom adjacent to the courtroom. When the door to the storeroom had been opened to remove the items, the stench of the dried blood—over a year and half old by this time—spread quickly in the courtroom. Many of the gallery occupants gagged at the ghastly smell. A court officer was instructed to close the storeroom door to stop the spread of the odor.

Defendant Nancy Kissel turned her head away as the evidence was paraded to the witness stand. The police constable, Cheung Tseung-sin, who had collected the evidence at the Kissel apartment, identified it as the property he'd recovered.

The next day Chong Yam-hoi, the police photographer at the murder scene on November 8, took the stand. He was part of the police evidence seizure team. He identified the photos for the prosecution.

In cross, defense counsel King pointed out what appeared to be "white powder" on the carpet in one of the photos. The policeman said he did not know what it was and no samples had been taken for chemical analysis. It was clear to all in the court that King had brought up the appearance of white powder to plant the suspicion that it was cocaine. Cocaine, along with alcohol, was claimed by the defense to have been what had fueled Robert Kissel's rage, which had led to the assault on his wife.

On Monday, July 4, the fifth week of trial, crime-scene investigator Tam Chi-chung testified. Tam said that even on his way over to the bedroom from the apartment he had been able to smell blood. He told the court how he had found blood spatter on the master bedroom walls, the headboard of the bed, on a picture frame, the top of a table, the side of a bureau and on the TV. Tam also conducted chemical analysis on a large brown stain on the bedroom carpet and determined that it was blood as well. Under cross from King, Tam admitted that the carpet stain had been the only one he'd tested for blood.

On July 11, the courtroom gallery's interest perked up noticeably at the testimony of government chemist Lun Tze-shan. He told the court he could determine, by the blood spatter pattern, size and height and where it was found, "what might have taken place."

"From the distribution of bloodstains," Lun said, ". . . my finding is that the attack could have happened at the end of the bed or the surrounding area."

Lun continued that the bloodstains were not "contact blood," explaining that that meant the blood was not smeared on the surfaces by a struggle. Judging by the low-lying level of the blood spatter, the victim was lying down and not standing.

In his cross-examination of Lun, Alexander King pointed out that there were bloodstains near the head of the bed that the investigator had purposely left out of his "expert's report" and did not submit for DNA testing. King asked him if there were any other stains he'd left out of his report, and consequently, omitted testing. Lun admitted there were, because he'd believed them to be out of the same blood pattern he had recorded. Lun also admitted he had since destroyed all the notes he'd taken at the crime scene.

King spent all of the next day attacking the credibility of crime-scene investigator Lun Tze-shan. Lun's conclusion that Robert Kissel had been killed without a struggle was questioned by King because of his failure to collect samples of all the bloodstains he'd found. It led King to proclaim that Lun's conclusions regarding the death of Mr. Kissel were "fundamentally flawed."

Lun replied that his conclusions were not "fundamentally flawed" and that it was "likely" and not "highly likely" that Robert Kissel was attacked without a struggle.

King then changed tack and referred to the photographs taken in the Kissel bedroom. He asked Lun about the quality of them, since Lun had relied on them to determine that the blood spatter pattern indicated no struggle. Lun hesitated with his answer. King pounced.

"Don't be shy, Dr. Lun. It's [the quality of the photographs] not good enough, is it?"

Lun countered with "It could be better," but that it was good enough for "basic information."

King continued to question Lun's lack of attention to other places in the room where bloodstains seemed to exist in the photos. Lun conceded that there seemed to be stains on a dumbbell and some on the bed that he hadn't taken into consideration.

King pointed out other apparently missed bloodstains. Pressed by King, Lun said the blood spatter appeared to have signs of smearing, which may have indicated contact patterns, or stains caused by a struggle.

On July 13, the jury learned that police officer Chan Kinwah had gone to the Kissel crime scene on November 12 and seized, along with other items, a white purse belonging to Nancy Kissel that was found to contain a pill vial that listed its contents as dextropropoxyphene. The prescription was made out to Nancy Kissel. There were fifteen pills left in the vial which had originally contained twenty. Another vial of the same drug was found in the wardrobe closet. It was missing nine pills. Chan also collected some white powder that was found on two corners of the bed.

In his cross, King again pointed out other locations in the bedroom where there had been apparent spots of white powder that were not collected.

The next day, Dr. Wong Koon-hung was called to testify. Wong told the court about items from the crime scene that he'd analyzed. He said that the blue tape used in binding the carpet that contained the body of Robert Kissel had

had Nancy Kissel's DNA on it. The cut end of the tape perfectly matched the cut end of the tape roll found in the Kissels' apartment.

Wong also showed how the ornament figurines and the base could be joined to be one piece. The prosecution claimed that the eight-pound ornament had been the murder weapon.

Wong said the force that had broken it was applied by holding the figurines, which caused their legs to bend upward and break off from the base. Asked by Chapman if a small child could wield such an object with the strength needed to break it, Wong answered that a five-year old could not muster the significant force.

When questioned by defense counsel Alexander King, Wong conceded that an "elongated object" such as a baseball bat could have been used to break the ornament.

King was subtly alluding to the bat that Kissel housekeeper Maximina Macaraeg said Mr. Kissel had kept in the master bedroom, which the prosecution said never turned up in any search of the apartment by the police.

Prosecutor Peter Chapman also read a statement by forensic scientist Billy Leung that the white powder found in the bedroom consisted of sodium carbonates that are usually found in household detergents. The sample did not contain any evidence of dangerous drugs.

Judge Michael Lunn asked for a clarification from the prosecutor. "Was the white powder cocaine?"

"No," said Chapman.

Next, DNA analyst Dr. Pang Chi-ming testified that the blood found on the alleged murder weapon was probably Robert Kissel's, with one chance in 429 billion that it belonged to someone else.

"You have any idea about the size of the population of the whole world?" Chapman asked Pang.

"It's about six billion," he answered.

Dr. Pang also testified that a penile swab done on the victim showed no traces of semen.

• • •

On July 19, Dr. Li Wei-sum was called by the prosecution. Dr. Li had examined Nancy Kissel when she was brought by police upon her arrest to the Ruttonjee Hospital on the morning of November 7. The prosecution's intent was to prove that the injuries she'd suffered were not a result of her trying to defend herself from an attacking husband.

Dr. Li had found abrasions on her lip, chest, knees and feet, and bruises on her upper and lower forearms, her shoulders and the backs of her hands. From the color of the bruises, she believed them to be one to two days old.

High levels of the enzyme creatine kinase in the blood and signs of damage to muscles in Nancy's arms, legs and ribs, Li said, indicated either physical injury, strenuous activity, a heart attack or some other medical conditions.

King took the floor.

"Given that the accused did not have a heart attack, does not suffer from any relevant medical conditions and had bruises in areas described in medical textbooks as being 'classic positions' for defensive injuries, a possible cause of an elevated CK [creatine kinase] reading is a result of Mrs. Kissel receiving blunt force injuries—is it not?"

"It can reflect Nancy Kissel had muscle injuries," Li replied, "but I cannot be sure she received blunt force injuries."

In re-examination by prosecutor Chapman, Li then conceded that the injuries may have been inflicted two to three days before her examination of Kissel rather than the one to two she had said earlier.

Chapman was able to elicit from the witness that the injuries could only have been caused on the morning of November 4, 2003, at the earliest, or two days after Robert Kissel had been bludgeoned to death.

Anthony Hung, Kissel's boss at Merrill Lynch, also gave testimony and confirmed that Robert Kissel was a prized employee and "very straightforward," who, like many of his colleagues, drank wine "on appropriate occasions, such as with dinner."

Hung said that when the police had seized Robert Kissel's property at his office at Merrill Lynch, they'd found copies of the e-mails his wife had exchanged with her lover in the United States, and also reports from the private investigator Robert Kissel had hired to spy on his wife while she was in the United States.

E-mails continued to be the topic of testimony the next day. In his opening statement on Wednesday, July 20, prosecutor Peter Chapman told the jury how Robert Kissel, suspicious of his wife, had installed "eBlaster" spyware on the family computers to track her correspondence and her web activity.

A forensic scientist from the Technology Crime Bureau, police officer Cheung Chun-kit, was then seated in the witness box.

Cheung told the court how he had found fragments of e-mails and website addresses on Nancy Kissel's purple Sony VAIO laptop computer, which was seized by police. Many of the e-mails were exchanges between Mrs. Kissel and her alleged lover in Vermont, Michael DelPriore.

Cheung testified that the spyware could not only capture what programs were being used, but also forward all e-mail correspondence to another designated address.

One part of an e-mail sent to DelPriore by Nancy Kissel was particularly revealing and seemed to confirm the prosecution's contention that she had been continuing her affair after promising to end it. It read:

> I am not quite sure how he feels about me . . . after hiring a private investigating firm to follow me . . . Are they going to be watching me forever? Hidden camera in the bedroom, tapped phone . . . I realized what the affair had to him . . . done trustwise.

Cheung also said that sleepingpills.com and medhelp.com had been viewed for between one and three minutes. Internet Explorer also indicated that Mrs. Kissel had made such searches as "sleeping pills," "overdose," "medication causing heart attack" and "drug overdose."

On November 5 and November 6, 2003, Cheung testified, nine temporary Internet files had been found on Nancy Kissel's Sony laptop indicating that HKPD webpages featuring "Wanted Persons," "Missing Persons" and telephone numbers of police departments were viewed.

Chapman also told the jury that one of the sites Nancy Kissel visited explained that the "date rape drug," Rohypnol, could not be detected by a person who drank a liquid that contained it. Nancy Kissel had obtained a prescription for Rohypnol and traces of the drug were found in the victim's stomach at the autopsy.

Defense attorney Alexander King followed the prosecution's computer evidence with some of his own. King told the court that the prosecution had provided the defense with the hard drive from the Kissel family's Dell desktop. The defense team had employed software to analyze the Internet activity between April 3 and April 5, 2003, when Robert Kissel was the only person home in the Parkview apartment. Nancy and the children were on a three-day trip away from Hong Kong at the time.

Displaying their findings on a monitor for the jury to see, the defense's software appeared to reveal search engine requests such as "anal," "cocks," "gay anal sex in Taiwan," "bisexual" and "male ass." King then asked witness Cheung if these were gay pornographic websites. Cheung confirmed that by saying, "Seems so, by looking at the names on the websites."

The software also turned up searches for "married and lonely in Hong Kong," "Mpeg sex," "wife is a bitch," "Taiwan female escorts" and "Taiwan companions." Robert Kissel often made short business trips to nearby Taiwan.

Defense lawyer King continued on the subject of Robert Kissel's web surfing of sex sites. He told how the deceased had made a search on the family computer of "gay sex in Taiwan" when his family was out of town. His personal IBM laptop, King said, would show that Mr. Kissel surfed sites that advertised "gay sex sites, sexual services and escort services."

King provided evidence of domestic tensions found on Mrs. Kissel's laptop that spoke of her husband's "harsh actions" and "blaming it all on me." There were other written words by Nancy:

> You see Rob, at the end of the day it seems like I am the only one making the effort. . . . But because of this fight and how uncontrollable you got in the car . . . How you are always telling me we won't fight in front of the kids . . . A fight and you give out an ultimatum . . . Who should be going to therapy? Whatever happens . . . to us? You never use those words anymore ever.

It was an apparent effort by King to bolster the idea that Robert Kissel could be an uncompromising and violent man.

Cheung, still on the witness stand, expressed "doubt" under cross-examination that the computers were used for cruising gay websites. He explained that it was possible that Robert Kissel may have simply made searches containing the letters "g," "a" and "y." The letters could actually have been in the middle of an innocuous search word that the victim had typed in.

King asked Cheung if Robert Kissel had not cruised such sites as www.boysgaypicnude.com, "free black gay porn," "black gay male pictures," "gay black men," "black males" and "ebony men." There were also searches of "Paris Gay," Paris Gay Massage," and "Male Cock Gay Sex," as well as escort services in Perth, Australia.

Cheung conceded that the addresses were a "result of searching."

King called up on a courtroom computer, for the benefit of the jury, one such site. He asked Cheung to look at a particular page.

"Do the boxes on the site," King queried, "appear to cater to a number of different tastes?"

Cheung answered, "Yes."

"Including gay males?"

Cheung replied in the positive again.

Having made his point, King took his chair.

CHAPTER ELEVEN

On the first day of the eighth week of the trial the prosecution presented some damning testimony to Nancy Kissel's defense when Senior Toxicologist Cheng Kok-choi was seated as a witness.

Cheng had received samples of contents taken from the victim's stomach and liver during autopsy that included antidepressants, hypnotics and sedatives. Two drugs, Rohypnol and the sedative Lorivan, had been prescribed to the victim's wife. Testing the deceased's alcohol level, he'd found it to be "insignificantly low," about the level of $1/100$ of a beer. Cheng added, when prompted by Chapman, that in the ten years he had been on the job he had never seen such a deadly concoction, "not even in suicide cases involving multiple drugs."

In a re-examination by the prosecution of computer expert Cheung Chun-kit, it was learned that most of the gay websites the defense claimed Robert Kissel had visited were Google results pages. Cheung said there was nothing to suggest that the victim had gone "beyond" those pages, or past the homepage of the sites, nor had Robert Kissel bookmarked the pages.

Chapman stated, "There is nothing to suggest . . . paid entry or membership to those sites?"

"That's correct," Cheung replied.

• • •

The following day the defense struck back with a toxicology report of their own that was written by well-known Hong Kong authority Olaf Drummer, associate professor of forensic medicine at Monash University in Australia. When asked by King if he was familiar with Drummer, Dr. Cheng admitted he had attended some of Drummer's Hong Kong seminars.

Drummer wrote that despite the combinations of drugs found in the body, the prosecution's report had failed to provide an "indication of the amount of drugs present, when they were consumed nor the root of administration."

In defending his own findings, Cheng contended that the body had already been five days old at the time of the autopsy, and had started the decomposition process, rendering the amount of drugs present in the victim not measurable.

Drummer had determined from the victim's hair sample that one of the hypnotics found, a sleep aid called Ambien, had been in Mr. Kissel's body two to three months before his death.

In re-examination of prosecution witness Cheng Kok-choi, he conceded that toxicology of hair samples was a "well-established method" in drug detection and based on Drummer's report, it appeared that Robert Kissel had been taking Ambien "habitually."

Cheng also said it was possible that the traces of different drugs found in the victim could have been present due to the chemical process in the decomposition of the body, and didn't prove the drugs were taken orally.

The defense got another huge concession from Cheng when he admitted that the best sources for testing the presence of alcohol in a cadaver were urine and the liquid from the eyeball. He had not received such samples.

Also, a test for the presence of cocaine had not been done. Cheng said no test was made because "Unless you have taken an overdose of cocaine, you can not detect it in the liver," since it would be hydrolyzed in the stomach because of the acid nature of the gastric juice.

Alexander King asked Dr. Cheng if any hydrolyzed product of cocaine was found in the stomach samples. Cheng replied that there was no universal screening procedure that could "detect everything under the sun."

Professor Yeung Hok-keung, an expert pharmacologist at the Chinese University in Hong Kong, was asked by Peter Chapman about the symptoms Robert Kissel had probably experienced after drinking the dangerous drug cocktail, allegedly concocted by his wife, Nancy, shortly before he'd been bludgeoned to death.

Yeung said Kissel was likely to have experienced drowsiness, slurred speech and memory loss, much like his neighbor, Andrew Tanzer, had testified he experienced after apparently drinking the same concoction. The effects Tanzer testified to have felt, Yeung related, were "consistent with the drugs found in the stomach contents of the deceased."

The sedatives Lorivan, Rohypnol, Stilnox, Amitryptyline and Axotal had probably been crushed into a powder and mixed into the drink, Yeung said. When asked by Chapman whether someone would be able to taste it in a milkshake, Yeung replied that there may have been a "bitter taste."

In his cross defense, counsel King told Professor Yeung that Robert Kissel had been captured on security video cameras playing with his son in the park at around 4:40 PM, or more than forty minutes after imbibing the milkshake. Video also showed Mr. Kissel making a phone call at 5:15 PM, over an hour later than when Andrew Tanzer had been experiencing the narcotic effects of the drink. King pointed out that Tanzer was a big man, bigger than Kissel, yet he had been affected within fifteen minutes of drinking the tainted milkshake. King asked why it would not have "the same pharmacological effect" on the deceased.

Yeung replied that the drugs do not always affect people the same way, so it was hard to make "direct comparisons."

King's implication was clear. He was insinuating that Robert Kissel had had a high tolerance to drugs. He laid the groundwork for further accusations on Kissel's drug use by asking a closing question of Yeung.

"But these drugs," King asked, "do what they tend to do quickly?"

Yeung replied in the affirmative.

King next read a statement to Yeung and asked him to comment on it:

> 'New cocaine users often use cocaine to increase productivity in their work, and other activities in their lives, so they can work longer and harder. Dangerous lifestyle choices often follow repeated cocaine use.'

Psychological addiction, paranoia and mood disturbances, replied Yeung, were possible with repeated cocaine use.

In re-examination of the witness by Chapman, the prosecutor stated that the effects of the sedatives found in the deceased's liver and stomach often are not felt for hours. He pointed out to Yeung that Kissel's fellow worker had called his colleague at 5 PM and testified that the victim was "generally non-responsive."

Asked to comment, Professor Yeung said, "Assuming that he was under the effect of the drugs, that wouldn't surprise me."

Theatrics finally reared its head in the murder trial of Nancy Kissel on Thursday, July 28. Not surprisingly, flamboyant defense attorney Alexander King was the lead in the drama.

Kissel housekeeper Maximina Macaraeg was recalled

to the witness stand by the defense. King asked her if she remembered the baseball bat in the Kissel master bedroom that she had mentioned in her previous testimony, given over a month earlier. She replied that she did. The house-keeper said she remembered the bat because she'd had to lift it when vacuuming the master bedroom, and that she recalled it as being wooden and of "medium weight."

When Macaraeg finished talking, King signaled the po-lice exhibits officer. The officer brought in an elongated object that was heavily wrapped. The jury leaned forward in their seats and watched with stretched necks as the ex-hibits officer carefully unwrapped the mystery object. It was a wooden baseball bat. The witness was asked by King to come forward and inspect the bat.

"Are you able," asked King, "to recognize whether that was the baseball bat you saw kept in the master bedroom between two pieces of furniture?"

Macaraeg studied it carefully before speaking. She spoke through an interpreter in her native Ilocano. "I cannot be sure," she replied.

Caught off guard by the defense's introduction of the baseball bat, prosecutor Peter Chapman had to downplay the surprise defense tactic. After a brief recess, Chapman called forensic pathologist Lau Ming-fai to the stand. At Chapman's prompting, Lau testified that five fatal blows to the head caused the skull to be pushed into the brain, caus-ing severe bruising.

"Each of these blows was potentially fatal," Lau added. "The combination was severely fatal."

Lau testified that the victim was prone, with his face turned to one side, adding that Robert Kissel "had little or no ability to move or defend himself at the time of the attack."

Chapman then asked Lau if the closely grouped blows to the victim's head were "not suggestive of people moving around."

"There's nothing in relation to the wounds themselves"

that could show that the deceased was not moving about, "but one has to look at the injuries as a whole."

Lau continued by explaining that a face-to-face fight where five fatal, closely grouped wounds could be inflicted was "unreasonable." Lau said that although a non-fatal wound that did not fracture the skull could cause unconsciousness and give the attacker the opportunity to inflict the fatal wounds, he did not find such an injury on the victim.

Chapman then asked the witness if Nancy Kissel could have inflicted the fatal wounds with the eight-pound ornament while fending off the baseball bat attack. Lau said it was unlikely.

King took the floor.

Stated as if a fact, King said that "repeated blows to one single area on the head could be inflicted in a short period of time."

Pausing, King then added that the blows could "be inflicted in a frenzy—bang, bang, bang, bang, bang!"

"Frenzy," said Lau was a psychiatric term and speaking as a pathologist, "it was impossible to detect the mental state of the assailant."

At King's prodding, Lau also held firm that he had found no defensive wounds or fractures on Robert Kissel's limbs.

After forensic pathologist Lau stepped down, the prosecution introduced the deposition of Bryna O'Shea that was recorded in the United States in May 2005. O'Shea was identified to the jury as Nancy's "best friend" and a "confidante" of Robert Kissel. It was read to the jury by senior government counsel Polly Wan.

In the deposition, O'Shea testified that she believed the Kissels had "the best marriage in the universe," only to find out later that it was really a facade to "hide the stress and disorientation of life as an expatriate in Hong Kong."

O'Shea claimed that Robert Kissel had confided in phone conversations and e-mail that he'd believed Nancy was trying to kill him. He told of his hiring of a private investigator to spy on her, and of the incriminating e-mail between Nancy and her lover that he was able to lift from her computer via spyware software he had secretly installed.

The absent witness wrote of how she'd first met Nancy Keeshin when the two of them worked in a trendy restaurant in New York City back in 1986. She related that they treated each other "like sisters."

By 2002, O'Shea couldn't help but notice the couple had become "distant" and that by April 2003, Rob had confided in her about his marital problems.

The court was adjourned and the deposition was to pick up where it had left off the next day on Friday, July 29.

Bryna O'Shea's words continued to be read. She told of how she'd gotten mixed signals on the marriage from Nancy. She'd thought Nancy's mindset was a result of the SARS epidemic that had uprooted and split up the family at that time.

In June 2003, O'Shea got a phone call late in the evening from an upset Rob Kissel. Sobbing audibly, he told Bryna he had called his oldest daughter in Vermont and she had told him that Michael DelPriore was over at their house with his daughter, and they were all watching TV. Rob told Bryna that it should be him there and not the TV repairman.

In July, Rob had written Bryna in an e-mail that he was upset Nancy had ignored his 40th birthday. The marriage was coming undone. O'Shea, when she asked about Rob in phone conversations, was told by Nancy, "Don't even ask."

O'Shea continued in her deposition by saying that Nancy had boasted in the past on what a great sex life she had with Rob, but Bryna had since found out they no longer made love with each other.

When Nancy and the children finally returned to Hong Kong in late July '03, Rob had e-mailed O'Shea that he was hopeful that his marriage could be repaired. Rob had spoken of them overcoming "the initial awkwardness" at the airport reunion and that Nancy had warmed to him and even held his hand. When they'd arrived home and sat and spoke about "us," Nancy broke down and cried.

Polly Wan read one of the e-mails written by Robert Kissel to Bryna O'Shea on August 17, 2003:

> 'It's mostly been me ... so fucking perceptive ... I had a pretty shitty summer ... especially when everyone is thinking we have the best marriage in the universe.'

Soon thereafter Nancy had found out that Rob was having an ongoing communication with her old friend, and expressed her feelings of betrayal to Bryna, claiming that Rob had stolen "the one thing she had"—O'Shea's confidence and loyalty.

O'Shea had defended her position, writing that she was just "concerned" and not acting as Rob's "cheerleader."

On September 30, 2003, O'Shea received a buoyant e-mail from Rob describing the events of the day before. He told of a counseling session with a marriage therapist in which Nancy had demanded a divorce, only to later recant at Rob's office. Nancy, Rob wrote, told him she still loved him and didn't really want a divorce.

In the deposition, the defense had queried O'Shea as to whether there had ever been any domestic violence between Rob and Nancy. O'Shea could only remember one instance: Rob had "slammed her against a wall" during an argument.

Later in October, O'Shea said, Rob had learned of Nancy's secret cell phone and how she was still speaking with Michael DelPriore in the United States after promising to stop communicating with him. He wrote her in an e-mail that "I can't wait to have a really big cry."

"He felt," wrote O'Shea, "that she was still lying to him." It was then that Rob had begun looking into instigating divorce proceedings against his wife of fourteen years.

Shortly afterwards Rob had spoken on the phone to O'Shea, who was living in San Francisco, and told her he planned to discuss the divorce with Nancy on Sunday, November 2.

On November 1, O'Shea said, she'd received an e-mail from Rob expressing Halloween wishes and that he was "signing off." O'Shea interpreted that as meaning she would not be hearing from him until the following Monday, after the divorce discussions with Nancy.

"That was the last time I had any communication with him," O'Shea wrote, adding, "I thought they were the happiest couple."

It wasn't until after attending Rob's funeral back in the United States that O'Shea had recalled another telling phone call she had gotten from Rob. He had said that Nancy had accessed some "dark websites" pertaining to drug overdoses. Rob had also asked Bryna if she thought Nancy might try to kill him. Bryna, shocked at such a question, answered with a humor that had been honed behind a bar for twenty-five years by saying, "If she's trying to kill you, put me in your will!"

O'Shea said Rob had laughed at her remark and then grown serious again, saying, "If anything happens to me, make sure my children are taken care of."

On November 2, after trying to reach her friend, and leaving numerous voice mails, Bryna got a message from Nancy on her answering machine while she was out of her house. Nancy said in a disjointed voice that she and Rob had had a fight when he'd insisted on having sex with her, and that her ribs had been injured in a scuffle. Rob had then stormed out of the apartment.

Thousands of miles away in San Francisco, O'Shea had tried frantically to reach Nancy and Rob for days, to no avail. She had gotten the frightened housekeeper Connie on the phone on November 3, but couldn't learn anything from her. She'd remembered Rob's friend and colleague at Merrill Lynch, David Noh, and called him on November 4. He'd told her Rob was nowhere to be found and that he had filed a missing persons report with the Hong Kong Police Department.

The court adjourned late in the afternoon until Monday, August 1, when the defense would present Nancy Kissel's case. The prosecution had rested.

CHAPTER TWELVE

On Monday, August 1, 2005, the trial of the pale and slender Nancy Kissel for the murder of Robert Kissel had entered into its ninth week. It was time for the defense to convince the jury that Nancy had bludgeoned her husband of fourteen years to death in self-defense. It was a daunting task for the high-profile barrister from Australia, and everybody, including the jury, knew it.

Wasting little time, defense counsel Alexander King called the now almost mousy-looking Nancy Kissel to the witness box. The local press, and there were many outlets covering the trial, never ceased to be amazed at the transformation of the once-glamorous blonde American expatriate to the now almost oriental-looking brunette dressed in the dowdy dresses and the plain-Jane eyeglasses. There was a tangible sense of anticipation as Nancy took her seat in the box. The press and the public gallery wouldn't be disappointed with what they were about to hear—if they could hear it. The defendant would have to be reminded constantly, not only by her lawyer, but also by Judge Michael Lunn, to speak up so that she could be heard by the jury.

Sitting behind her in the courtroom were the victim's father, Bill Kissel, and sister, June Clayton, staring intently at her. Nancy's mother, Jean McGlothlin, sat motionless nearby.

Asked by Alexander King about the state of her marriage, the defendant quickly broke down in tears as she told the court how she didn't know how "to talk about such things." Coaxed soothingly by attorney King to describe in detail the history of abuse, Nancy got ahold of herself and took a deep breath, then continued.

She spoke of how her marriage had been coming apart because of her husband Robert's alcoholism, drug addiction and his "ultra-stressful job." Nancy blamed the stressful job for his Jekyll & Hyde–like transformations.

In 1997, Nancy testified, her husband had landed a job at Goldman Sachs.

"It was the biggest firm in the [distressed debt] industry, everyone wanted to work with Goldman Sachs." It was a step up, position-wise, and it paid "a lot of money."

According to Nancy, the job is what made Rob "tick" and "he thrived on it . . . the power of it all, succeeding."

The new job meant that the family had had to move to Hong Kong in 1998. Just prior to the relocation from New York to the Far East, Rob had been prepared to work both the U.S. and Hong Kong stock markets, which had meant being on call twenty-four hours a day. The "accumulation nightmare of stress" had led the hard-charging investment banker to abuse of alcohol and drugs, said Nancy.

At first Rob had been a social drinker, Nancy claimed, drinking wine, beer and vodka tonics, but over time he came to indulge in expensive single malt scotch. "It became his drink," she said.

Once the family was settled in their new home, the defendant related, she'd gotten involved in volunteer work at their children's new school, the Hong Kong International School. It became a stressful job for her. At the school she worked forty hours a week, sometimes sixty hours when a special event was scheduled.

Her husband had complained, Nancy testified, about all the hours she worked at the school and how she did not spend enough time at home. He wanted her to give up the job. But he approved of her volunteer work at the United Jewish Congregation, since, Rob claimed, "it improved their social status."

"I needed to focus on being his wife and being at home for him. The fact that I wasn't getting paid for any of this bothered him tremendously. But payment wasn't why I did it."

Nancy told of her husband's constant scrutinizing of her spending habits and how he cut her credit cards from five to one.

She said Robert's addiction to cocaine had started in 1989. Nancy testified that at that time she had been working three jobs in New York to support Robert as he worked his way through postgraduate school at New York University. Elaborating, she told of his growing impatience and roughness towards her:

"When we arrived in Hong Kong, our marriage changed. He was starting up new businesses. He was never really home, and it took its toll when he got home. He became rougher with me and he drank all night."

Nancy said she never told anyone about her failing marriage because, she related, "You just don't . . . it's humiliating."

She told the jury how her husband had insisted on engaging in aggressive sodomy after her first childbirth because she had put on weight and "her breasts began to sag," as her husband had said. As a result, she came to believe that he no longer found her attractive.

Nancy Kissel recounted the first time that Robert had struck her. It was in 1999 after she'd refused to have doctors induce labor when she was pregnant with their third child. She explained he'd wanted to be at the birthing, but had planned a trip to South Korea on the natural due date.

"He took a punch at me . . . I hit the wall and it happened again . . . He hit me, and I was seven months pregnant. To induce labor was nothing to him. . . . He said I was disrespecting him."

Nancy claimed that the first punch was so powerful, it had broken through the wall. The next day Rob had come home with a cast on his hand.

The witness, in her own defense, told of how her husband had forced her into sex after the birth of son Reis, the Kissels' third child, in 1999. She told the riveted courtroom that after the child was born, Rob's personality had changed.

"It was a routine of coming home, drinking and sex. . . . it made me nonexistent. Sex became a routine of oral sex for him and anal sex for me." She said she'd broken her ribs on two occasions when she tried to stop him.

Nancy claimed it became a power game for Rob. He would say "things to me so he could do anything he wanted." She said that she would often find herself trapped between his legs with him pulling on her hair to perform sex acts on him.

He would force her to lie on her stomach so that he could do as he pleased. Once "he tried flipping me over. I didn't want it. He grabbed me by the hips, just twisting. I felt something pop. . . . he was just so angry. It was like I wasn't even there. It was just something he did. He never even had to look at my face."

Nancy went on to say that she'd later gone to the hospital, where she learned that he had broken her rib.

"It was just the start. It was just always a struggle," Nancy added.

In 2000, Robert Kissel had switched jobs. He'd left Goldman Sachs for a position at Merrill Lynch. Asked by her lawyer why he'd made the change, Nancy answered, "Money. It was a move to a more controlling position." By then, "everything was based around money."

On her second day of testimony, Nancy Kissel related how she'd attempted suicide when she and her children were staying in Vermont while the SARS epidemic raged in Hong Kong. She had started up her car in the garage of their Stratton home and waited for the carbon monoxide to overcome her.

"I don't know how long I was in the car, then I got scared of leaving [the children], then I turned off the engine and went back into the house."

Alexander King brought up the issue of the Internet searches on drug overdoses that she'd apparently made on her computer. The accused said it was she who'd wanted to die, but that she'd also wanted to be careful. She claimed that she'd wanted to give the appearance that her suicide was the result of a medical condition, since she didn't want to burden her children with the stigma of having a mother who had killed herself.

"I wouldn't want my children to be affected going through the knowledge of their mother committing suicide . . . I wouldn't want them to ever know about it," she managed to say in between the sobs.

Two days after Christmas in 2002, Nancy claimed, Rob had started another argument with her because he thought she was "fussing over the tree," and he had brutally slammed her against a wall. The abuse and the aberrant sex, she said, just kept escalating.

Rob had also begun to browbeat his children as well. On a visit to his family in Vermont in May of 2003, Rob was a tyrant.

"Everything bothered him, the way they were sitting at the table, Elaine [the oldest Kissel child] not eating her vegetables. He grabbed her and started shaking her, and she said, 'Daddy, you are hurting me,' and he wouldn't let go."

Nancy Kissel explained that she'd sought refuge during the months of June through August 2003 in Vermont in the arms of a lover whom she'd met while he was doing audio/visual/security work at their vacation home. She called Michael DelPriore "a reliable confidant who was a great source of emotional support."

"It was very easy, very comfortable," the defendant testified. "I could cry, I cried a lot . . . He [DelPriore] was very open and honest to me about his childhood with a mother and father that abused him, and that he had alcoholics in his family."

Nancy told of how she'd been able to tell him how superficial and money-obsessed her life was, living as an expatriate in Hong Kong, where people were "more interested in what you're wearing and how big your diamond ring is, and your car."

She claimed that the relationship with DelPriore had included three sexual encounters when their relationship evolved into a more intimate one. She had written in a diary how he offered her unconditional love and that he was the only person who brought her true happiness.

The accused also told how DelPriore had gone with her when she'd gotten tattoos of Chinese characters symbolizing the births of her three children, something she claimed that Rob had not approved of. But the accused testified that she had been determined to make her marriage work and never contemplated divorce.

Back in Hong Kong, she'd kept in touch with DelPriore and saved his love letters to her. Her husband had found them and Nancy said, "He ripped them to pieces in front of my face."

Rob had become more controlling back in Hong Kong, she claimed. He'd told her to stop calling her father, and had taken away the children's passports. Nancy admitted to surreptitiously slipping drugs into his scotch, simply "to calm him down," but claiming it had no effect on him.

Explaining how she'd obtained the drugs, Nancy said they'd been prescribed to her by a Dr. Fung, a psychiatrist. She had gone to see him at the end of August because she was mentally and physically exhausted from never knowing when the sexual abuse would occur, which had made her feel "on-guard all the time."

Nancy said Dr. Fung had prescribed Lorivan, Stilnox and amitriptyline. The prosecution had presented evidence earlier in the trial that these drugs were three of the five found in the victim in the post-mortem.

Previously the defendant had seen another doctor who was one of the first people she had met in Hong Kong. Kissel said she'd made an appointment to see Dr. Annabelle

Dytham because she just wanted to talk to another woman about what she was enduring in her marriage. Dr. Dytham had prescribed Rohypnol for Nancy, and since she did not know what it was, she'd looked it up on the Internet on her Sony laptop.

When the couple had gone to a second marriage therapy session, Nancy told her husband she wanted a divorce. Rob stormed out of the therapy session and later came home "drunk and angry."

"Who do you think you are?" Nancy testified that he'd yelled at her. "You'll never divorce me. If anyone's doing the divorcing around here, it'll be me!"

On the third day of her testimony Nancy Kissel was to tell her side of the story of what had happened the night her husband was killed. Cross-examination by the prosecution was also expected to start. Every Hong Kong newspaper, many foreign ones and most of the wire services were represented. There was standing room only in the gallery. The trial watchers had all been waiting in anxious anticipation for this day. They would not be disappointed.

At King's prompting, Nancy recalled how the evening had degenerated from an argument, to rape and then murder.

On the events of the day prior to the fatal encounter on November 1, Nancy claimed that her memory was "a little patchy." She recalled how her neighbor Andrew Tanzer and his daughter had visited them in their apartment and how the children had wanted ice cream but decided on making ice cream shakes. Because it was Halloween, the little girls had decided to add some red food coloring to the mix of bananas and ice cream. The girls then took the drinks to their fathers. After Tanzer and his daughter had left, the confrontation with Rob began. (There was no theory ever publicly given as to the motive for Nancy spiking Tanzer's drink, although there was speculation that it would make the incident appear more random and perhaps a result of accidental product contamination.)

But Nancy Kissel denied spiking the milkshakes with drugs:

"It was a milkshake that I made for my children and for someone else's child. I wouldn't harm my own children. I wouldn't harm someone else's child."

In tears, and trembling uncontrollably, she told the High Court how Rob had informed her he was divorcing her, that he had talked to his lawyers and it was a "done deal." Since she was in no condition to have custody of the children, he would be taking them.

Rob had been standing in the doorway of their bedroom at this point, claimed Nancy, tossing a baseball bat from one hand to the other. Walking toward him, she'd picked up the statue and asked him what he meant by her not being fit. She'd wagged her finger in his face, something he hated, with him slapping it away two times. On the third time, he'd grabbed it and wouldn't let go.

"I spat in his face. He hit me across the mouth and I fell down and dropped the statue."

According to Nancy, Rob then dragged her into the bedroom. In a whimpering, barely audible voice, she described what happened next:

"He grabbed my ankles and pulled me and wouldn't let go . . . He said, 'I am not finished with you yet.' "

Nancy said that Rob then threw her on the bed and attempted to sodomize her, but she managed to get away from his clutches. Nancy remembered they both ended up on the floor.

"He kicked me in the stomach and he wouldn't stop . . . I was on the floor, and I reached for the statue and swung it back at him. I felt I hit something and he let go . . . I saw his head was bleeding . . . and he said, 'I am going to fucking kill you, bitch.' "

Continuing the testimony Nancy described how Rob then attacked her again with the baseball bat as she defended herself with the statue, swinging it at his head. She couldn't remember striking him on the head five times or anything else after the violent encounter, except for her sitting on the floor next to the bed in a daze when it was all over.

The accused was asked by King to inspect the baseball bat on the court clerk's desk. She rose slowly and held on to the witness box for support. Looking at the bat, she identified it as the one her husband had held the night of November 2. It was, she claimed, one of her last memories of that horrible evening, saying, "He was going to kill me . . . and he was going to."

King asked his client, "Are you able to tell us the last thing you remember going through your mind during this incident?"

"I just wanted him to stop swinging the bat at me," she said.

Her lawyer then asked her if she remembered anything else about the fight. The accused said nothing, and sobbing, bowed her head.

Pausing a moment, King then raised the subject of her appearing on the security camera in the Parkview's parking lot at 2 AM the next day. He quietly asked her to explain.

"I got in my car and drove down the hill. I don't know where I went. I just remember being in my car."

She remembered doing work the next day, but had no memory of any phone calls she'd made or e-mail correspondence she'd received.

King asked his client about the evidence the prosecution had presented on the "cleaning" that was done in the master bedroom after Rob was dead.

"What was your recollection of that?" King asked.

"No, I don't remember," Nancy answered.

Next the defense attorney asked her when she'd realized Rob was dead. Nancy said it had come "in bits and pieces . . . fragments of memory came back.

"Maybe six months or so later in Siu Lam [a Hong Kong psychiatric hospital]. The first month I was there I don't

Left–right: unidentified, a glamorous Nancy Kissel, and Bryna O'Shea, New York, 1994. *Photo courtesy of Bryna O'Shea*

Nancy Kissel (left) and Bryna O'Shea (middle) at O'Shea's 1986 wedding in New York. *Photo courtesy of Bryna O'Shea*

The Kissel boys on the slopes of Stratton Mountain, VT, circa 1985. Robert, third from the left, Andrew, far right. *Photo courtesy of William Kissel*

Robert's graduation from the University of Rochester, 1986. Left–right: Robert, Elaine, unidentified, Andrew, Jane. *Photo courtesy of William Kissel*

Kissel family get-together, 1989: Jane, Robert, William, Elaine, Andrew. *Photo courtesy of William Kissel*

Carlos Trujillo, Andrew Kissel's man Friday.
© *Kevin McMurray*

Kissel's private investigator, Frank Shea. *Photo courtesy of Frank Shea*

Robert and Nancy's Stratton, VT, home and Nancy's love nest. © *Kevin McMurray*

Andrew and Hayley's swank Upper East Side apartment in New York. © *Kevin McMurray*

Kissel family plot with Robert's headstone in the foreground, and Andrew's temporarily marked grave to Robert's immediate left. © *Dan Burns*

Close-up of Robert's headstone. © *Dan Burns*

Left–right: Nancy Kissel and Bryna O'Shea, New York, 1994. *Photo courtesy of Bryna O'Shea*

Left–right: Ira Keeshin, Joanne Keeshin, Nancy Kissel, and Robert Kissel in Hong Kong, circa 2000. *Photo courtesy of Bryna O'Shea*

Phillip Russel, Andrew Kissel's Greenwich, CT, attorney. © *Jennifer Soffayer*

Above: Robert and Nancy flanking former President George H. Bush in a Hong Kong benefit one month before Robert's murder, 2003. *Photo courtesy of William Kissel*

Robert Kissel and daughter, June, Hong Kong, 2003. *Photo courtesy of William Kissel*

The young Kissel family, New York, 1969. Left–right: Andrew, Robert, Jane. *Photo courtesy of William Kissel*

really remember much. I started to remember things, of where I was in January [2004], because I remember the holiday, which is when I was able to be let out of where I was, and I don't have a clear memory of the beginning when I was there."

King interrupted Nancy by asking, "On November third, did you know he was dead?"

"I don't remember," Nancy replied.

Nancy offered no explanation on how her husband's body had come to be wrapped in the carpet and stashed in the storage room in the basement of the apartment building. She couldn't explain her fingerprints on the packing tape, the boxes of bloody bedding, cleaning the master bedroom after the altercation with her husband, or calling to arrange the disposal of Rob's body.

Prosecutor Peter Chapman took to the floor, obviously relishing the cross-examination of Nancy Kissel that was about to begin. Several members of the jury leaned forward in their chairs.

Chapman got right to the point.

"Do you accept," he asked, "that you killed Robert Kissel?"

The defendant replied in a firm voice, "Yes."

Chapman told Nancy that he'd noticed that the accused had passed notes back and forth with her lawyer continuously during testimony by witnesses. He asked, "Can you help us please, with which of those evidence do you dispute?"

She replied that there was so much that she couldn't remember all of them. Pressed by Chapman, Nancy did remember one instance. She disputed the observation of her housekeeper Maximina Macaraeg that she, Nancy, was "hot tempered."

Nancy also confirmed, on being queried by Chapman, that she'd bludgeoned her husband to death with a heavy ornament, which she identified for the jury.

But she couldn't recall the events that had followed shortly after the fatal fight: her report to the police of the beating she'd gotten from her husband, or her father showing up at her apartment.

Chapman asked Nancy Kissel about drugging her husband, specifically spiking the bottle of scotch he'd kept at home. She told the High Court that she'd spiked the scotch just once with Stilnox when they were staying in Vermont. Nancy said she'd done it because Rob had been "aggressive" with the couple's children and she'd just wanted to calm him down. She claimed it had no effect on him.

Once back in Hong Kong, she'd tried it again. But she'd noticed sediment formed at the bottom of the bottle, so she poured it all out, bought a new bottle and poured half its contents into the old bottle to cover her tracks. Nancy claimed that she "never thought of it again."

Under questioning from Chapman, the defendant admitted that there may have been times when she cried out from the abuse administered by her husband.

"Did anyone ever hear you in the household, Mrs. Kissel, in those five years?"

"I don't know . . . a lot of the time, I cried." She explained that her domestic help left for the day at 7 PM and wouldn't have been there to hear her cries.

Chapman also asked the witness if she had ever been tested for HIV infection, since she'd testified that her husband had forcibly had anal sex with her and that he'd traveled a lot. He suggested that her husband may have had anal sex with other women on those business trips—did she know if that were true? Nancy said she did not.

Again the prosecutor asked if she had ever been tested for HIV or AIDS. Again she replied that she had not since they'd both been tested before they married in 1989.

Chapman asked Mrs. Kissel if she had a history of memory problems. Had she ever seen a psychiatrist about the problem, other than the memory loss after her husband's death? She replied no and that she had been on anti-depressants during the events of November 2003.

Chapman moved on. He asked about her life with her husband in New York when he was a postgraduate student at NYU.

"You were supporting him, you were giving him money. How much would he spend on the drugs?"

Nancy Kissel replied that "It would vary," but it was around $100 a day and "sometimes more." Chapman tried to get her to specify a monthly amount, but she claimed she didn't remember since he'd sometimes gotten drugs from friends or hadn't had to pay for purchases. She was paying for his drug habit only at the beginning of their relationship. Peter Chapman asked her to explain how she could come up with that kind of money on a steady basis. Chapman reminded her that the couple was able to rent an apartment in a fashionable part of Manhattan.

She said that she worked at the restaurant, and did "outside catering" at various jobs—here and there.

There wasn't any need for further questioning on his part. He looked at the jury and smiled.

"While he was in Hong Kong," Chapman asked, "where was he getting his cocaine from?"

Nancy claimed, once again, that she didn't know. Chapman asked her if she'd ever warned her husband about the draconian punishments meted out in Asia for drug possession. She said she'd only lectured him on the health issues of drug use.

Did she ever see his stash of cocaine in Hong Kong?

"I have never seen bags, mostly bottles."

Chapman dropped the line of questioning and then asked her if the frequency of anal sex had increased after they moved to Hong Kong.

"It increased tremendously," the accused replied.

"How often each month would you be having forced anal sex with Robert Kissel?"

She claimed she'd never counted.

When prodded for a number by Chapman, Nancy Kissel said it wasn't about the number but the "progression of sexual activity" and how there was force involved. He then asked if she'd ever told anybody about it. She said she hadn't because it was something that happened gradually in her marriage and "forceful sodomy was not something you brought up at the dinner table or during social events."

"Did Robert Kissel ever wear a condom?" Chapman asked.

"No," replied the defendant.

"Did he ever use any lubricant or gel?" Again, Nancy said no.

"And he never had a problem effecting anal entry throughout this period?"

Nancy replied that she had had anal bleeding two times, each time for "maybe a day or two."

He asked Nancy Kissel if she'd ever seen a doctor about the anal bleeding.

Nancy said no, because "it was too humiliating."

On Monday, August 8, prosecutor Peter Chapman continued his cross-examination of the witness.

It still wasn't clear to trial watchers what tack the defense would take in trying to spare Nancy Kissel a life sentence in a Hong Kong prison. Speculation ran rampant in the enthralled city. "Temporary insanity" and "diminished capacity" were the odds-on favorites. Standing room only in the courtroom was still creating problems. The court had to employ two crowd control marshals. People who left their seats for a break were routinely not let back in the court.

Courthouse rumors had it that Nancy's psychiatrist, Dr. Henry Yuen, would not be permitted to testify in court. It seems he had found that his patient did not have suicidal tendencies or problems of memory loss.

• • •

Chapman opened his questioning about the so-called "abusive behavior" Robert Kissel had exhibited toward his three children.

Choking back tears and noticeably shaking, she uttered, "I still love him . . . he was my husband . . . he was my husband!"

With that emotional outburst, Judge Lunn called for a brief recess so that the accused could compose herself. Nancy Kissel remained seated in the witness box for several seconds. Turning to the judge in tears, she said, "He's my husband . . . It's so hard."

Back on the stand Nancy Kissel related how shocked she was to learn of her husband's apparent interest in bisexual and gay sex, as suggested by Internet searches that were discovered by police when they examined the home computer.

"It put things in perspective . . . why he did what he did with me . . . It's quite shocking to find out he was somebody I didn't really know."

The prosecutor suggested that she was just slandering his name to serve her purpose. She replied by saying, "I still love him deeply."

Chapman pressed the witness about why she had not told her family and friends about the mental, physical and sexual abuse she was suffering. Chapman suggested it was "because it wasn't happening."

In her defense Nancy said that her husband's confidante and her best friend, Bryna O'Shea, and the Hong Kong expatriate community did not like to face up to such distasteful issues as physical, mental and sexual abuse.

Chapman countered, "The alternative, Mrs. Kissel, is that there is nothing to tell."

The prosecutor brought up the issue of the defense not permitting her psychiatrist Dr. Yuen to testify. He asked if that was because she did not have any psychiatric problems.

Surprisingly Nancy replied "Yes," but added that the doctor's report was given in the context of whether she was psychiatrically fit enough to be granted bail. No, she didn't suffer from schizophrenia or any other disorder according to the Mental Health Ordinance that would prevent her from being free on bail.

"Did you tell Dr. Yuen about the cocaine, the sodomy, the suicide attempt?" Chapman asked.

"No. He was mostly interested in my medication and my day-to-day life in Siu Lam." That said, Nancy's voice picked up an angry tone. "They have no idea of what you've been through in your life and you just can't go in there and say, 'Hey, this is what happened to me.'" With that, she burst into tears.

Composing herself, Nancy Kissel went on to explain that she had to contend with the language barrier at Siu Lam, the isolation and the loss of the comfort of her children.

She then made a stunning revelation: "There's nothing psychiatrically wrong with me. I'm not suffering from any mental illness. Depression—yes. Feeling sad, feeling remorseful—yes. Suffering from something tragic—yes!"

Chapman asked Nancy why, in her public life at the Hong Kong International School and at the United Jewish Congregation, no one had noticed her alleged bruises, and why she hadn't told anybody about her husband's abuse of her.

"I didn't think of approaching anyone."

"Because it wasn't happening?" Chapman interjected.

Kissel explained that she hadn't told anyone because she was ashamed.

Asked about her husband's abusive behavior toward the children, Nancy got very emotional and claimed she didn't mean to portray him in a bad way, because she still loved him. It had been the "isolated instances of violence" that had frightened her.

Chapman asked the defendant about the vacation in

Thailand where their daughter had been treated for a in-jured elbow, allegedly a result of the roughness of the de-ceased. Nancy's story differed dramatically from the one her housekeeper Connie had testified to.

"Who's making up the story, you or Connie?"

"Connie," Nancy replied.

Next Chapman asked whether she'd ever been tested for AIDS, considering her husband's "fascination for gay sex." She answered that she had not. (This was a surprising ad-mission in light of the tragic AIDS-related death of her friend Ali Gertz.)

"Because you don't believe it yourself, do you, Mrs. Kissel?"

Nancy did not respond. Chapman asked Kissel about her lover back in Vermont.

Michael DelPriore, she said, was five to ten years younger than she, and "he was the best person to talk to about life." She said they'd had "good times" together back in Vermont.

Asked by Chapman if DelPriore still spiritually sup-ported her, she replied, "I don't know. I have not main-tained contact with him."

Chapman suggested that the reason Nancy had readily accompanied her husband back to New York for his back surgery so soon after her return to Hong Kong was so she could see DelPriore.

Nancy said she had met DelPriore "briefly" in New York's Central Park, but that, she claimed, was not the rea-son she'd made a trip halfway around the world. She'd gone because Rob had asked her to.

Chapman posed another question to her. How could her husband abuse her while being treated for the debilitating back injury?

Nancy Kissel said that that was what the painkillers were for. Her husband was still mobile, and still demanding oral sex. "He was capable of that at any time," she added.

Chapman's retort was poetic: "You sneaked out behind your husband's back, while he lay on it."

Chapman proceeded to read the love notes between Nancy and her paramour.

In one of them Nancy professed that, "I will always love you." In another DelPriore wrote: "I love it when you call my name. It makes me melt."

Visibly embarrassed, Nancy, with as firm a voice as she could muster, lamely replied, "He's a person I had a relationship with."

Chapman continued, stating to the full courtroom that Nancy had had no intention of saving her marriage and that Michael DelPriore "was the man you loved . . . the man in your life."

Chapman asked if her lover lived in a trailer park. He received a negative answer.

"In a stationary mobile home?" he suggested.

"I believe something like that."

"And you represented a potential goldmine to him, didn't you, Mrs. Kissel?"

"No, he had an understanding of what my life was about," she answered back rather firmly.

She said DelPriore had not judged her by what she had, but solely on what kind of a person she was, and she'd never spoken to him about her drug prescriptions or her suicidal tendencies.

Chapman told the court that the accused had made fifty-two calls from Hong Kong to DelPriore in the United States in September 2003. In October she'd made 106 calls, seven of them on the 23rd before and after going to her doctor to get the Rohypnol prescription. Two days before her husband had returned to Hong Kong after back surgery in New York, Nancy had made her incriminating web searches on drug overdoses. That very same day she had spoken to the audio/visual installer for over three hours. The prosecuting attorney suggested that she "was well aware that divorce was in the cards."

"No," she answered, "He [Robert] was very clear . . . with me that divorce was not a solution."

Chapman didn't let up.

"This man called you back, spending hours on the telephone, spending hundreds and hundreds of U.S. dollars, which a resident of a trailer park can ill afford."

"He worked," Kissel tersely replied.

"I suggest to you," the prosecutor said, "he considered that a good investment."

Nancy admitted that her husband had called her in Vermont from Hong Kong in the summer of 2003 and told her he knew she was having an affair. Chapman then asked if the charge of adultery in a divorce action had concerned her.

"No doubt your thoughts turned to money? And another issue might be custody of the children?"

Nancy skirted around the question by answering that she'd focused on the children's "well-being and life in Hong Kong."

Chapman asked the defendant how her husband had found out about her "secret" cell phone. Nancy said she did not know.

"So he didn't come and confront you and beat you up? This would seem a bit out of character, wouldn't it?" Chapman asked sarcastically.

"Yes, it would seem so," she replied forthrightly, and added that she had no idea why there wasn't a confrontation over its discovery.

Chapman addressed the jury and reminded them of Frank Shea's testimony of September when Robert Kissel had told Shea of his suspicion that he was being poisoned by his wife.

The jury listened as Chapman related that on October 28, Nancy had gotten a prescription of twenty tablets of the painkiller dextropropoxyphene and two days later was prescribed Lorivan, Ambien and amitriptyline by another doctor. All of these drugs were found in the contents of Robert Kissel's stomach in the post-mortem.

When asked if she'd told the second doctor of her prescription to Rohypnol, Nancy claimed she didn't remember.

"You were shopping for drugs, weren't you?"

She denied it.

Kissel was asked about a trip to San Francisco she had planned in early November. The accused said she was going to have a breast lift and liposuction because it "was very important to my husband." She said she had to cancel the trip because it conflicted with her daughter's dance recital.

Chapman produced a photograph taken just one month before Rob's murder that showed a smiling Rob and Nancy flanking George H. W. Bush at an event held in honor of the former president while he was visiting Hong Kong. Nancy, in a stylish dress, cradled a drink in her hand. She appeared not to have any bruising on her exposed flesh. Another photo, Chapman said, was, taken when Nancy was on vacation in Canada, just a day after her husband had attacked her, according to her allegations. Again she appeared happy and unmarked.

Nancy Kissel said she'd just been putting on a "brave face."

"Happiness on the outside has nothing to do with what you are feeling inside," she said.

Kissel also claimed that the injuries inflicted by her husband could have been masked with cosmetics and tanning cream.

Chapman challenged Kissel on the different accounts of the fatal fight that she'd given to two doctors. Dr. Annabelle Dytham reported that Mrs. Kissel had told her two days after the events of November 2 that the couple had been running around the bedroom when Robert grabbed and kicked her. Nancy had defended herself with a fork, clutching it upside down. Chapman suggested Nancy had said that so she could explain the puncture wounds in her hands that had been caused by the broken statue that she was actually wielding. In January at Siu Lam Hospital the attending psychiatrist had written that Mrs. Kissel claimed her husband had been beating her with a baseball bat and she had defended herself with a metal statue.

Chapman said that at the November 4 appointment there was no indication that Nancy had trouble recalling the fight specifics, yet she'd testified that she did not remember that visit to the doctor.

Chapman paused and then asked, "Your claim here of memory loss is . . . a lie, isn't it, Mrs. Kissel?"

Nancy Kissel was quick with her response: "I was not aware at that time that I had memory loss."

Chapman pressed the witness, claiming she was employing "three levels of deception" on Dr. Dytham, the police and her father. The prosecutor hypothesized that when her father, Ira Keeshin, had flown to Hong Kong on November 6 to be at his daughter's side, Nancy had surprised him with the truth only once the police had arrived on the scene and insisted on searching the storeroom. That explained why the police had heard Mr. Keeshin cry out, "Oh, my God, I don't believe it!"

"I don't know," the defendant said. "There are things that I don't understand. That's a part of my life that was taken away from me."

Chapman quickly added, "The person who has had a part of his life taken from him is Robert Kissel, because you killed him. And in order to achieve that purpose, you had to drug him first."

"He was going to kill me," Kissel protested, "and I defended myself because he was going to kill me. I fought for my life."

"You just forgot to mention that to Dr. Dytham, thirty-six hours later. You remember not putting drugs in the milkshake, but remember Robert Kissel threatening to kill you."

Chapman questioned the defendant about the "furious fight" she had described in earlier testimony. Mrs. Kissel had claimed that the fatal wounds she'd inflicted on her husband were a result of defending herself against her bat-wielding husband.

"It did not happen, Mrs. Kissel, it just did not happen," Chapman said. "Those five grouped accurate fatal blows were delivered by you from above, weren't they, Mrs. Kissel?"

Kissel insisted that she had been on the floor defending herself with the statue while her husband was on top of her.

It was now 4:29 PM. Prosecutor Chapman asked Judge Lunn if this would be a convenient time to adjourn. Before the judge could dismiss the jury for the day, Nancy Kissel cried out from the witness stand: "He was going to kill me. Oh God, oh God, he was going to kill me."

That said, the accused dropped her head to her folded arms resting on the desk and sobbed uncontrollably.

On August 11, Nancy Kissel's time in the witness box was drawing to a close after eight days of tense and emotional testimony. Peter Chapman, in his cross-examination, was not about to let up.

When Nancy Kissel was asked what explained the cur-vature in the base of the statue that was originally flat, she claimed it was the swinging baseball bat that had caused the damage. Chapman said the force required to damage it would surely have knocked the ornament out of her hands, leaving her defenseless to her husband's attack.

The accused shook her head and claimed she had been holding the statue with both hands "with some strength to protect myself."

The prosecution claimed that at 7:41 AM, November 3, Nancy Kissel had called her lover back in the United States and spoken for twenty-four minutes.

"By this time, you're unlikely to need a sympathetic ear about an abusive husband," Chapman intoned. He continued.

"During this phone call, did you tell Michael DelPriore you had solved the problem with your husband?"

Nancy said she didn't remember the conversation.

Chapman said that on November 4, two days after the murder, she'd called DelPriore six times. It was the same day she'd been examined by her doctor, who'd described her as being "tearful," "slow to move" and having "total body pain" after being physically and sexually assaulted by her husband.

Chapman said it was also on November 4 that Nancy Kissel had gone on "three different shopping expeditions" and been caught on the Parkview security camera lugging a rug and a suitcase into her building when she was allegedly injured from Mr. Kissel's assaults.

The accused claimed she'd never stopped her activities because, she said, "Your body is on autopilot . . . I do it for my children."

She added that she'd had to buy new bedsheets to replace the ones that had been bloodied from the anal sex Rob had forced on her.

"Eventually," Chapman said, "the rug containing Robert Kissel's body and various items is removed from the apartment into the storeroom. While all this is going on, you're continuing to speak to Michael DelPriore."

"Yes," Nancy replied, stating the obvious since the prosecution had her telephone records.

Kissel also admitted phoning DelPriore up until the time she was arrested. When asked if he had been in touch since, she'd answered, "No, he hasn't contacted me."

Defense counsel Alexander King took to the floor again and began his re-examination by emphasizing that the bail application had been heard in the context of mental stability and did not cover the issue of memory loss. But, said King, since that bail hearing, Mrs. Kissel had been diagnosed as suffering from "dissociative amnesia" after being seen by Dr. Desmond Fung, who was called to testify.

The psychiatrist said he'd attended to Nancy Kissel in August and October. He related that Mrs. Kissel had said that arguments between her and her husband often "erupted into physical violence." When asked by King how she'd "presented herself," he answered, "She's describing every-thing in . . . sequence. I did not detect evidence that she was making up a story."

Fung told the court that on the first visit, when she'd claimed she was getting little sleep, he had prescribed Mrs. Kissel ten tablets of Stilnox or Ambien. On the second visit Mrs. Kissel complained that the pills were not effective, and mentioned that her marriage had "deteriorated." Dr. Fung then prescribed three types of sleeping pills and anti-depressants—Stilnox, Lorivan and amitriptyline.

Chapman claimed in his cross-examination of Dr. Fung that the psychiatrist was "totally reliant" on what Nancy Kissel had felt like telling him. Dr. Fung conceded the point.

On Friday, August 12, the defense called Dr. Annabelle Dytham to the stand. Dytham had treated Kissel on November 4, 2003, two days after Robert Kissel had been murdered. She told the court that Mrs. Kissel had come to see her at the Wan Chai Clinic in "total body pain," and with restricted body movement.

Dr. Dytham, who had treated Mrs. Kissel several times since 2002, said the accused had called the clinic at 8:30 AM for an appointment. She'd walked in a half hour later all "hunched over." Usually, the doctor related, Mrs. Kissel was well-dressed, but this time she was plainly attired and wore large sunglasses.

The defendant told the doctor that her husband had tried to have sex with her, but she had refused. Mrs. Kissel said Robert had punched and kicked her and that she'd defended herself with a fork, which she'd held the wrong way. She had swollen and cracked lips, swollen fingers and small puncture wounds on the inner crease of her right hand. Dytham thought that made sense, considering Nancy had said she'd used a fork to fight off her husband.

Mrs. Kissel had been bruised on her right arm, and her left arm was painful to the touch and did not have a full range of motion. She'd claimed she had pain in her rib area, chest and collarbones. She'd also had decreased movement in her spine and upper thigh. Bruises had been found on her legs. At first Dytham thought she had broken some ribs, but the X-rays were negative.

In cross-examination by Peter Chapman, Dr. Dytham admitted that she'd "felt a little frustrated that everywhere I touched," Mrs. Kissel was pained, even "in places with no physical injuries."

She added, "I am not used to dealing with psychosomatic pain—patients who have pain where there is no actual physical injury."

Chapman had the security video played which depicted Nancy Kissel carrying the rug and suitcase from her car. The prosecutor asked the doctor if the video surprised her.

"I can't see the speed in which Nancy's moving [in the video stills] . . . I don't know how heavy the suitcase was. There's no facial expression. People are known to be able to struggle through all sorts of injuries. I can say I am a little surprised. However, if Nancy had come to me to report injuries on November fourth. I could understand a possible exaggeration of the pain, given that she had been assaulted and she might want to make a court case out of it."

Phone records indicated that Nancy Kissel had received a call from the United States while she was at the clinic. Asked about that, Dr. Dytham recalled that a call had come in on Nancy's cell phone when the doctor was examining her. Nancy had said, "I am with Annabelle at the moment."

Dr. Dytham said she had heard a man's voice on the phone. Finished with the call, Nancy explained that it was a friend from the States on the other end who had called to voice his support.

Chapman asked Dytham if she'd advised Mrs. Kissel to call the police. She replied that since Nancy hadn't mentioned anything about rape, she had not made that suggestion. But the doctor added that she had given Nancy a copy of her notes, since they might be needed in the event of divorce.

"During her course of description of events," Chapman

asked, "did she mention to you that Robert Kissel had used a weapon to assault her on Sunday [November 2]?"

Dr. Dytham replied, "No."

Chapman asked the witness if she thought the accused had had any memory lapses when recounting what had happened to her two days before. The doctor said she had not seemed to have any difficulties in that area.

The doctor was asked about a previous office visit by Nancy Kissel on October 23, 2003. Dytham had complimented her on how well she looked when she came in for her appointment. Nancy had surprised her by complaining about insomnia and the "marital problems" she was enduring, and elaborated by saying she had been constantly assaulted sexually by her husband for the last year. She claimed injuries from being sodomized.

Chapman asked Dr. Dytham about the Rohypnol she'd prescribed Nancy Kissel at that October visit. The doctor explained she was not in the habit of prescribing such a strong hypnotic, but she had made an exception because Nancy'd told her the Stilnox did not help her sleep. She did, however, warn Nancy that the sedative could cause black-outs if the user drank alcohol.

On Monday, August 15, Dr. Dytham continued to give testimony. She told the court that it was possible that after the fight with her husband, Nancy Kissel could have been suffering from intense pain despite the fact she showed no visible injuries.

Defense attorney King told the witness that the blood tests later showed the possibility of "skeletal muscle injury." Hearing that, Dytham said that the blood finding "would definitely have been a matter of consideration" and it might indicate that Nancy's "expressions of pain were not exaggerated."

"Deep tissue injuries," said Dytham, "do not necessarily show up as bruises."

Dytham was shown pictures of the body wrapped in the carpet and asked her opinion whether Nancy Kissel, in the pain she'd claimed to be in, could have carried that carpet by herself and rolled her husband's body in it.

"Nancy was very distressed when I saw her. If it now seems that she's admitted she had killed her husband, then I could imagine how frantic she must have been and desperate to destroy or remove any evidence under those circumstances. Given how she presented herself to me, I am surprised. Given how she was exaggerating her injuries, then I am not surprised."

King then presented a possible scenario that he wanted Dytham's opinion on.

"If someone was holding the ornament to protect herself from the blows of a bat and the bat came in contact with the ornament, would the shock transfer itself to the joints of the elbows and shoulders?"

The witness said it was possible that there could have been injuries to the ribs without fractures.

Chapman in his cross-examination of Dr. Dytham noted that her report made no mention of a memory disorder, baseball bat or nine or ten places on Nancy's body which the defense had called "classic areas of defensive injuries."

Dytham, although claiming no expertise in psychiatry, had detected no problems with the patient's memory. She said she may have seen the injuries, but made no note of them, and about the mention of rape, she said, "Rape is very serious, and if it had been mentioned, I feel I would have explored that at greater depth."

Chapman asked the doctor what kind of wounds she would expect to see had a man attacked a patient of hers with a baseball bat. She answered, bruises, possible bone fractures, and, if struck on the head, possible loss of consciousness. Dytham continued by saying there were no areas of Nancy's body that showed "serious forceful blows."

• • •

On Tuesday, August 16, the first witness to take the stand was Nancy Kissel's half-brother Brooks Keeshin. He testified that he'd arrived in Hong Kong on November 8 after hearing of Nancy's arrest. He had come to help pack up the kids for their return to the United States with his father. After looking around the apartment with lawyer Simon Clarke, they'd found a baseball bat.

Chapman, when it was his turn to cross-examine the witness, accused Brooks Keeshin and Simon Clarke of being an "expeditionary force" there to conduct searches to help Nancy in any courtroom defense. Their "reinforcements" were Ira Keeshin and Alexander King, who would later show up "armed with cameras."

Brooks Keeshin defended his actions, telling the court that he and Clark had moved only one piece of furniture, made only general searches and brought just one disposable camera with them. Their main goal, he said, was to pack the children's things and look for Nancy's personal belongings.

Ira Keeshin took the stand in the defense of his daughter Nancy that afternoon.

He told the court that he and his son-in-law Robert Kissel had gotten along well, describing him as a "good guy, pretty industrious and bright." Keeshin, 63 years of age, said the two men would bond discussing their mutual interest in business over glasses of scotch and cigars. He said it was a "nice relationship" and that he was unaware that Rob had used drugs.

Keeshin said it was around September of 2003 when he received a call from Nancy telling him that Rob was jealous of their tight relationship and that he wanted her to stop calling her dad on a daily basis. Keeshin said he'd told his daughter that her marriage was more important and for her to bow to Rob's wishes. He added that "as Rob made more money, worked longer hours, traveled more, Nancy's life became more lonely." Keeshin then related the events of early November 2003.

The father of the accused said he had received a call from Nancy on November 3, the day after she had killed her husband, and she'd told him, "Dad, I've been beaten up pretty badly" by Rob.

Nancy also told her dad that Rob had fled the apartment and had not returned.

Telling Brooks [a son from his second of three marriages] of the phone call, his son advised him to book a flight to Hong Kong as soon as possible, saying, "Dad, this is a defining moment in your relationship with Nancy. When men beat up their wives, sometimes they come back to kill her and their children."

Ira Keeshin valued his son's opinion, since he was a medical student and often did volunteer work at women's shelters. He called his daughter back and told her to lock the doors.

When he arrived in Hong Kong on November 5, he was shocked to see how "terrible" and "beat-up" she looked. Keeshin said she was shaking, had a cracked lip, a bruised hand and a Velcro strap girdling her ribs. Nancy also was "spacey and erratic" and said she didn't remember what had happened the day before.

Keeshin, who was staying at a nearby hotel, quickly returned to his daughter's apartment at 11 PM on the 6th, when he was alerted to the presence of the police. The officer in charge took him aside, showed him the search warrants and asked for the key to the storage area. Keeshin testified that the officer was "pretty sure" they knew where his son-in-law was.

It was at that time that he'd uttered the "Oh my God" exclamation, because it was then that he'd realized something might have happened to his son-in-law other than just his disappearance. When the police had informed him that they'd found the body, it was the first time he realized that Rob was dead.

Nancy was shaking so "violently" that he'd asked the

police to get an ambulance for her. He recalled looking out the window of the ambulance at a surreal sight.

"I . . . saw a parade of cops." Seeing more vehicles following them, Ira continued, "I thought, who could this be at one AM? And there was the press. I remember Nancy screaming when they went into the custodial ward . . . I broke down. It was very, very sad."

Chapman asked the dapper gray-haired Keeshin if his daughter had ever mentioned that she had been physically abused by Robert in the last five years. He replied that she'd never mentioned it to him.

Had he, asked the prosecutor, ever asked Nancy's domestic help where his son-in-law was? Keeshin replied that it had never occurred to him to ask that question of the two Filipino women.

Chapman asked Keeshin if his daughter had told him that she had made arrangements with the Parkview staff to store the carpet containing Robert's body in the building's storage area. Keeshin claimed he did not recall if she had told him that. Questioned whether he had made any queries about the location of his son-in-law following the call his daughter had made to him in Chicago on November 3, he replied, "I wasn't investigating anything. I was handling things, which I ended up doing the rest of the week."

Keeshin also claimed to have been a little fuzzy on details at the time, as he was jet-lagged from the long flight from Chicago and also "in shock."

With the cross-examination completed, Ira Keeshin stopped by the defense table, bent down and kissed his daughter goodbye. Two days later he caught a flight back to Chicago to take care of his baking business.

Nancy Nassberg, a friend of Nancy Kissel, was the next witness to testify for the defense. She said that in February

1999 she had asked Nancy why she was wearing dark sunglasses inside the apartment during a birthday party for the children. Nassberg related that Nancy had lowered the glasses to the tip of her nose, exposing a black eye, and said matter-of-factly, "Rough sex." Nancy Kissel had broken the embarrassing silence by nervously laughing, and changed the subject.

There was another time in late 1998 at the Hong Kong International School that Nassberg had noticed bruising on Nancy's face. When she asked what had happened, Nancy Kissel had dismissed the question by saying that the bruising was a result of horsing around with the kids.

Geertruida "Trudy" Samra was an employee of the U.S. Consulate in Hong Kong, and had provided the guarantee for the defendant's bail application. She told the court she had visited Nancy Kissel at the Siu Lam psychiatric center during "the very early days" of the accused's stay there. Samra recalled being shocked when Nancy asked her, "How's Rob?"

The consulate official told the defendant, "Honey, Rob's gone, you know that, right?" Samra said Nancy had replied that she "didn't remember much."

Samra also said she remembered times over the course of the five years she had known the Kissels that Rob had been critical of Nancy. Once Rob had been "on edge" at social gatherings at the Aberdeen Marina Club and reprimanded Nancy in front of everyone about her having no control over their children.

Pressed by defense attorney King, Samra recalled that she had seen three injuries to Nancy in 2002. All of them had been attributed to rough play with the children.

Samra described rushing to the Kissel apartment—she lived at the Parkview as well—on November 8 upon hearing that the police had found Rob's body. At first she'd thought Rob had had a heart attack.

"The door was wide open and I walked in." There were no guards outside the door, she testified. She saw policemen moving about the apartment and dogs searching the rooms.

It was clear what Alexander King was insinuating. In previous testimony given by Connie Macaraeg, she'd said that the police had not cordoned off the crime scene and that police, family and friends had been free to come and go as they pleased. Had the crime scene been tainted or compromised?

Chapman, in his cross of Samra, asked her if she'd been aware of her American friend's alleged suicidal tendencies and her affair with a younger man back in the States. Had she known of the plethora of sedatives Nancy had been prescribed? Claiming she had not known any of these things, Samra did say she'd known that Nancy was having "sleeping problems."

Pressed for an explanation on how she could not have known such things, considering her "close and enduring relationship" with the accused, Samra explained that she had not wanted to pry about what went on "behind closed doors." Samra reasoned that "the expat community in Parkview is very gossipy" and that Nancy may have wanted "to protect herself and her family."

The consulate official admitted that when she'd arrived at the apartment, Nancy had told her that "something terrible has happened to Rob."

A small procession of Nancy Kissel's friends testified on her behalf. All testified to her "level-headedness," to her being very involved in her children's school activities and that she was a wonderful mother. Two of them recalled having seen Nancy with a black eye.

Benedict Pasco, a computer expert for the defense, was called to the stand. He confirmed that the deceased had searched the Internet using the words "gay anal sex in Taiwan" on the family's home computer. The search was done when Nancy and the kids were not home in April 2003, a few days before a trip that Robert was to take to the island nation off the east coast of mainland China.

After a detailed explanation by Pasco on how his search had been conducted and what software was used, he said Mr. Kissel had apparently gone through several pages of Google results of his search. "Gay sex," "anal sex," "wife is a bitch," "twinks"—gay slang for attractive young or young-looking males, usually of slender build, only slightly muscular, with little or no body hair—and "Paris gay massage" were some of the searches that were made on the Internet.

Chapman, in cross-examination, asked Pasco if he had been instructed by Mrs. Kissel's defense team to look only for homosexual sites that may have been visited by the victim. He replied that that was the case. Chapman suggested that the analysis of the computer's hard drive was "incomplete."

The prosecutor also suggested that it was a possibility that a house guest, not necessarily Mr. Kissel, had made the web searches. Pasco agreed that it was.

The prosecution's cross-examination of Benedict Pasco continued on Monday. Chapman took note on the report in his hand, written by Pasco, that there seemed to be only two days out of two years of available data that was considered "relevant." He also asked if any gay pornographic web searches had been found on the deceased's IBM laptop. Pasco replied that he had found none.

The prosecutor asked Pasco about the installation of "porn-dialer" software, which allowed a user to dial up pornographic sites at faster speeds. Pasco noted that it had been installed on the family desktop on September 14, 2002. Chapman showed Pasco Mr. Kissel's travel itinerary and it showed that he had been out of town at that time.

"Whoever is responsible for installing the software . . . cannot be Robert Kissel?"

Pasco agreed.

In re-examination, Alexander King asked whether, if no

gay sex websites were found on Mr. Kissel's laptop, did that mean there hadn't been any? Pasco explained that he had found 226 pages of web searches on the family desktop, but only 15 pages on the IBM laptop. What that could mean, he said, was that the Internet history files on it could have been deleted by the user or someone who had access to it.

King pointed out to the jury that in the two days of "relevant material" found by Pasco that the user—Robert Kissel—had been on for an hour and a half each day.

Was it not true, King asked, that there was a large number of similarities on "anal sex" between the searches done on the family desktop and the deceased's laptop? Pasco said there were. Again the victim's travel itinerary was introduced, but this time it proved that he had been in town when those searches were made.

With the re-examination of Pasco complete, Alexander King made an announcement and set the court press corps scribbling frantically in their notepads when he told Judge Michael Lunn that the defense had presented their last witness. King had never disclosed at the beginning of the trial how many witnesses he was planning on calling, possibly to keep the prosecution off-balance and wary, making them subject to mistakes.

Judge Lunn turned to the jury of five men and two women and told them they would hear that same afternoon the prosecution's rebuttal evidence on the roles of the baseball bat and the metal statue seized by the police from the Parkview apartment.

DNA profiling expert Dr. Pang Chi-ming testified that there had been no blood found on the baseball bat allegedly wielded by Robert Kissel. There was also no "human material" found on the handle that belonged to the victim or the accused. He did, however, find some that belonged to an unidentified female.

King asked Judge Lunn for an early adjournment to

give him more time to consider how he was going to continue to cross-examine Dr. Pang. Lunn granted the request.

In his cross, King suggested that there may not have been more human material found had the bat not sat in storage for six months. Pang disputed that, saying it was likely that some human material would have been found. King then asked, "Are you saying, then, in the history of that bat, only one person has ever held the handle?"

Pang quickly replied, "I did not say that."

The next rebuttal witness called for the prosecution was Dr. Wong Koon-hung. Earlier in the trial Dr. Wong had been asked to determine if the indentation in the lead base of the alleged murder weapon had been caused by the blows of the bat.

From his most recent tests Wong concluded it was "doubtful" the bat had caused the indentation on the base of the statue that had delivered the fatal blows to Robert Kissel, although he could not definitely rule it out.

Dr. Wong said he would have expected to find wood grain patterns, paint or varnish smears on the ornament base and traces of lead on the bat. He found none. Also, in controlled experiments using lead sheets to re-create the bat blows on the ornament base, he found it unlikely that the baseball bat had caused the indentation.

In cross-examination by the defense, Wong was asked to produce the lead sheets from his first tests. He said that they couldn't be presented since the sheets had since been re-used.

Defense counsel King was able to get Dr. Wong to concede that if his tests on the baseball bat were flawed "in any significant way" then his conclusion would be, as well.

Wong, under withering questioning by King, admitted that he had not checked to see that the bats he'd used for the tests were made from the same wood as the Kissel bat. He said he'd chosen the test bats by relative appearance and weight. King pounced on the concession.

"You would agree, would you not, different woods, like different metals, have different hardness?"

Wong agreed that the type of wood possibly could make a difference, but disagreed with King's implication that his tests on the lead base indentation were skewed by poor testing criteria. Wong said he was pretty sure that those tests were valid.

On the 26th of August, gallery hopefuls lined up early on this Friday morning for a seat at the trial of the decade in the free-wheeling capitalist enclave of communist China. Hong Kong was all a-dither at the drama that had been going on for nearly three months and was drawing to a climactic ending. The prosecution was up first. Peter Chapman's task was to sum up the evidence given in the long drawn-out trial and convince the jury of seven that Nancy Kissel had planned her husband's murder to escape a "messy divorce," get his money, keep their children and be with the new "man in her life."

Chapman asked the jury to return a "true verdict" by finding Nancy Kissel guilty of murder. Chapman disputed the defense claim that the five fatal blows to Robert Kissel's head had been a result of a defensive "frenzy." It had in fact been a premeditated act committed when her husband was unable to defend himself.

"There was no provocation, no baseball bat. This is a cold-blooded killing."

The central issue in this case, according to the prosecutor, was Nancy Kissel's credibility. Chapman pointed a finger at the quiet and still lady in black, sitting next to her lawyer, and accused her of not being the picture of a compromising, self-sacrificing, and abused wife she portrayed herself as. She was not the victim of five humiliating years of sexual and physical abuse of a controlling sex-obsessed substance abuser. They were outrageous claims that not even her father could testify to.

Chapman referred to testimonies by witnesses early in

the trial who spoke of Robert Kissel as a loving, kind, soft-spoken husband who was well-regarded by his company.

The prosecutor said that the starting point of the "cold-blooded" murder case had begun on a family skiing vacation to the Canadian resort of Whistler near Vancouver, British Columbia, in December 2002. It was then that her friend and Robert's sister, Jane Clayton, had noticed how Nancy had distanced herself from her husband of thirteen years and had left early to return to Hong Kong. It was just a month later that Robert, suspicious of his wife, had installed spyware on the family computers to monitor her activity.

Chapman claimed it was on August 20, 2003, that the idea of poisoning her husband had come to his unhappy wife. It was then that the spyware had detected Internet searches made by the accused using such key words as "drug overdose." Chapman argued that it was her lover back in the United States, Michael DelPriore, who was the "catalyst" in the series of events that had led to the brutal bludgeoning to death of a drugged, defenseless Robert Kissel.

It was Frank Shea, the private investigator, who had confirmed the victim's worst fears. Robert Kissel's wife was indeed having an affair back in Vermont where she had gone to escape the SARS epidemic in Hong Kong in the spring of 2003. Just one month later, in June, Robert had begun to look into instigating divorce proceedings against her. The accused knew a "messy divorce" that involved adultery could last a long time, certainly long enough for Robert to change his will and the beneficiaries of his estimated $18 million estate. Her lover regarded Nancy Kissel as a "gold mine," something she certainly did not want to jeopardize.

Chapman said it had been proven that Nancy Kissel had gotten "four drugs in seven days."

"There was no possible medical reason for her to take them together. Whether the drugs were intended to kill or to subdue him was an open question, but they were employed successfully by Nancy Kissel."

Chapman claimed that Nancy had taken advantage of an opportunity when a neighbor, Andrew Tanzer, visited their apartment on November 2, 2003. It was then, the prosecutor said, that Nancy had drugged her husband. Said Chapman: "There was no life-or-death struggle. No one heard screaming, nor yelling, nor was there evidence of defensive injuries on the deceased."

On the alleged history of abuse, Chapman mused, "How well did they know Nancy Kissel?" He was speaking of her father Ira Keeshin, brother Brooks Keeshin, and friends Bryna O'Shea and Trudy Samra, all of whom had pled ignorance to Nancy's supposed suffering. They, her closest family members and friends, also had never known of her torrid affair with Michael DelPriore.

It was a "fabrication," Chapman said, about the forced and injurious sodomy perpetrated on her by her husband. Nancy Kissel had never sought out medical attention for the supposed attacks. What could the reason for this be? asked the prosecutor. He answered his own question: Because "It never happened."

Then there were the two different versions of the fatal encounter on the evening of November 2, the one she'd told her doctor, and the one she'd testified to in court. The one she'd given in court months later was calculated to conveniently explain the discrepancies of her earlier explanations of what had happened.

On the days following that fatal Sunday, Chapman said, "The purchase of the new rugs and boxes" spoke "so loudly, so incriminatingly, of her intent to cover up."

Noting that it was now 3:30 PM on a Friday and how it was "the worst time to start," Alexander King nevertheless outlined his closing arguments for the jury. It would give the panel of seven an inkling of what they could expect on Monday.

"We say she is not guilty because in the course of events, Mrs. Kissel acted in lawful self-defense." The "circumstantial evidence," he said, pointed conclusively in the direction of the defense and, like a rope, "when you put all the strands together, it's strong enough to rely upon."

Alexander King took center stage in Hong Kong's High Court of the First Instance on Monday morning, August 29. For the entire day he would have it to himself.

Dressed in her usual black, Nancy Kissel watched intently as her lawyer laid out the defense's case in front of the standing-room-only crowd. Occasionally she would dab her eyes with a tissue. She was the picture of innocence, or at least she tried to be.

King's task was to explain why his client had pleaded not guilty by reason of self-defense to murdering her husband. He asked the jury to use their "common sense" and realize that the prosecution was trying to portray the case as a "colliding of universes."

Apparently William Kissel, the father of the victim, had heard enough. He got up from his seat and stormed out of the courtroom.

King continued.

"The prosecution would have you believe," he said, that the "cheating, ungrateful, plotting, scheming wife" had laid down a murderous plan.

He said that at the same time, Robert Kissel had been planning to tell his wife that he was going to divorce her. This, the prosecution claimed, culminated on the fatal night of November 2, 2003, when Nancy Kissel had sprung her trap.

King called the motive attributed to his client by the prosecution "a classic—money, love, lust and sex."

King feigned umbrage when he spoke of how the government's case attempted to paint Nancy's lover, Michael DelPriore, as "someone living a wretched life, eyeing up wealthy people" as a mark. DelPriore, according to the prosecution, had tacitly encouraged this pre-meditated murder of his rival. "Pure speculation," King uttered indignantly.

King also pointed out that Michael DelPriore had never even been captured on the surveillance video shot by Rocco Gatta, the investigator who had been hired by Robert Kissel. All the video showed was a "beautiful countryside," a "very expensive home" and an unattended van parked in the street.

The defense counsel put forward that Robert Kissel had been looking for an excuse to divorce his wife of fourteen years in a way that would not cost him so dearly. That is why he obsessively spied on her. King claimed that the deceased knew that if his wife filed for divorce on the grounds of spousal abuse, the proceedings would get "ugly, dirty and messy." His career as a prominent, successful American expatriate in Hong Kong would come "crashing down." Because of his controlling nature, King said, premeditation had to be ruled out by common sense. The argument that night had escalated from a yelling match over custody of the children into a deadly struggle in which Nancy Kissel had defended herself, killing her husband in the process. Yes, the accused had dealt five fatal blows to the head of the crazed investment banker, but only when she'd realized he intended to harm her.

King harped on the fact that a "family heirloom" was the murder weapon. He asked whether such an instrument of death would have been picked had the murder been premeditated.

Where in the e-mails, the attorney asked, was it indicated that Nancy Kissel and Michael DelPriore were nefariously planning on a life together? King didn't recall either of the two writing, "Oh my darling, we will soon be together."

Nancy Kissel did not kill her husband for money, claimed King. It was "nonsense" to say she'd planned to maintain that her husband had simply disappeared. No insurance company would be stupid enough to pay off on such a claim. "Their investigation would be a lot more thorough than the investigation conducted in this trial."

King claimed that if Nancy Kissel really had wanted a

lot of his money, she would have simply stayed in Vermont at their expensive retreat in the mountains, saying, "Sorry, Robert, I'm not coming home, I'm filing for divorce." But she didn't. When her husband called and asked her to come home, she "quickly" did.

About the disposal of the body, the defense counsel said that the "bizarre" actions by the defendant proved the killing wasn't pre-meditated, but that she'd had a "meltdown in her mental condition."

Why the rug? he asked. King said no one would ever do as Nancy had done, and festoon the carpet with such brightly colored cushions, making it unforgettable, if she'd had the intention of hiding it. King mocked the idea that after a pre-meditated murder, Nancy Kissel would spend two nights in a bedroom with the decomposing body of her husband.

On the other hand, King said, Robert Kissel wanted to be in "total control" at all times.

Had he not known that his marriage was in trouble as early as December 2002?

"Did he use his usual energy to say, 'Right, let's go to marriage counselors and sort it out'? What did he do? He installed spyware so that six times a day Robert Kissel could check on his wife."

King then pointed out to the jury that the spyware had been installed in the family computers before Nancy had even met Michael DelPriore.

"The truth," King insisted, "is unpleasant, is brutal." He was a man, who, according to Internet records, "in advance of traveling to destinations, is looking to procure gay sexual services."

Robert Kissel was a man who had became incensed when he was on the unfamiliar receiving end of a beating, screaming, "I'm going to fucking kill you, bitch!"

The jury listened intently as King told them that they could not rely upon the police investigation beyond a reasonable doubt because they'd acted as if it "was an open-and-shut case," making only "cursory glances," which had resulted in unanswered questions and tainted evidence.

The police had not given the accused "a simple application of legal rights," forcing them to maintain "the stupid and ridiculous story about investigating a missing person." This was despite the grilling cross-examinations Nancy Kissel had been forced to endure.

King claimed it had been a "substandard" investigation that missed crucial evidence, failed to secure the crime scene and was run on the false pretense of being a missing persons investigation.

King, in a self-congratulatory mood, claimed that if he had not discovered the baseball bat, it would not be available to consider as evidence. Continuing, he said there had been no fingerprinting tests done on the bat because it was covered with police latents, as they had examined and discarded it.

On Tuesday, Alexander King continued to attack the prosecution's case against Nancy Kissel.

King said that the police were so sure of Mrs. Kissel's guilt that a proper investigation was not done, and therefore one was not presented to the jury. Calling it an investigation that lacked coherence, King cited the botched blood stain analysis and poor photographs of the crime scene as reasons to doubt the state's investigative conclusions. He also faulted the prosecution's toxicology findings, saying it could not prove if the victim was "one, unconscious, or two, so severely impaired that he could not defend himself."

The testimony of witnesses and the security camera, King said, should make the jury conclude that the victim was not "drugged, unconscious, or severely impaired," since he'd been seen, apparently sober, just prior to the deadly argument. King concluded that "evidence all points to the direction that [Robert Kissel] didn't receive the same dose as Mr. Tanzer."

The prosecution, King said, claimed that the accused's shopping spree for drugs proved that the doping and murder of her husband had been planned. The sedatives Rohypnol, Lorivan and Stilnox and the anti-depressant amitriptyline had not been requested by the accused, but prescribed to her by her doctors.

"But of course," King said, "they didn't call Dr. Fung or Dr. Dytham to explain why they had prescribed those drugs."

King, to cast any lingering doubts aside, reminded the jury that doctors Fung and Dytham had testified for the defense that they'd prescribed the sedatives for Nancy Kissel's sleep problems and depression from marital abuse.

The "abusive relationship in which Robert Kissel inflicted physical violence on his wife," claimed King, was substantiated by Nancy's friends, who'd seen the bruises, black eyes and signs of rib injury.

After a day and a half summarizing his defense of Nancy Kissel and casting doubt on the prosecution's case, Alexander King asked the jury of seven to return a "true verdict" of "not guilty to murder."

He took his seat at the defense end of the table just before the lunch break.

Judge Michael Lunn wasted no time. He turned to the jury and began with his instructions.

Lunn told the jury that before they returned a verdict of guilty of murder they had to be individually sure that the defendant had the intention to kill, before and during the fatal event, and that she did not do so in lawful self-defense.

First Judge Lunn summarized the prosecution's case.

Nancy Kissel is accused of killing her husband by "smashing his skull with five separate blows to the upper right side of his head, each one of the blows fatal. Fractured skull bone was driven into the brain," causing "massive spillage of brain substance."

Judge Lunn said the jurors could also consider a reduced verdict of manslaughter by reason of provocation if they believed the victim had caused his wife to "suddenly and temporarily lose her self-control."

He continued by saying that the prosecution had claimed that the accused could do this because Robert Kissel and a neighbor were "sufficiently impaired by a cocktail of drugs" disguised as milkshakes and served to them by Mrs. Kissel.

The Internet searches by the accused, the prosecution had claimed were proof positive of Nancy Kissel's intent to kill, as were the drugs prescribed to her, which were found in the victim's stomach. So, too, was the fact that the amorous relationship between Nancy and Michael DelPriore and the victim's enormous estate of $18 million were at stake, and the incriminating actions by Nancy Kissel after the fatal struggle, including her testimony in court, which the prosecution contended were evidence of her "spinning a web of lies."

As to the defense of Nancy Kissel, Judge Lunn said, they'd claimed Nancy Kissel had killed Robert Kissel in lawful self-defense when her husband had made "taunting and provocative statements" and attempted to forcibly have anal sex with her while threatening her with a baseball bat.

Judge Lunn recapped how the defense's premise was that the defendant had feared for her life and killed Robert Kissel with the statue, which she'd first used to defend herself from the blows of the bat.

Lunn also noted that the defense had made much of Robert Kissel's perusal of gay sex sites on the Internet when his family was out of town. This buttressed the defendant's contention that her husband had routinely "forced anal sex on her."

Judge Lunn reminded the jury that the prosecution did not have to prove a motive in a charge of murder, but it can suggest an explanation "to satisfy natural curiosity." He advised the panel of seven that killing in self-defense can at times be lawful and that it can even make "good sense," so long as it is done with "such force as reasonably necessary to defend [oneself]."

The jury was instructed that if they did not believe the

victim had brought on the deadly attack by his conduct, they should convict the accused of murder. But, he added, if the victim's conduct could "cause the defendant of such age and sex to do what she did," a verdict of manslaughter should be returned.

The good character of the accused, as testified to by friends at the Hong Kong International School and the United Jewish Congregation, could be taken into consideration by the jury in determining the credibility of the evidence given. He added, "If you think self-defense may be true, you may acquit."

The credibility of oral testimony by its consistency was important to consider, Lunn said. He cited Ira Keeshin's seemingly conflicting statements on first learning of his daughter's alleged abuse. In an early police statement, he'd said he first heard of it in a phone conversation on November 3, 2003. Yet in court just a month ago, Lunn said, Keeshin had testified to having heard of it back in 2002. When the discrepancy was pointed out to him by prosecutor Chapman in cross-examination, Keeshin had said his oral testimony was incorrect.

The judge mentioned that the toxicologist for the prosecution had testified that he'd never seen such a combination of drugs in the stomach contents of a victim. But Lunn added that the government lab could only test for trace elements, and there was no way to know what effects the drugs may have had on Robert Kissel.

On his second day of summation of the trial, Lunn said that the alleged "meltdown" of Nancy Kissel, according to the defense, had to be viewed in light of the way she'd carried out what the prosecution called her "cover-up" activities. Lunn cited the defendant's shopping spree after the killing, the witnesses' accounts of her behavior, i.e. wearing dark glasses, her "normal," but "a little loud" manner, the visit to the homepage of the HKPD on missing persons, and the ordering of the moving boxes. There were also the phone calls with her American friend Bryna O'Shea, who'd described Nancy as "forcing herself to sound upset" when she claimed that she had been beaten and Rob had disappeared. Lunn also reminded the jury that the accused had refused to cancel her breast lift surgery as suggested by O'Shea.

The judge made a point that no one questioned the generous time the defendant gave to her children's school and their house of worship, the United Jewish Congregation.

It was time to hand the case to the jury. At 12:30 PM they were asked to decide whether Nancy Kissel was a cold-hearted and calculating murderess or the victim of, as the Hong Kong tabloid the *Guardian* wrote, a "cocaine-snorting, whisky-swilling, abusive, workaholic monster who frequently forced her to have anal sex."

At 8:30 PM, on Thursday, September 1, 2005, the jury filed back into High Court #33 ready to reveal their decision regarding the guilt of the accused. It had been eighty-six days since the start of the trial and twenty-two months since the death of the victim. The jury had only taken seven hours to reach their decision.

No one in the packed courtroom stirred or even cleared a throat as the foreman of the seven-person panel stood to read the verdict.

When asked of the jury's decision by Judge Michael Lunn, the foreman simply said, "Guilty."

Nancy Kissel, sitting next to her attorney Alexander King, showed no emotion as the verdict was read.

Judge Lunn wasted no time in sentencing the felon. Nancy Kissel stood before him and he addressed her:

"As I am required to do so by law, I impose a sentence of life imprisonment upon you."

With that, the lady in black lowered her head, and was handcuffed and led away by four officers of the Correctional Services Department. She wasn't permitted by the officers to embrace her mother, Jean McGlothlin, as she usually did upon conclusion of the day's proceedings.

Judge Lunn then thanked the jurors for sitting with patience and care while listening to the "gruesome details of the circumstances in which Robert Kissel met his death." He then proceeded to reward them an extra HK$280 (U.S. $36) a day for their service and exempted them for jury duty for fifteen years.

CHAPTER THIRTEEN

Defense counsel Alexander King left the building without giving a statement, but did say when asked that an appeal was likely.

Prosecutor Peter Chapman was inclined to agree with his opponent's assessment: "It's only chapter one of the Kissel case. Chapter two will start on the third floor of this court building—the Court of Appeal. The fat lady has not started singing yet."

Whether King would be the lead attorney in the appeal was an open question. It was rumored that he had been paid $1.5 million for his services in the sixty-six-day trial. The money had reportedly come from Nancy's father, Ira Keeshin.

A small throng of people, mostly family and friends of the defendant and of the deceased, reporters, photographers and the curious waited in the stuffy lobby outside the courtroom on the thirteenth floor. The edginess in the air was almost palpable for what one Hong Kong journalist called "the OJ Simpson murder trial and the Michael Jackson child abuse drama rolled into one," and "a wild American soap opera transplanted to Asia."

Adding to the tension of the crowd was an earlier exchange between Bill Kissel, father of the victim, and former American reporter for ABC TV Jim Laurie. Laurie, now a guest lecturer at the University of Hong Kong had acted as an informal advisor to the defendant. His wife was a friend of Nancy Kissel and a potential character witness for the defense.

Laurie had asked Bill Kissel in a loud, accusatory voice if the Kissel children would be permitted to visit their mother.

"What do you think?" hollered back Kissel, "She's killed her husband and now she's condemned her children" to an unhappy life. Kissel also accused the defense team of attempting to portray his son as a sodomist and a drug and alcohol abuser. Just because Laurie had lived in the same building, it didn't mean he knew Robert Kissel, Bill said. "What puts you in a position to judge?"

Laurie shouted back that it was "impossible to know what happened" in the relationship.

"Are you going to write a book now," replied Kissel, "and say Nancy is innocent?"

Mr. Kissel had also told the assembled press that his daughter-in-law was "not a moral person," adding, "This is a coward."

Bill Kissel seemed to be relieved when he spoke publicly about the trial outcome:

"That's justice. All the allegations [by the defense] made in court are false, untrue. And Robert, I pray, can now rest in peace and his children can go on with their lives in peace knowing their father loved them and they are his dear children."

Mr. Kissel was more unrestrained about the ordeal in an e-mail to the author:

Dear Mr. McMurray,

I sat in a courtroom for four months and listened to a pack of lies and ravings from a woman who said she killed my son, Robert. She then went on to say that she loved him, and would not do anything to hurt her children.

She then commenced to malign the father of her children, and her husband in a most vile and calculated way to save herself.

The trial lasted for 66 days. In less than one-half day, the jury returned with a unanimous vote of GUILTY. This mandated life in prison. . . .

She went for the whole enchilada because she was advised that this would make her the "poster girl" for "abused women." . . .

Was a life sentence too much? Yes, you are correct in one sense. Had this been under Chinese law, they would have taken her outside and shot her . . .

This woman has ruined all the lives around her; her own, her children, her father, her mother, mine and many more.

She now refuses to see her father [and] never talks or seems to care about her children.

What is there to say? It has been said. We, the world, do not need anyone to judge for themselves. There has been a judgment.

William J. Kissel

After the verdict was handed down, Mr. Kissel was asked by the Hong Kong reporters what his immediate plans were. He answered that he planned to visit his son's grave back in New Jersey, "where he can now rest in peace."

Trial pundits were as unanimous as the jury in concurring on the verdict. Barrister Kevin Egan was quoted in the *Standard* as saying that to get a different verdict would have taken a jury of "cuckoos from Connecticut and neurotics from New York."

Jean McGlothlin, Nancy Kissel's mother, when approached by the press for comments, admitted to being "a little stunned." She was embraced by her daughter Nancy's friends, some of whom had testified on her behalf. Mc-

Glothlin thanked the press "for the respect you have shown me and my family."

Two stunning revelations were made upon the trial's conclusion that couldn't be divulged while it was in progress for fear of prejudicing the outcome. One was the revocation of Nancy Kissel's bail back on August 11, after she had finished testifying. No reason was given, but it was assumed it was done because she had finally admitted killing her husband. The Hong Kong authorities didn't want an admitted killer freely walking the streets of their city.

The issue of entering the baseball bat into evidence by the defense was the other. It was midway through the prosecution's case when it was revealed that the bat had been found and removed from the Kissel apartment by the defense team and kept in their offices without notifying the police or the prosecutor's office. Apparently Judge Lunn was none too happy about the surprise submission of the evidence in the midst of an ongoing trial. He announced that he had ordered the trial transcripts that pertained to the "mystery bat" to be sent to the director of public prosecutions "for directions as he sees fit."

Without the jury's knowledge Judge Lunn had noted his astonishment that the defense had not notified the court until that stage, given "the significance of the baseball bat."

According to trial watchers Nancy Kissel had gone to great lengths to appear the traumatized, battered wife that she claimed she was. Seated in court, her shoulders were always slumped forward with her eyes cast downward. At opportune times she would quietly weep and dab her eyes with a tissue and avoid making eye contact with anybody. According to one witness, during a break in the trial one day, Nancy Kissel let her guard down.

Outside the courtroom were two glassed-in conference rooms that flanked each side of the entrance doors. The room to the left was used by the prosecution team and police, the one on the right by the defense team. The large glass partitions were tinted to afford some privacy to the occupants—if the glaring overhead lights inside the room were off. This particular time they were not.

Nancy, as per her usual routine, sullenly walked into the room in a dejected slouch. Once the door was shut, out of the public view—she thought—she straightened up and began to aggressively and accusedly point her finger at her defense team. She appeared to be haranguing them over something that had happened in court. Either it was pointed out to her that the lights were on and she could be seen, or she realized it herself. She abruptly ended the scene and sat down in one of the chairs and hunched forward in the familiar slouch.

Although it was never revealed in court, the *Sunday Morning Post* reported that Nancy Kissel may have been planning to clandestinely ship her husband's dismembered body back to the United States three days after his murder. Nancy had contacted Links Relocations, a moving company, for a quote on shipping the contents of her Parkview apartment and storage room. An employee of the company confirmed that Nancy Kissel had indeed called them on November 5, the same day she'd had Robert's body taken down to the storage area.

After the discovery of Robert's body and Nancy's arrest, the contents of the apartment were prepared for boxing and removal back to the States. A butcher's saw and a heavy duty clipper were found in Reis' closet under some clothes. Speculation had it that Nancy had planned to cut up Robert's body and ship the dismembered parts back to the United States in the boxes she had purchased the day after the murder.

There was also a videotape of a tryst of Nancy's, shot in Vermont by Alpha Group investigator Rocco Gatta, that was never shown in court. In the video an unidentified person walks onto the Kissel property late at night after parking his van down the street, slips in a side door of the garage and climbs the stairs to the guest bedroom over the carports. He is joined there by Nancy Kissel, who has come in from the house entrance. Minutes later Nancy's bare feet and legs can be clearly seen stretched up into the air in a sexual pose.

The prosecution decided against showing the tawdry video to the jury.

"It wasn't necessary," said someone who had seen the tape. "The testimony of Rocco Gatta watching the house was sufficient to establish that she wasn't baking a pie."

As for Michael DelPriore, he was home free, literally and figuratively. On September 6 the Western District Police Commander David Madoc-Jones dismissed as "incorrect rumors" that the HKPD was continuing its investigation of Michael DelPriore. Having found no evidence of his direct link to the murder, the police never filed charges against him, convinced from immigration records that he had never visited Hong Kong before or after the murder.

Telephone records, however, did show the two had talked prior to and after the murder, but what was said remained a mystery. Said Madoc-Jones, "Unless they decide to tell us what was said in those conversations, and in the absence of any direct evidence, there is nothing we can do."

One of the puzzles of the case was how Nancy had known to purchase, then wrap Robert's battered body in, polypropylene to prevent body fluid leakage while inside the carpet. Investigator See later found out that poly-wrapping animal carcasses was common knowledge in Vermont when transporting them in motor vehicles. It was proven by telephone records that Nancy had called her lover, who lived in Vermont, the day after she bludgeoned her husband to death.

After his brother Michael's affair with Nancy Kissel was exposed, Lance DelPriore was bombarded with interview requests from newspapers, magazines and TV tabloid shows, which descended on Brattleboro for scoops on the romantic link that may have turned Nancy into a murderer.

Lance had had no communications with his brother since he'd fired him. He'd heard from the grapevine that Mike had again married. But when the articles began to appear in the papers where Lance was, according to him, "misquoted," Mike showed up at his house.

Lance told his brother to get off his property. Mike said he hoped Lance had been misquoted, because he didn't like what the papers claimed were Lance's words. Lance told him to "shut up and leave." Mike left without uttering another word.

If the murder of Rob Kissel had been committed in the States, Lance was convinced Mike would have been arrested as a potential accomplice. He had remembered something his brother Ronny had told him. Some months before Mike had said he would be able to retire with plenty of money by the time he reached his early forties. Since Mike was already 41 at the time, and knowing how much he made working, this raised the question of where all the retirement money was coming from—Rob Kissel?

Lance and Mary are certain that Mike was somehow, perhaps even unwittingly, involved in the murder of Robert Kissel. The convicted murderer doesn't call her lover the day before the bloodbath and the day after without involving him in some form or another.

Lance and Mike's relationship remained strained for other reasons as well. Lance was annoyed that his brother never apologized to him or his wife for anything—and he had stolen from them. Mike had told their brother Ronny that the reason for his thefts from the business was that Lance had underpaid him. Lance believed he treated his brother "too well." He was generous with pay and benefits, had helped him relocate north, put him and his wife up in his and Mary's house for nine months, loaned him the down payment for a home and even given him one of Lance's prize possessions, a 1971 Corvette sports car. How did Mike repay them? He stole money and time from Lance, lied and had an affair with a customer's wife.

An experienced investigator who attended the trial and wishes to remain anonymous, because at the time of this writing the case is under appeal, took a jaundiced eye on Nancy Kissel's defense tactics. On her alleged sexual abuse, he told the author:

"The problem with her testimony [on the forcible anal sex allegation] was that she never went for any medical treatment and she never confided in any friends or her mother. Although it is not uncommon for sexual assault victims to keep the details to themselves, the events as described by her would have necessitated treatment."

He also thought the testimony by the defense's computer expert would have been laughable had it not dealt with so serious a crime. He drew from considerable forensic computer experience in his analysis.

"If a person were to put in a search term such as 'boys' the returns would have included everything from little league to pornography—in other words, the search results can be manipulated by the examiner. When presenting the results to the jury, Nancy's attorneys displayed only the highly explosive sexually referenced returns, but did not disclose that the evidence was highly questionable, if not unethical. The prosecution rebutted and explained how the searches had been conducted and was successful in making it clear to the jury how biased the defense presentation of the search terms were."

This expert's opinion certainly could be construed as prejudiced since he'd worked on the case for the prosecution, but it cannot be said that it transcended common sense and Internet literacy.

The question that begs for answer is, if it was Nancy Kissel's intention to murder her husband to get all his money by avoiding a messy divorce, how could she—an intelligent, educated, sophisticated woman—be so sloppy in committing the crime? A source close to the investigation has an opinion, which was shared by many of the trial watchers, on why Nancy had bludgeoned Robert to death.

"Clearly her initial intent was to slowly poison her husband so that his death would appear to be a result of a heart attack. It wasn't working. She was losing her patience and was rattled by frustration. An impending divorce would draw scrutiny and would lend motive for murder. She had to act fast, so she beat the unconscious man to death and concocted the spousal abuse defense. Thankfully the jury didn't buy it."

Nancy Kissel was turned over to the Hong Kong Correctional Services Department. She was interned in the top-security Tai Lam Institute for Women, one of five prisons in the system. There are 600 inmates in the prison near the China border, with eighty-one of them being "other nationals." She is in a seven-by-seven–foot "cellular accommodation" and is allowed a daily hour of outdoor exercise. Hong Kong prisons, although spartan and overcrowded, are considered to be quite safe compared to their American counterparts. The overcrowding has been blamed on the huge influx of prostitutes from the Asian mainland.

On September 28, the firm of Mallesons Stephen Jaques, which represented Nancy Kissel, lodged an appeal against the High Court ruling that found their client guilty of murder. Among other things cited, the appeal challenged the summing up of evidence and the directions Judge Michael Lunn gave to the jury.

If Kissel is not granted an appeal, her life sentence will automatically be reviewed every two years thereafter by a government board. The board then would recommend to the city's chief executive that the sentence be commuted to a fixed term. The inmate can then seek an early release after serving two-thirds of the term.

Nancy Kissel can also seek, after any appeal, to serve out her sentence in a U.S. federal penitentiary. Bryna

O'Shea believes Nancy is better off in the Hong Kong prison, saying she would "never last" in the predatory U.S. prison system.

Jane Clayton and William Kissel want her to remain in Hong Kong prison as well—but not for humanitarian reasons. They believe Nancy's incarceration in a faraway prison is best for her children.

If Nancy Kissel had pled guilty to manslaughter, she would have been sentenced to 25 years and be paroled out after 8 years, when she would be 49 years old.

In Tai Lam, Nancy Kissel can receive visitors twice a month for fifteen minutes each. When she is taken to and from the claustrophobic cell, she is always reminded of her fate, because on the door a sign in English and Chinese reads "Lifer."

CHAPTER FOURTEEN

"It was the worst feeling in the world," Bryna would later say, "testifying against my friend." But, as she said, she had to look at the "big picture." She had to do what she believed was right and she didn't have any options. Bryna does not believe that Rob beat Nancy, nor that he tried to have sex with her while still recovering from back surgery. She also didn't believe all the "stupid stuff" that was being said at the trial by the defense. Bryna loved and knew Nancy, but couldn't stand up for her. She remembered the conversation she had had with Rob weeks before, when he'd told her he thought Nancy was trying to kill him. After Nancy's arrest, Bryna recalled that conversation and how it was "freaking her out" that she was the only one who knew that. She knew she would have to tell the Hong Kong authorities.

Bryna misses her friend terribly and can not get any information from Jean McGlothlin about how "Nan" is holding up in prison. Bryna used to "hang" with Jean and her husband when they visited New York, and they were great friends. Now Jean refuses to talk to Bryna.

"I'm the bad guy," Bryna said, "for having to have to testify against Nancy."

Bryna wonders what they would have done if they'd been in her situation, speaking to both sides—Rob and Nancy—knowing that one was lying.

Bryna doesn't care what "middle America" thinks about this case. To the people who knew and loved Rob and Nancy, they were great people, a loving couple and wonderful parents who had a tragedy befall them. She doesn't know how Nan could live with herself.

"Nan was as far away from being evil as one can ever think," Bryna said.

In retrospect, Bryna O'Shea can only think of one reason why Nancy Kissel killed her husband. "She had to be crazy," she reasoned. The only cause for the insanity, she believes, is postpartum depression.

Vivien Burt, M.D., is the director of the Women's Life Center at the UCLA Medical Center in Los Angeles, California. She is a nationally recognized expert in postpartum depression and is often consulted by attorneys on the subject when preparing for trial.

Dr. Burt says most of the cases brought to her involve infants turning up abandoned or found dead in Dumpsters. Public defenders usually handle these cases where the mother is charged with the abandonment or murder, and think that postpartum depression may often be the reason for such an unfathomable offense. Her answer is almost always that they will have to go elsewhere for help.

"Postpartum depression begins during the first month following childbirth and generally lasts for the same time span as major depression occurring at other times . . . about nine months to eighteen months, usually around twelve months. Postpartum psychosis arises during the first few days and has a variable course . . . generally involves auditory hallucinations, delusions (fixed beliefs not based in reality) of paranoia, persecution, etc.—postpartum psychosis is presumed to be a variant of bipolar disorder (manic depression)—often patient exhibit strange behavior, a mixture of depression alternating with grandiosity and psychosis (hallucinations, delusions, etc.), inability to sleep, super-surges of energy, irritability, racing thoughts, agitation."

Simply put, postpartum depression is a major depression occurring after childbirth. Major depression, Dr. Burt explains, is a clinical uni-polar depression that needs to be treated with anti-depressant drugs and psychotherapy. According to Burt, one out of six Americans suffers from clinical depression. Pessimism, guilt, lack of motivation, or suicidal thoughts are symptoms of this mental disorder.

Longitudinally, over the years if this depression is alternately mixed with manic episodes of euphoria, elatedness, social inappropriateness, racing thoughts, sleeplessness and grandiosity, the prognosis is postpartum psychosis.

In case studies of postpartum psychotics, bi-polar disorders were often never diagnosed. To date, neither Nancy Kissel nor her family have ever admitted to her being treated for any mental disorder. According to Burt, that was the case with Andrea Yates and her intentional drowning of her five children in Texas. It was a psychotic episode in a postpartum state, a classic case of postpartum psychosis.

Regarding the murder of Robert Kissel, Dr. Burt says, considering the circumstance surrounding the homicide, and that Nancy left Rob's body in the bed for three days, it smacks of being a "psychotic episode."

"It is so bizarre," says Burt, "that it defies understanding."

The fact that Nancy Kissel was carrying on an affair adds a "curious wrinkle." If this was out of character for her, Dr. Burt would attempt to put it together with what later happened. If Dr. Burt had been treating her as her psychiatrist, she would have asked if Nancy was going through long periods having difficulty sleeping, experiencing "super-surges of energy" and felt more beautiful and sexual than she had ever felt before. The cause for such behavior could be that Nancy Kissel was bi-polar.

Dr. Burt explains that the postpartum time in a woman's life is a vulnerable time for them. Of all the illnesses that put women at the greatest risk with postpartum difficulties is bi-polar disorder or manic depression. The common manifestation of it after childbirth is depression mixed with feelings of grandiosity. Women who are in this mania or mixed state typically make poor judgments, they are impulsive, spend money frivolously, feel very "sexualized" and engage in affairs that they would never normally consider.

Nancy Kissel's behavior once she returned to Hong Kong in the days leading up to the events of November 2 makes Dr. Burt wonder if she was indeed suffering from postpartum psychosis. If Nancy's affair and murderous rampage was totally out of character, she may have become increasingly psychotic and delusional.

There is one major flaw in the postpartum depression/psychosis theory. Nancy Kissel's youngest child, son Reis, was two years old. Dr. Burt said this about that:

"PPP arises within days following childbirth and would not be ignored for years, only to be discovered years after delivery. Of course, if the woman with PPP was actually bipolar, it is true that her illness would be lifelong."

Dr. Burt thinks there may be another explanation. Nancy Kissel may have been a woman filled with a lot of rage. Once she acted out her rage, she could have become "paralyzed with fear," and then three days later, when faced with the reality that the body would have to be removed, wrapped it in the rug and had it carried to the basement.

Dr. Dominic Lee, a professor of psychiatry at the Chinese University of Hong Kong, has another theory on why Nancy Kissel committed such a heinous, unconscionable act. Dr. Lee has studied the expatriate community and, although many expatriate families are quite happy, the eighty-hour work weeks and spur-of-the-moment business trips to Tokyo, Bangkok and New York can put "enormous strain on family life."

Certainly the benefits look too good to be true, says Lee, with "the $1 million paychecks, luxury cars and up-scale apartments staffed with maids and cooks, but the high-flying lifestyle often requires serious sacrifice." The sacrifice can take the form of depression brought on by a sense of isolation. Lee wrote:

"The single most important issue is that many expat families don't have family or friends in Hong Kong. This is particularly depressing for the wife."

Lee says advancing computer and Internet technology enabling cheap telephone and video conferencing with home easier and faster has helped alleviate some of the problems; but in Nancy's case it might have aggravated them. It may have been the e-mails and cell phone calls between her and her lover, Michael DelPriore, that put her into the mindset that ultimately led her to murder her husband.

Bryna got a surprise e-mail from 8-year-old June, the middle Kissel child, not long ago. In a few brief sentences she asked:

> *"Do you love my mommy?"*
> *"We're you and my mommy best friends?"*
> *"Do you miss my mommy?"*

At first Bryna thought some prying journalist had gotten hold of her address and was trying to worm some information out of her. Bryna called Connie, the kids' nanny. She told her about the strange e-mail and her suspicions, but Connie assured her that it had come from June and put June on the phone. Bryna then answered the little girl's questions, saying that June's mommy would always be in her heart and that she loved her. She didn't go into anything else.

It broke Bryna's heart trying to make sense of such an out-of-character, heinous act by her beloved friend to a child who was the progeny of this evildoer. She knew it was an impossible task. Saying good-bye, Bryna slowly returned the receiver to its cradle, hung her head, covered her face with her hands and wept bitterly.

PART THREE

DOWNWARD SPIRAL

CHAPTER FIFTEEN

Nancy Walkley, an intense-looking woman on the long side of 40, has a focused stare framed by conservative, no-nonsense spectacles that gives one the impression that much doesn't escape a sharp eye for detail. An unfailingly polite and pleasant demeanor masks a self-described "suspicious nature" honed, she says, by a ravenous appetite for true crime books and detective novels that are rife with red herrings and convoluted plots. Her suspicious nature, no doubt, serves her well in her profession: a title attorney. Nancy Walkley was the one who brought down Andrew Kissel's mansions of cards.

Walkley initially began her career in law as a real estate attorney at the height of the land boom in the 1980s. She found it satisfying and financially rewarding, and she never had to stand in front of the court's bench. Courtroom appearances were confrontational and she "hated it." Then came the collapse of the market in the early 1990s. Developers went bankrupt, banks went under and that wasn't good for any lawyer in a real estate practice. Walkley found herself in court pursuing foreclosure actions. She did not like the work.

Fortunately one of her clients was Chase Manhattan Bank, which at the time was taking over two failed banks

in Bridgeport, Connecticut. Chase, she learned, was opening a subsidiary corporation to liquidate the assets of the
failed banks for the Federal Deposit Insurance Corporation
(FDIC). Walkley applied for the job of in-house lawyer,
and got it. She stayed for three years, until Chase decided
to move the operation into New York City. Walkley
dreaded the prospect of a long commute from her home in
suburban Trumbull, Connecticut. She knew it would certainly upset the routine of her other job, housewife and
mother of two school-aged children. She left Chase to run
a title company office in nearby Stamford. After six years
she left to oversee a Fidelity Title office in her hometown.
It was while there that she became familiar with the name
of Andrew Kissel.

Title insurance is a fairly complicated business best left
in the hands of attorneys with expertise in real estate law.
By statute in Connecticut, unlike most states, title agents
must be attorneys. Walkley had a stable of attorneys/title
agents throughout the state of Connecticut who brought her
real estate titles to insure. Developers, real estate investors,
speculators and banks, by the nature of their business, tend
to stay with one, sometimes two, title agents. They develop
a business relationship and a trust that they nurture. It's a
comfort factor business-to-business that is common in the
fast-moving world of real estate.

One of Walkley's agents, just engaged by a real estate
investor by the name of Andrew Kissel in May of 2005,
heaped praise on his new client, who had been referred to
him by a builder–architect friend. He gushed on how
Kissel was a "great guy with a great net worth." The agent
assured her this would be "an easy loan" for him. The lot
was a "tear-down," real estate business-speak for a lot
where the older home has been demolished so it could be
replaced by a larger, modern-equipped domicile with a
staggering price tag. Large new homes were routinely
snapped up quickly in toney Greenwich.

Initially the search came up clean. There were no

mortgages on the property. It was not unusual to find a free and clear property title in Greenwich, where investors had the wherewithal to pay large sums of cash. To Walkley it looked like a "plain vanilla deal," and she expected it to close quickly. But then something happened.

Andrew Kissel went into Manhattan to close the deal instead of staying in Greenwich. Kissel overnighted the signed documents to the agent in Greenwich. This particular agent had an arrangement where, instead of him recording them in the Town of Greenwich's land office, Walkley's office did it themselves. A title searcher for Walkley ran the search, dated from a week before when the search was ordered, and then was to officially record the documents. According to Walkley, most agents will run down the title the day before the closing, assuming the usual—that nothing had been recorded in the intervening days between title order and title search. Others are more "anal," says Walkley, obviously including herself and her employees in that category. The recorder found an intervening mortgage of $1 million recorded days before on the same property. He double-checked his property information and found it correct. The new mortgage lien was also recorded properly. He dialed his boss in her office in Trumbull to ask what he should do next. Walkley told him to sit on it, and then made a call of her own to Kissel's lawyer.

The lawyer said, "Wow, that's news to me!" Her next question was whether the money had gone out for the new mortgage. The lawyer replied that the bank had wired the $1 million to Kissel's private account. Walkley had the attorney call Mr. Kissel to find out "what was going on" and then dialed her waiting title recorder at the Greenwich land office to go ahead and record the deed, but to subject it to the found mortgage, as Fidelity Title was committed to insure the bank's title on the property that they had already funded.

Kissel was supposedly out of the country, but was

exchanging e-mails with his lawyer via his BlackBerry. Kissel claimed it was a mistake and the newly found mortgage was attached to the wrong property. Kissel's lawyer thought it sounded reasonable because his client owned a number of properties in Greenwich, and the bank in question had funded many of them. The lawyer ended the call by saying he would get the first mortgage off it. It was a Friday and Nancy Walkley did not get much sleep over the weekend.

On Monday Kissel's lawyer called Walkley and told her that he had gotten a release from the bank that had the first mortgage. Walkley requested that he fax it over to her before he recorded it himself, as the lawyer was right there in Greenwich. When she got her hands on the fax she thought it looked "a little strange." She noticed it was from a New York bank, but that it had been witnessed and notarized in Connecticut. Walkley thought that, since Mr. Kissel was such a "big hitter," and his banker may have lived in Connecticut too, he must have gotten the release taken care of in his home state over the weekend. Since her client bank was now the first mortgage holder, it was a done deal as far as she was concerned.

Just two weeks later another loan from the same lawyer came across her desk with Kissel's name on it. It was an apartment building in Woodbury, sixty-five miles northeast of Greenwich. Walkley used a different title searcher and dispatched him to Woodbury. He found a large mortgage on the property attached to the deed. Walkley immediately called the lawyer and informed him of the discovery. The lawyer called back minutes later and told her Kissel had said that that mortgage had been released. Perplexed, Walkley sent the searcher back to the land office the next day. The searcher didn't bother to call his boss, faxing instead a revised title search with the bank release on the first mortgage. Walkley studied it closely.

She remembers thinking how the form in her hand did not look like a real bank release. Most banks use pre-printed forms with fancy script. This one looked like it had been typed up on a computer word processing program and printed at home. But Walkley knew that didn't necessarily mean anything, since she was seeing more and more of this type of quality document from other banks, especially on commercial properties. The thing she found curious was that there was no other mortgage on the property, a multi-unit apartment building. That was very unusual. Commercial property owners rarely leave a piece of property completely free and clear. They frequently take out loans against the property to fund other ventures.

The commercial property funds were to flow through her employer, Fidelity Title, with the $7 million being wired in from a bank in California. Walkley had to pay for "a laundry list of services" that was performed in the process of obtaining the title. The balance was to be wired from Fidelity to Kissel's personal account in Manhattan. Walkley told the lawyer that Kissel would not get a dime until she was satisfied that the new mortgage documents were of record and were in first position on the property deed. Walkley was still remembering the "funny business" over the property in Greenwich two weeks before.

Kissel overnighted the original signed documents to Walkley. She placed them in the hands of a lawyer colleague at the end of the working day with instructions to drive up to the Woodbury land office the first thing the next morning.

In Woodbury the lawyer ran the title search from the first day it was ordered, pulled the documents and literally waited there with cell phone in hand for word from Walkley that the wired money from California had reached the Fidelity account. Once Walkley confirmed the wire delivery she told the lawyer on the cell to record the mortgage. All it would then take was a touch of the button on her computer to transfer the $6 million–plus into Kissel's personal account. But she hesitated, remembering that, just to be extra safe, she should have a disbursement authorization from Mr. Kissel. The disbursement authorization would grant Walkley the right to pay for all the services rendered in securing the title. Kissel's lawyer said he would fax it over, but Walkley had left her office for the day.

The next morning Walkley studied the fax. It was a Power of Attorney authorization giving Kissel's lawyer permission to disburse the funds. Since the lawyer was her agent, in effect, it gave Walkley power of disbursement. Walkley remembers thinking that maybe she was being paranoid, but something struck her as strange. Kissel signed his name "Andrew" with a large sweeping "A" that was quite distinctive. In the front of her file was the release from the prior bank, signed by the bank officer, whose first name was "Arthur." Comparing his signature to Kissel's, she noticed the oversized, sweeping A's were identical. Walkley's caution antenna went up. She didn't like how all these dealings with the Greenwich real estate entrepreneur were adding up.

Walkley called her title searcher in Woodbury and asked her to look back over the history of the property and see if she could find anything "fishy." The title searcher called back to report that there had been three mortgages on the property. She sensed her boss's nervousness, and suggested that Walkley call the banks and get verbal confirmations on the three mortgage releases.

Walkley had the loan numbers of the mortgages and Kissel's Social Security number, and with the help of the Internet she found, after checking with the bank about the status of the most recent bank loan, that there was still a $5.3 million balance.

After thanking the bank officer she hung up and then immediately phoned the agent/lawyer handling Kissel's loan and told him the mortgage she had the release on was "still alive." Walkley told him that "all bets were off and we're not closing."

Kissel e-mailed Walkley to say that the loan had been, according to his memory, paid off by his business partner. Walkley responded that she "didn't care for his excuses"—the fact remained that the loan had not been paid off,

according to her research. What followed was a frenzied
exchange of e-mails between Walkley, the agent and Kissel,
who was again supposedly out of the country and communicating via BlackBerry. Finally Kissel told the agent to
"just pay off the loan" with the ample funds in the closing
account. Walkley e-mailed back that she would not do it.
Since it was 8 AM Walkley had to wait several hours until
the California bank was open for business to notify them of
the problem loan. In the meantime she instructed her title
searcher in Woodbury to make copies of every loan and release on the Greenwich mortgage she had worked a few
weeks prior and drive back to Greenwich with them. There
were seven loans with releases. Walkley and her colleague
called each bank to inquire about the status of the loans. To
Walkley's dismay, every single mortgage loan was "alive."
According to Walkley, the dollar amounts were in "the
multi-multi-millions," and way more than the market value
of the property.

The California bank finally returned Walkley's call and
insisted they wanted to process the Kissel loan. Flabber-
gasted, Walkley said, "What are you talking about, you are
not the first mortgage!" The bank said there must be some
kind of a mistake, and to just go ahead and close the deal.
Walkley suspected someone at the bank was just thinking of
their commission. Walkley refused to close the loan. The
California bank was not very happy with her.

Walkley re-confirmed with the banks that their loans on
the Greenwich property were still alive. She faxed each
bank a copy of the mortgage releases, writing that she believed the loans were still alive, but these releases had
been recorded at the land office. Walkley wanted confir-
mation about what she already knew—the releases were
fakes.

From Kissel's web page, Walkley got a list of LLCs
(Limited Liability Companies) that he did business under
the name of and notified every agent in the tri-state area—
New York, New Jersey and Connecticut—of a blacklisting.

There was one other suspicious detail in the loan documents that got the attention of the title lawyer: all the releases were notarized by one notary public. What was the chance, Walkley thought, of all seven banks using the same notary? As it would turn out, the notary public was a former employee of Hanrock who had inadvertently left her notary stamp behind when she'd left her job.

Other things about Kissel's methods of operation rankled Walkley. She found that he used different lawyers. From her vast experience Walkley knew that real estate investors and developers usually used one attorney for all their legal work. Kissel also was always out of town for closings and relied on e-mails and faxes for communicating with the principals in any deal. Perhaps Kissel did not want people to see him actually sign the documents? The puzzle was all coming together for Walkley.

Within days one of the swindled banks notified the FBI of Kissel's real estate fraud. Andrew Kissel's empire was about to collapse.

In retrospect, according to Walkley, there is really very little that could have been done to prevent Kissel's fraudulent practices. Says Walkley, "The public record system that we all rely on presumes the honesty and integrity of the system itself and the people filing in it, and that's what he [Kissel] relied on and abused."

Explaining her statement, Walkley said the standard in the industry, especially in the tri-state area, was, you order a title search and rely on what the search shows—and the search generally only shows open financing. If a release was filed, the financing the release pertains to will not usually show up. Any prospective buyer or lender is then led to believe the property is free and clear of liens.

It is surprisingly easy to file a release or transfer of title in Connecticut. The documents are available on the Internet and at many stationery stores. You could also use an existing one as a model and just type it up. All one then needs to do is get two witnesses' signatures and have the document notarized. As it turns out, Andrew Kissel was his own notary. Creating the bogus documents was as easy as a click of the mouse. If it hadn't been for Nancy Walkley's "suspicious nature" and her sharp eye for detail, Andrew Kissel would probably still be perpetrating his real estate fraud.

He also might still be alive.

CHAPTER SIXTEEN

As if the trial of their mother for murdering their father was not bad enough, the three Kissel children—Elaine, 11, June, 8, and Reis, 5—had another very public legal proceeding to endure. Who would care for the children and oversee the $18 million estate that was left to them?

Battle lines were quickly drawn. At first, just as with the murder trial, they were along family lines, but it was later to be intra-family—Kissel vs. Kissel. The legal drama would also have a different venue: the United States. Just as the Hong Kong press breathlessly covered the sixty-six-day murder trial, the New York papers would have their own field day with the custody battle over what one paper called "the three little millionaires."

After Nancy was arrested for the murder of her husband on November 6, 2003, the children were flown to Chicago with their nanny on the 22nd, where they were cared for by Ira Keeshin, Nancy's father, and his third wife. In a concession to Nancy, Rob had designated her father as guardian of the children and co-executor of his will, mainly because Nancy didn't like Bill, Andrew or Hayley. That arrangement lasted all of two weeks when their

63-year-old maternal grandfather complained to friends that he and his wife were not equipped, due to their age, to care for such young children.

Keeshin took his grandchildren and their nanny to a hotel in Cincinnati while arrangements were made for them to be cared for by his second wife and their son Brooks Keeshin, who was an unmarried medical student, with no experience in child-raising.

Ira wrote Andrew assuring him that the children would be raised in a "loving and nurturing environment" and that he hoped it would not prove to be "a source of conflict." He could have not been more mistaken.

When Bill Kissel caught wind of the questionable care arrangement, he was outraged, calling it "not normal." The way he saw it was, the Keeshins were doing everything in their power to keep Rob's children out of the hands of the Kissel family. Andrew petitioned a Connecticut court for custody.

Brooks Keeshin claims that Bill Kissel personally threatened him.

"He was pretty malignant. He threatened that he would ruin me and everyone that was close to me, bankrupting my father, making sure I never practiced medicine. And he gave the impression that he meant it."

Ira Keeshin felt the full-court press being made by the Kissels. He could not deal with Bill Kissel, directly, finding him too difficult. Andrew, on the other hand, was at least civil, realizing that Ira was "not the enemy."

Keeshin conceded care of the children to Andrew, and as the year 2003 was drawing to a close, Andrew chartered a private jet to fly him to Cincinnati to pick up his nieces and nephew. Andrew billed the $8,000 charter fee to his brother Rob's estate.

From her maximum security cell at the Hong Kong psychiatric hospital that she was housed in after her arrest, Nancy Kissel protested Andrew's custody of her children.

She issued a notarized statement on December 18 asking that custody be given to her young brother, adding that "in no event shall my children be placed under the care, direction or supervision of Andrew Kissel." Nancy did not elaborate as to why.

Andrew's custody of his nieces and nephew was granted after a consensus of the lawyers involved recognized that, besides being their uncle, his wealth and business success made him the obvious choice. Also working in his favor was the fact that he had two children of his own, Ruth 5, and Dara, 3, and that they were living in Greenwich, Connecticut. One of the lawyers advising Jane Clayton, Robert and Andrew's younger sister, called Greenwich "a privileged community where the kids were likely to be raised well." Andrew promised the court that he would provide "a stable, loving home they needed while their mother's case was resolved."

When Andrew Kissel's legal problems came to light and his opulent lifestyle began to unravel, temporary custody was then turned over to Andrew's wife Hayley. Hayley by this time had started divorce proceedings against her husband.

But as *The New York Times* pointed out, due to the fact that her husband was facing criminal charges, it would be difficult for Hayley to continue in her "picture-perfect home in Greenwich . . . while battling to preserve any semblance of the life she has led."

On September 15, 2005, just two weeks after Nancy Kissel's murder conviction was announced, Jane Clayton petitioned the New York State Surrogate's Court for custody of the three children. Jane, her husband—an executive with Microsoft—and their two children lived on Mercer Island, Washington. Randy Mastro, attorney for Jane Clayton, made the following statement:

The purpose of this filing is to provide the children with a stable family and a loving environment to ensure their growth into productive and happy individuals.

It was also pointed out that Jane had been named in her brother Rob's will as the co-guardian of the children. Despite his wishes, sister-in-law Hayley was dogged in her pursuit to keep the kids.

When the custody battle began, Jane was torn as to what to do. She had two babies—one was one and a half and the other was just born. She did not want to battle Andrew, but she felt it was her duty. Her father was concerned whether she was physically up to the task of climbing aboard a plane repeatedly for a cross-country trip, alone with two small children. It would also cost Jane about one million dollars for legal fees.

Jane Clayton wrote the following affidavit, submitted to the Stamford (Connecticut) Superior Court on September 23:

> Hayley has represented to me that she and Andrew's legal problems have left her in a desperate financial situation and that she intends to fight for custody of Robbie's children—even though she admits that it is not in their best interests to remain with her—in order to benefit from the considerable assets.

Hayley responded with the following statement:

> I take my role as custodian very seriously, care deeply for the welfare of the Kissel children and am happy to continue as temporary custodian.

Jane Clayton had seen to it as a co-executor of Robert's estate that Andrew did not have a managerial control or a fiduciary role over her murdered brother's will or the children's trust.

Court records showed that Andrew and Hayley had received $170,000 in 2004 for the care of the kids. The estate allotted $8,000 a month for the children's expenses, and all major bills, such as school tuition and medical care, were paid directly by the estate.

Jane had called the custody situation "bleak and problematic." She also accused Hayley in court of "using the children as pawns to solve her own deepening financial woes." Randy Mastro was even more disparaging of Hayley's attempt to keep Robert's kids.

Hayley Kissel has demonstrated blatant financial self-interest in seeking to maintain custody of the Kissel children and a disregard for their best interests.

Jane further claimed that these "deepening financial woes" had forced her sister-in-law to renege on the agreement of turning over the children to her care when the school year was over. In court, Jane referred to her notes of her conversations with Hayley, testifying that her sister-in-law had stated:

"I am going to do what is best for myself. If I keep the children, it may not be the best thing for them, but at least I won't be out on the street. I have nothing left."

The patriarch of the family, William Kissel, sided with his daughter: "Andrew is in deep trouble," he said, "and it wouldn't be appropriate to have the children in a house without a mother and a father, where the wife needs the children to support her lifestyle."

Further reasons for granting custody to Jane surfaced when it was learned that Robert's estate worth had been lowered from $18 million to $15 million. The reason? Rob had invested some of his money in his brother's real estate ventures. That money was lost. The estate's lawyers were considering joining a lawsuit against Andrew for the fraud.

On October 3, the Manhattan Surrogate's Court denied Jane Clayton emergency custodial care of Robert and Nancy Kissel's children, saying that although the environment may be "unstable," the kids did appear to have been well cared for and had bonded with their custodial family.

Hayley Kissel was livid with the Kissel family. She felt she was unappreciated for taking in Rob's kids when nobody else would. Andrew was of no help. If they thought the kids were a boon to her, then they knew nothing.

"It's brutal work taking care of five kids," Hayley had vented to a friend. "I get impatient, stressed, frenzied and am prone to the occasional rant."

On top of all that, Hayley also had a full-time job in New York, although she was able to engage a housekeeper.

After Andrew's criminal arraignment in Manhattan over the co-op fiasco on October 6, 2005, Nathan Dershowitz, Hayley's lawyer, said he did not think it would affect his client's chances in the custody battle.

On October 18 Judge Eve Preminger reversed her own ruling and gave temporary custody of the children to Jane Clayton, citing the recommendation of court-appointed lawyer Michael Collesano, who represented the interests of the children in the family feud.

In a written statement from prison, Nancy Kissel argued against granting custody to her sister-in-law and thereby uprooting her children once again. It was quite an about-face for the children's mother.

"The fact of the matter is my children are not in harm's way emotionally or physically right now," Nancy wrote. "Children understand love. They don't understand change," adding that "Loving families don't turn on each other. They support one another."

But the Manhattan Surrogate's Court dismissed the plea of the biological mother of the three children by stating that her murder conviction rendered her judgment questionable.

"She is the lone voice for that position," said Judge Preminger, "and would seem to have forfeited my belief in her good judgment based on the actions she was convicted of."

Hayley Kissel was not in court for the judgment, but attorney Dershowitz stated that she would abide by the court decision. A teary-eyed Jane Clayton said she was "thrilled" by the ruling.

"This story finally has a happy ending after two years of hardship for this family," proclaimed Clayton's attorney Randy Mastro. On December 13, after negotiating, Hayley Kissel and Jane Clayton agreed on the transferral of custody of the warred-over orphans. It was decided that the kids would be flown to Seattle to live with their aunt Jane on December 21, when school closed for the Christmas break. Thus ended another trying saga for the star-crossed Kissel family.

There was, however, more tragedy to come.

CHAPTER SEVENTEEN

There was no hint of trouble on the horizon in May 2005 when, convincing himself he was in need of some R&R, Andrew made plans to spend some time in Florida. The extended weekend extravaganza was the brainchild of Andrew's old high school buddy Brian Howie, one of whose off-Broadway productions, called *Pieces*, Andrew had invested in in 2004. The trip was to be a working weekend, or so Andrew told his wife, where he and his associates would be looking into various real estate ventures in Florida. At the same time Andrew would be shopping around for a new boat.

According to the *New York Post*, there was also a woman named Alison Statler by Andrew's side. Statler did public relations and marketing work for Hanrock. Howie also knew a lot of actresses, several of whom would be in attendance.

For three days Andrew had a wild time aboard the *Special K*, a $4 million ninety-four-foot Italian yacht. The *Special K* cruised around the Keys with Howie, several other men, Statler and a collection of young and attractive actresses. Witnesses said Andrew had a cocktail in his hand before the morning had ended each day he was there. There were dinners at expensive South Florida restaurants and clubbing in

Miami's chic South Beach. The floating party would have continued had not a call to Andrew's cell number interrupted the festivities. To make things particularly sticky, the call was answered by one of the invited female guests. Shocked to hear the feminine voice at the other end of the line, Hayley reportedly screamed into the phone, "Who are you and why are you fucking my husband?"

After a heated argument over the phone, Andrew announced to fellow revelers that the weekend was over. He had to return to Connecticut. The aborted party was a harbinger of things to come.

Philip Russell's law offices are on the ground floor of a modern glass-and-steel office building across the street from Greenwich's sprawling town hall. It's apparent from the staffing, the list of partners and the décor of the richly appointed offices that the senior partner of Greenwich Legal is successful at what he does. According to fellow criminal lawyer Lindy Urso, Russell is "the quintessential defense lawyer, will go right to the limit—and perhaps beyond, for the client. He is well-regarded by the defense bar, not so by the prosecutors."

Bald, bespectacled and well-dressed, Russell is as articulate as one would expect of a former assistant district attorney in New York, now a top gun in the lucrative game of criminal defense. He is also not one to leave out a choice expletive in his otherwise precise and proper English where needed. Russell is well-known for having a wickedly droll sense of humor.

The 47-year-old lawyer had never heard of Andrew Kissel until he was brought to Russell's attention by a real estate attorney toward the end of June 2005. The attorney was representing the bank at a Kissel property closing when he noticed some "questionable documents" in the chain of title, and confronted Kissel over them. The lawyer, according to Russell, basically "unwound" the closing he was in the middle of and "returned the money to the bank, the title insurance money to the title company and he sent Andrew Kissel to see me."

Within one day of their first sit-down, Philip Russell had Andrew Kissel report himself to the United States Department of Justice. Russell and his real estate lawyer colleague advised Andrew that turning himself in was the "prudent thing" to do in light of the enormity of his actions and the inevitability that he was going "to get snagged." That same day they learned that attorney Nancy Walkley of Fidelity National Title in Trumbull had also reported Andrew Kissel to federal authorities on another fraudulent real estate closing in Connecticut.

It must have become apparent to Hanrock partner David Parisier that Andrew was in trouble. Parisier had been fielding calls at the company's Stamford office of late from mortgage refinance agents about loans he did not know existed. He asked about them and was shocked to have Andrew screaming, "How dare you question me?" at him, and threatening to kill him.

It had been a mystery to some why Parisier, a former neighbor of Andrew at East 74th Street, had stayed with him after the co-op flap. Claimed one mutual acquaintance: "David was looking at dollar signs and thinking that Andrew was the ticket for him."

To a builder who worked with the two partners on some property constructions, the two "spent most of their energy going at one another," calling them "the most dysfunctional group I was ever with.

"I don't think they trusted each other," the builder added. "I don't think Andrew trusted anybody."

If Andrew was stealing, and apparently he was, he had good reason not to trust anyone.

Philip Russell and his client were directed to meet with Assistant United States Attorney Cathy Seibel for the Southern

District of New York. Within days there was a meeting between Andrew Kissel, the attorneys and FBI agents assigned
to investigate the case. Kissel related to them what had occurred with the various real estate deals he was involved in,
some of which had come to the attention of the feds.

On July 17, Andrew Kissel was charged by complaint
and was arrested the following day at 8 AM at his vacation
home in Stratton, Vermont. He spent the night in jail. The
next morning, Hayley and attorney Russell were at his
side. Since Russell did not have a personal check on him,
Hayley had to pay the court clerk's $180 fee so that Rus-
sell, who is admitted to the New York and Connecticut
bars, could argue his case in a Vermont court. Hayley also
assumed responsibility for Andrew and would see to it that
he appeared at his next court appearance.

It was a bit of an embarrassment for the Vermont U.S. attorney, as he had told the court the previous day that he understood Kissel's wife wanted to have nothing to do "with
the son-of-a-bitch," leaving Kissel with no place to go and
a risk of flight. He wanted the accused jailed. Hayley's
presence and fee payment debunked the red-faced U.S. attorney's assertion. Andrew signed a personal surety bond
in court and was released into the custody of his wife. The
judge ordered Andrew to appear at the New York federal
court in White Plains for arraignment the following day.

In White Plains, Magistrate George Yanthis placed Andrew Kissel on electronic monitoring. The conditions for
his house arrest were determined in open court and for the
record. According to Philip Russell, there was no real ob-
jection to the electronic monitoring from the U.S. attorney.

"House arrest," said Russell, "is a fairly standard procedure. What happens is that the device is hooked up to a
dedicated phone line inside the individual's house. Then a
computer telephones that number and the gadget which
they install in the house finds the ankle bracelet within 500
feet of itself and reports back to the computer that, 'Yeah,
the dude is here.' The device is smart enough to know if it
has been cut off the ankle."

There are, of course, prescribed times when the felon is off monitoring. Andrew was allowed to visit his lawyer and doctor and to pick up his kids at school.

Initially it was estimated that Andrew Kissel had bilked a total of $25 million from Washington Mutual ($1.6 million), Hudson Valley Bank ($4.5 million), Independence Community Bank ($1 million), Fairfield County Bank ($4.5 million) and private investors, but that was revised down to $6.4 million in the federal charges. Russell had a plan.

"There were a number of things," he says, "that we did to try to make this criminal case . . . to minimize the damage to himself, to his family and to his finances. Of course, it's like trying to survive an atomic bomb. It was a very difficult case, but we did make a substantial amount of headway."

The defense of Andrew Kissel was able to marshal about a million dollars' worth of assets for the benefit of the creditors. But, according to Russell, because of the "obstinacy of some of the lawyers involved in the collection cases," the defense was not able to distribute all of the million dollars to the victims directly.

The problem arose when Andrew became the target of four separate lawsuits: two were title companies, one represented the investors of Kissel's failed company (Hanrock) and one was Hayley's divorce suit. To further complicate things, Andrew's partner at Hanrock, David Parisier, had seized $10 million of Hanrock's assets by legal writ. They were all trying to be first in line when the assets were divvied up while there still were some assets to be had. In each one of the lawsuits there were court orders to lock up all of Andrew's assets to prevent him from disposing of them.

Russell was able to work out an agreement for distribution of some of the assets among the four litigants. They broke it out in five equal parts, leaving a "small amount" for Andrew's legal defense. Attorney Russell said asset money would go to pay for the forensic accounting work and the psychiatric evaluations so that the defense could make an intelligent presentation for mitigating his sentence.

"It was always going to be a guilty plea," Russell related, "because we really did not have much of a choice about that. It was impossible for him to say that he did not commit the crime. We were never going to try to deny it."

After the first payment was made, a problem arose with lawyers from one of the title companies. Russell said that they'd acted so "nasty" in scrutinizing the every sale of assets that it bogged down the whole process. Russell's reaction to the obstructive title company was "Go to hell." If they didn't approve the sales, Russell would just turn the assets over to the government on a forfeiture order. Russell related that the title company, and later Hayley Kissel's lawyers, became so difficult to deal with rationally that their legal fees wound up eating into the settlement sums their clients would receive. Some $500,000 went into the government's coffers.

Philip Russell thought the federal government did a "superb job" in prosecuting Andrew Kissel, a surprising statement from a defense attorney. The FBI agents were experienced, intelligent and sophisticated. They had taken their time figuring out where the money had gone. According to Russell it was a "very difficult, laborious job." The defense team cooperated, but the FBI really didn't trust Kissel, so they got the job done in a couple of months despite him. Russell also found the government "pretty reasonable" in terms of conditions of bail, not overcharging the case and working towards what Russell thought would have been "a reasonable resolution of Andrew's criminal liability."

"It's rare in my business," said Russell, "that we get to deal with prosecutors or [FBI] agents that are as mature and sophisticated as this group happened to be."

Working with Andrew Kissel was another story. Russell remembers Andrew as an interesting guy who was able to compartmentalize and "was able to make you think that he was feeling whatever way you wanted to make him think that he was feeling." In other words, he could project any image that he thought would work for him. He had an affable and cooperative demeanor about him and he was agreeable to just about everything suggested to him by his legal team.

Yet Russell was never sure Kissel followed their advice "to the letter" about anything, from getting his financial records together to finding certain documents or contacting individuals, do this, don't do that. Added Russell:

"I don't think Andrew Kissel listened to anybody. I think he did whatever the hell he wanted to do. He always seemed to be helpful and cooperative, but a lot of the times he just wasn't being honest, and that was helpful to nobody."

Andrew gave Philip Russell only one clear instruction in regard to his case, and that was not to have anything to do with his father William Kissel. Russell found it strange, but respected Andrew's wishes, thinking the gulf between father and son was none of his business. As far as he knew, Andrew had no communications with his father. Russell saw that Hayley was similarly distanced from Andrew.

The Greenwich lawyer is convinced that Hayley had no knowledge of her husband's criminal activity. The reason he is so sure, besides what he learned about Andrew's dealings, was his take on Andrew's nature. Andrew was a liar, and basically "incommunicado" as far as his wife was concerned. Hayley did not know where her husband was half the time.

Little had been done over the two years since the Manhattan DA's office was alerted to Andrew Kissel's financial irregularities while treasurer of his co-op board. As Barbara Thompson, a spokeswoman for the Manhattan district attorney's office was reported as saying in reply to a question from a *New York Times* reporter, "White collar investigations are time-consuming cases that we have to do our own investigation despite the perception that much of the preliminary work had been done."

It wasn't until September 2005 that a Manhattan grand jury handed down an indictment of Andrew Kissel for grand larceny and other crimes that he'd perpetrated in his seven-year tenure as board treasurer of 200 East 74th Street.

Charles Clayman, lead attorney for Kissel in the Manhattan case, was disappointed that the DA's office had proceeded with criminal charges against his client after two years. Charges were formally brought against Kissel the week of September 12, 2005. Just one week before, Manhattan District Attorney Robert Morgenthau had announced to a cheering crowd of supporters on his election night victory that "nobody is above the law . . . people who are profiteers, big shots; they're not immune from prosecution." Andrew Kissel fit the bill perfectly. It wasn't long before an indictment for grand larceny was handed down by a Manhattan grand jury. Kissel was given two weeks to put his things in order and surrender to authorities or face the public humiliation of an arrest.

Charles Clayman complained publicly that he and his client cooperated "fully" with the DA's office and that "everybody knows" that Andrew had "paid back all the funds that were allegedly misappropriated."

There were grumblings uptown on East 74th Street. Swifter prosecution might have prevented Kissel decamping to Connecticut as a loan-worthy real-estate tycoon. Jack Haber, president of the co-op board, made the following statement to the press:

"A lot of the frauds that Mr. Kissel is reported to have committed in the last year and a half would not have happened if the district attorney in New York had done his job. Why didn't law enforcement officials make this case a priority? Yes, the co-op got its money back, but guess what? If somebody stole fifteen dollars from Duane Reade [a New York pharmacy chain] and got caught and gave the money back, they'd still get arrested."

His wife Hayley and his father were just two investors Andrew duped.

"Andrew took money from everybody possible," his father was quoted in the *Times* as saying. "From his father-in-law, from friends, from Robert, from everybody, and they're all holding the bag."

* * *

On Thursday, October 6, Andrew Kissel, attired in a grey suit, dejectedly walked into the state supreme court in downtown Manhattan, looking, according to one reporter on the scene, "dazed." He was accompanied by Charles Clayman and Philip Russell. Under federal house arrest and wearing his ankle bracelet, he stood before Justice Brenda Soloff. After listening to attorney Clayman tell the court how his client had posted a $1 million unsecured bond and surrendered his passport on federal charges, Judge Soloff ordered Kissel to pay an additional $10,000 cash bond and he was released. Andrew Kissel was facing 25 years in prison if convicted.

PART FOUR

SECOND-PLACE FINISHER IN A TWO-BROTHER RACE

CHAPTER EIGHTEEN

By the time he was 38 years old, Carlos Trujillo realized he had no future in his native Colombia. He had grown up in the teeming city of Cali, which was well known to the federal Drug Enforcement Agency (DEA) as the capital of Colombia's lucrative cocaine trade. Cali and the surrounding countryside had long ago been staked out by the narco-terrorists, and their grip is one the Colombian Army had been unable to break. But exploiting the narcotics trade is not what brought Carlos Trujillo to America, even though he was a truck driver without a future.

It was an established practice in this South American country for transportation companies to let older employees go and then rehire them on contract for short periods of time, with six months being the usual length of employment. This way the companies were not obligated to pay pensions and benefits once their employees reached retirement age. Trujillo had an aging mother, an estranged wife, two kids and a girlfriend to support. His future lay to the north.

In April of 1998 Carlos joined his younger brother in the United States. George had been living in the Bronx for almost ten years. The extent of Carlos' English was "good morning" and "thank you," he recalls with a laugh.

There were jobs for immigrant labor to be had, but they

did not pay well. Since Carlos wanted his 22-year-old girl-friend to stay home with their young daughter, he worked two jobs, six days a week. He somehow managed to get in three hours of sleep a night.

His relationship with his girlfriend lasted only a year in this country. She left him for a man with more money, money gotten from dealing drugs.

Carlos, of course, was aware of the "easy life" that some of his compatriots were living in America. The easy life was fueled by the cocaine trade. But Carlos had made a pact with himself to stay on the right side of the law in the United States. He knew a drug dealer only ended up one of two ways—dead or in jail.

His brother George was working as a driver and a handy-man for an elderly woman in nearby Westchester County. The woman had a Colombian housekeeper who was also working for a wealthy resident of Manhattan who needed a driver. Since his employment with the woman looked as if it was ending, the housekeeper put in a good word for her fellow countryman.

Andrew Kissel, of East 74th Street, hired George as a driver in March 2000. Eventually, impressed with George's work ethic, Andrew moved him up to a property manager of some of his real estate holdings in New Jersey. He needed a new driver, and George recommended his equally hard-working brother Carlos.

Despite his long love affair with automobiles, Andrew was too busy for the mundane tasks of chauffeuring his wife and kids around the perpetually traffic-snarled streets of the city, where parking places were almost non-existent. Carlos jumped at the opportunity to supplement his work at a rent-a-car agency with some afternoon chauffeur work. Andrew agreed to pay Carlos $550 a week with the use of the family SUV, which he could drive back and forth to his new apartment in Queens. Carlos had one problem: he still had not learned to speak English. Andrew paid for Carlos to learn English at a local community college at night.

Carlos was immediately impressed with Andrew Kissel. Unlike many rich people who treated their employees like "shit," said Carlos, Andrew was a very nice guy. He even gave Carlos a credit card to charge gas and expenses to Andrew's account. Andrew allowed Carlos to dress casually, "except no jeans," Carlos added, just thrilled he didn't have to buy a suit. Andrew reminded Carlos of his father back in Colombia, a friendly man who liked to help everybody. But Andrew had a temper.

"He would yell and scream at you and throw things around," recalled Carlos, "but five minutes later, all would be forgotten."

Hayley was very different. According to Carlos, unlike her husband, she was more reserved. She also was an impatient woman who curiously was always late for engagements. She often took her frustrations out on her husband's hired hand. Carlos would quietly sit behind the wheel of the big SUV feeling the kicks on the seat as Hayley vented, again late for another appointment.

Carlos had little contact with the Kissels outside of the car. On the Upper East Side of Manhattan, parking places are a commodity, and with street cleanings and commercial traffic, constant jockeying of a private vehicle is de rigueur. The fact that the Kissels' Denali was a pricy vehicle, with all the accoutrements that a car aficionado like Andrew demanded, meant that Carlos was always by the car, which was prized by thieves.

The first whiff of scandal Carlos got about the co-op's missing money was when he was accosted in the street by a resident of the building the Kissels lived in. The elderly woman railed about how he could work for such a man "who stole people's money." There was also scuttlebutt on the scandal amongst the building employees, who for the most part were Hispanic immigrants like himself.

In 2003 when Andrew relocated to Connecticut, Carlos stayed behind with Hayley and the two children and continued to chauffeur them around Manhattan. Carlos was convinced that Hayley had no knowledge of her husband's embezzlement. He was in a position to know.

Andrew had Carlos remove any incriminating mail from their postal box in the lobby before Hayley could retrieve it. He even ordered Carlos to remove all flyers from the co-op board that were left at all the doors of floor neighbors, for fear of Hayley coming across one. Since Hayley had no friends in the building, it wasn't too surprising that she was ignorant of the financial scandal brewing around her. Carlos knew it was wrong to keep it from her, but he couldn't refuse Andrew, a man who had been so generous to him.

Hayley and the kids joined Andrew in Greenwich at their first rented home there on Pecksland Road. Carlos was tasked with keeping Andrew's many cars cleaned and in running order, to run errands for him and to drive his kids to and from school.

Since the Kissels were now in a suburban house, as opposed to a city high-rise, Carlos got closer to the family both literally and figuratively. He was no longer out in the busy streets looking after the Kissel cars; he was constantly in and out of the house.

Eventually Hayley found out about Andrew's problems with the co-op board at their former residence. "Hayley went crazy," Carlos said. From that moment on, their marriage was in a tailspin. Carlos remembered that when the two were in each other's company, they argued incessantly. It was a reprieve for Andrew when Hayley left each morning to catch a train into Manhattan, where she worked as a stock analyst for Merrill Lynch.

Carlos also got to know Andrew's brother Robert, who often visited Greenwich. Carlos would shuttle him to and from the airport when he was in town. Robert, said Carlos, was "very nice, polite but quiet." He was just the opposite in temperament from Andrew, who was gregarious and outgoing. Carlos could tell that the two brothers were close.

After Robert was killed, a change came over Andrew.

He seemed to be sad all the time and not his usual fun self. But there was an upswing in his mood once he and his wife got temporary custody of Robert's kids. Despite the fact that his late brother's progeny's addition to his household brought him some comfort, he wasn't prepared for the problems that surfaced.

Carlos said the new tribe of five fought a lot among themselves. As Carlos said, "it was just kids being kids, but it drove Andrew crazy." Andrew began to make himself scarce around the house, and it was about this time when Andrew confessed to Carlos that he had a girlfriend. Andrew started missing the family dinners and often didn't come home until late at night. The fighting between Hayley and Andrew increased and intensified.

When the federal indictment was announced on July 13, Andrew disappeared. He was gone a month when Hayley summoned Carlos and told him she didn't have the money to pay his $850 weekly salary. David Parisier, Andrew's partner at Hanrock in Stamford, gave him some bad news as well. Since he was an employee of Andrew, Parisier felt no obligation to pay him what he was owed for cleaning their office suite in Stamford.

Carlos had some money he had put aside for a trip back to Colombia to visit his mother. He managed to survive for two months on the squirreled-away money.

After Andrew made his appearance in federal court, Carlos heard that it was Hayley who had somehow made good on the $1 million bond so that her husband didn't have to wait for his trial behind bars.

Soon after his court appearance, Andrew called Carlos and told him he couldn't pay him a salary. He *could* give him some money for doing odd jobs, since Andrew's mobility was limited by the terms of his house arrest. Andrew told him that Hayley was not to be made aware of their little arrangement. Carlos agreed and put in a couple of hours two to three days a week making runs for Andrew to the bank, to his lawyer's office and to pick up mail at the Hanrock office in Stamford. Andrew paid him in cash when he could. Carlos would get $500, sometimes $1,000 every couple of weeks. He picked up a morning job as a delivery man for a company in Stamford to make ends meet. Between the odd jobs for Andrew and the delivery job, Carlos was getting by.

CHAPTER NINETEEN

On February 28, 2006, at the State Superior Court in Stamford, Connecticut, Hayley Wolff Kissel filed divorce papers. It had been almost a year since she'd first applied for the divorce.

Among other scandalous revelations she made about her husband was that he had been in and out of drug and alcohol rehabilitation programs, but ". . . has resumed drinking alcohol, consumes alcohol on the property . . . and has been belligerent and argumentative especially when intoxicated including in the company of children."

Hayley also wrote about Andrew committing fraud against her, which included "forging powers of attorney to transfer property she owned in Vermont and converting assets for his use in violation of court orders."

Hayley was still living with Andrew in the house on Dairy Road, and she tried to keep up appearances for the kids, but it was difficult because all the couple did when in each other's company was quarrel. Hayley had moved into a spare bedroom after Andrew refused to vacate the master bedroom. In her divorce petition she asked that her husband be thrown out of the house.

Up to this time, lawyers who represented the couple contended that the divorce had gone from being amicable to contentious. Andrew was even representing himself. The next day he hired divorce attorney Howard Graber.

Graber said that his new client had been "very surprised" that Hayley filed the eviction request. From what Graber had learned, he didn't feel the litigants were acrimonious.

"He didn't present," said Graber, "as someone who was bitter or hated his wife or kids, like ninety-nine percent of the people who come into my office."

Hayley was staying in Vermont a lot, in an obvious attempt to avoid her husband. The big screen TV wasn't working there, so she called Lance DelPriore. Lance was pleased to hear from her and told her he'd be happy to help. Lance then called Andrew. Andrew was pleasant and chatty; he seemed to be happy to hear from a friend. The subject of his brother, Mike, and Rob's wife, Nancy, never came up. They talked about what needed to be done at the Kissels' Stratton home. As always Andrew wanted top-dollar equipment—in other words, the latest big-screen plasma TV. When Lance discussed the selection later with Hayley, she laughed and said she didn't know how her husband was going to pay for it, since he was "broke."

Lance DelPriore was, of course, familiar with Andrew's legal difficulties. In March 2006, Andrew had phoned Lance regarding the work, and Lance told him that he and his wife were praying that he would get through the legal trouble okay. "Pray harder," Andrew quipped. The two had a good laugh over that. Andrew went on to explain "it didn't look good," and that he was probably going to jail. Lance assured him that that was "okay." He would be out eventually, and he could get on with his life. That's how Lance remembered his last communication with Andrew Kissel.

Carlos Trujillo got a call from Hayley not long after he'd begun to work for Andrew again. She asked him if he was "aware of their situation" and that Andrew was going to jail. Replying that he was, Hayley explained that she had to let go their housekeeper, who had also been seeing to the needs of the children. Would he be willing to help around the house and watch the kids until they moved out? He was, and they agreed that he would quit his delivery job and that Hayley would pay him $600 a week. Hayley made it clear that he was working for her and not Andrew. It was understood that, besides driving the kids, he would help maintain the spacious house, and that Andrew would help.

Carlos recalled that Andrew wasn't much help. He would beg off from doing the mundane chores with him, promising some extra money to Carlos if he did the work himself, which of course he did. He had not really expected Andrew to pitch in anyway.

Under house arrest, Andrew was subject to some fairly liberal guidelines that his criminal defense attorney Philip Russell had negotiated for him. Andrew was free to go to the supermarket, his kids' school and to the doctor during the week. On weekends he had to stay within the walls of the estate. None of his "friends" visited him.

Andrew Kissel now wore the veil of an untouchable. After his arrests and indictments, those rich Greenwich friends who were approached by the press for a knowledgeable or pithy quote would beg off by explaining that they were just "acquaintances." His Hanrock business partner, David Parisier, avoided the press altogether in regard to his problematic associate. Parisier had filed suit against Andrew to the tune of $25 million for misappropriation of company funds.

No longer able to travel and to socialize, Andrew and Carlos Trujillo grew closer. It was understandable why the two men bonded: Andrew loved companionship, and all of his business associates and the Greenwich country club set he'd once socialized with now shunned the disgraced real estate mogul. Carlos was the only one left.

Carlos recounted that there were moments when Andrew lamented how his life had turned out. He would tell the Colombian expatriate that he didn't know why he'd done what he did, why he'd cheated so many people, including friends and family. All he could offer in his defense was that he thrived on the excitement of the deals, and how they produced money. He loved the boats, the airplanes, the world travel, the fast cars and the fast women it bought. "But," he would point out, "look what I got now." He would then stare at his ankle bracelet. It was a side of Andrew he'd never seen before. Carlos found himself feeling sorry for this man who had seemed to have had everything, a lovely family, money and a successful career. "Now," Carlos said, "his life was shit."

Andrew was brokenhearted about the collapse of his marriage. Carlos said that Andrew would constantly tell him how he "had fucked it up," what a good woman Hayley was and how much he still loved her. Carlos commiserated with him, but reminded him that it was Andrew's own fault, that he had done "lots of bad things to kill that love." Andrew would sadly nod his head in agreement and change the subject.

After his indictment, Andrew lost his source of income from the various bank accounts he had used for his real estate transactions. All the accounts were frozen by the federal courts. Then came the loss of income from his murdered brother's estate for taking care of his kids. Andrew was forced to sell off his possessions to pay the lawyers, the rent, the private school and other expenses. When the boat, the airplane and cars were gone, he began to sell off jewelry. Carlos became the middleman in those transactions.

Last to go was Andrew's collection of expensive watches. Andrew had phoned an upscale jewelry store in Greenwich and worked out a deal. Since Andrew couldn't accept a check written to him, they would write a check to Carlos for the agreed-upon sum when he delivered the piece to the store. Carlos would then cash the check at his bank, and give the money to Andrew. He wasn't comfortable with the arrangement, but he couldn't say no to the man who had been so generous with him in the past. Carlos brought "three or four" watches to the store; none of them went for less than $5,000. Andrew would always give him a few hundred dollars for his troubles.

Carlos was assured by his employer that the jewelry was Andrew's to sell, since he had bought all of it on his many trips to Europe. He was emphatic that the expensive pieces were not Hayley's—but, he cautioned, she wasn't to know about the sales. One of the watches did not belong to him.

His father had entrusted Andrew with an expensive antique wristwatch that his late wife had bought for him during a family holiday in Switzerland in 1979. William Kissel told Andrew he wanted him to hold it for Robert's son Reis, who was in their care at the time, and who was too young to appreciate and care for it. When Mr. Kissel learned of Andrew's legal problems, he called to have Andrew return it to him so it wouldn't wind up in the hands of a creditor or the government. Hayley had taken the call. The family patriarch explained to her that the watch was very special to him. Hayley replied, somewhat cryptically, that it was "special" to Andrew too. William Kissel never got the watch back.

Carlos had been planning for a trip to Colombia, but he was holding off until he got his green card. Because of his non-resident alien status he wasn't assured of being permitted back inside the country when he traveled abroad. In February 2006 his papers came through. Carlos then approached Hayley about a convenient date for him to take some time off. Hayley told him March would be good, since the kids would be out of school for spring break. He made plans to leave on March 18 to visit his family in Colombia for the first time in eight years.

When Carlos returned to work on March 27, Hayley

told him not to clean the house anymore. He was told to buy moving boxes and they would start packing the family's belongings.

The owner of the red-brick mansion on Dairy Road where the Kissels were residing was threatening an eviction notice. Jean Wurtz claimed Andrew Kissel had not paid her the monthly $14,300 rent in six months. The Kissels agreed to move out of the house by the first of the month, April Fools' Day.

It was a painful week for Andrew, Carlos remembered. It was becoming all too real to him that his family was breaking up before his eyes. He had lost the house, his wife and children were deserting him and he was destined for a jail cell.

March 29 was Hayley's birthday. A gift for her arrived at the house as Andrew and Carlos packed. It was from her new boyfriend. Andrew was hurt by the display of affection from his wife's new man, and he groused to Carlos about why the gift had to be sent to her here, right under his nose.

Carlos had known that, during the winter months when Hayley and the kids were away in Vermont for weekend ski trips, Andrew had "partied." He had confessed to Carlos that since he was estranged from his wife, he'd "go crazy" if he didn't have some female companionship. So Andrew had some professional girls come and visit him over the otherwise lonely weekends. Carlos warned him that if Hayley found out about his parties, she'd kick him out of the house for sure, and then where would he go?

On Friday, March 31, Hayley called the JB Moving company in Stamford and made hasty arrangements for the movers to come to her house the next morning. Contents of the house had been packed and were ready to be carted off to a temporary storage facility until she decided on what she and the kids would need for her new domicile. It was a problem Andrew would not have—he was due in court in a few days, and it would be there that he would learn where he would be incarcerated for many years to come.

♦ ♦ ♦

On Saturday Carlos was at the Dairy Road house early and proceeded to pack the last of the Kissel belongings. The moving trucks from JB Moving arrived shortly afterward. The packing and the loading of boxes into the truck continued all morning and into the afternoon. Eventually they would fill three trucks, but not before Hayley and Andrew got into an argument in front of the men.

By the end of the day the only thing left to move was the master bedroom set, but Andrew insisted on staying at the house through the weekend, and he needed a bed to sleep on. He complained that he had no place else to go. The vitriolics lasted an uncomfortable few minutes in front of the workmen. Eventually Hayley threw up her hands in exasperation and stormed off, remarking that he could have his way, since he'd be going to jail soon anyway. Andrew told her that the moving men could come back first thing Monday morning to pick up the bedroom set. The movers called their boss, Doug Roina. He reluctantly agreed. Roina had wanted to get this job over with on Saturday. Now he had to tie up his men for a few more hours on Monday to accommodate Mr. Kissel. Rich people were such pains in the ass, he thought.

Andrew pulled Carlos aside and told him about a big fight when Hayley had found the money Andrew had gotten from the watch sales—$18,000 in cash. She demanded to know where he had gotten it from, accusing him of stealing it from her. Andrew had lied and said he'd been putting it aside, little by little, over the last six months. He claimed he had forgotten where he had put it, probably because he had been drunk. Hayley didn't believe him.

Finally, at about 5 PM, the sad moment arrived. Hayley told the two kids to get into her car because it was time to go. They knew what was going on. They had to say their good-byes to their dad. Everyone broke down in tears, including Carlos. Andrew stood in the courtyard and watched silently as Hayley and the kids drove onto Dairy Road and disappeared down the wooded drive.

On Sunday, Carlos returned to the house early in the evening to pick up a few items for Hayley. He also wanted to check on Andrew and see how he was holding up, and if he needed anything to eat. Andrew had just emerged from the shower and was eager to tell his only friend about the previous evening. He had had some feminine company over, and he gushed how beautiful she was and "what a great time they had." Carlos politely listened as Andrew gave him the details of the debauched evening. Andrew didn't have to tell him about the cocaine. Andrew knew Carlos didn't approve of drugs, so he didn't mention his use of them. Carlos had cleaned his room enough to know that Andrew was a habitual user. After his weekend parties, there were always the little plastic Baggies with the residual white powder in them that had to be collected from under the bed before Hayley could find them.

Carlos didn't stay long. He drove back to his home in Queens. On Monday Hayley wanted him to stop by the house of a friend she was staying with in Stamford and pick up her dog Molly. The friend's children were allergic to dogs, so Carlos had to take the dog to Hayley's mother, who would meet him halfway in Springfield, Massachusetts, and take Molly back to Vermont with her.

Andrew Kissel was supposed to be waiting for the movers at the estate's security gate between 8 and 8:30 AM on Monday, April 3. When the movers got there, the black metal gate was closed and locked—and was no Andrew Kissel. The men waited outside the gate on the bleak, grey and cold early spring day, drinking coffee and intermittently honking their truck's horn. With no sign of life inside the house, the job foreman called the moving company offices at 8:30 for instructions. Doug Roina fielded the call.

After calling the house on Dairy Road and getting no answer, Roina dialed Hayley Kissel at the house she was staying at in Stamford. Hayley gave Roina the security code to the gate and he in turn called his job foreman on his cell phone and gave him the numbers to punch in. Minutes later the white moving van was inside the courtyard in front of the stately mock-Tudor home, with its ramp down, ready to receive the master bedroom set—the last of the material goods the Kissels had accumulated over the fourteen years of their marriage.

The men knocked on the door and waited for a few minutes. Finally the foreman tried the doorknob. The door was unlocked, so the men let themselves in, announcing their arrival as they did. They immediately went upstairs and, finding no one there, began disassembling the bed, then carried it out to the truck. One of the movers took the staircase down to the basement for a last search of any more items that were to go. He was greeted by a gruesome sight.

In the middle of the floor, surrounded by a dark brownish pool of congealed blood, was Andrew Kissel. He was seated in a chair, his hands bound behind his back with plastic Flex-Cufs. His ankles were also bound to the legs of the chair and his mouth was gagged. A bloodied T-shirt was pulled over his head, obscuring much of his face. His body was slumped forward, restrained by his extended arms. Andrew Kissel was still wearing the court-ordered ankle bracelet.

At 10:25 AM Marina Cepeda, a 51-year-old housekeeper in a nearby home, peeked out a window that fronted onto Dairy Road. She was drawn to the window by the wail of police sirens, a rarely heard sound in these secluded, wooded acres.

In just minutes, there were half-a-dozen sky-blue squad cars, emblazoned with "GREENWICH POLICE" on the panels, with lights flashing, wedged into the gravel courtyard of number 10.

Curious and unused to such excitement on the quiet road, Marina thought it might be an opportune time to take the family dog out for a walk. As she approached the gated entrance to number 10, police officers were in the process of stringing yellow crime-scene tape around the front of the property. Dour-looking men in suits appeared to be searching the grounds and a backyard shed. Marina, with the dog in tow, hurried back to her house.

A server for the Norwalk, Connecticut, housing court clerk showed up at the Kissel home amidst the tumult of police activity. In his hands he had documents signed that morning authorizing the forcible eviction of the Kissel family. Andrew Kissel owed $100,000 in back rent and damages to the property. Richard Witt, attorney for the house owner, was notified by the owner that the papers couldn't be served, saying "something was going down on the property."

Word of Andrew Kissel's murder spread fast. Print reporters and TV news crews were out in front of the Dairy Road house that morning scurrying about for interviews, but crime-scene gawking was way too bourgeois for this moneyed neighborhood. There were few willing to step in front of a camera. Most of the media stayed to get the obligatory shot of the victim's bagged body being trundled out of the house on a gurney by a coroner's employee later in the afternoon.

New York radio programs and the evening TV news programs led with the story. The next morning the *New York Times* Metro section ran it as the front-page story, complete with a color photo of the property draped with crime-scene tape. Ever since the murder of Robert Kissel, the high-profile indictment of Andrew for multi-million-dollar real estate fraud and the intra-family custody battle over Robert's kids, the star-crossed Kissels were big news.

Eileen Wolff met Carlos at the appointed time in downtown Springfield on Monday, April 3, early in the afternoon. She told Carlos there was a change of plans. He was to take Hayley's dog up to Vermont and stay there with Eileen's dog. She had to drive down to Connecticut right away.

Carlos wasn't sure he understood her correctly. He asked Mrs. Wolff why she had to drive down to Connecticut. "Carlos, Andrew is dead!"

Stunned, the 45-year-old broke down in tears. "What happened?" was all he could utter. Eileen Wolff told him that Andrew had committed suicide. Carlos couldn't believe it. He had just seen him the day before and, despite his predicament, Andrew was in fairly good spirits. It just couldn't be, he repeated over and over.

Carlos did as instructed and drove up to the house in Vermont with Molly the dog. Carlos didn't remember much of the two-hour drive; he was in shock.

Carlos had been told to stay in Vermont until he heard from Mrs. Wolff. For several of the longest hours of his life, he stayed at the Vermont house alone with the dogs. He finally got a call at 4 PM from Mrs. Wolff and was told he was to stay in Vermont and continue to take care of the dogs. Carlos objected. He wanted to be in Greenwich near the Kissel family; he might be needed. Andrew was like family to him; he had to be there, he pleaded. Mrs. Wolff relented. She told him to bring the dogs and pack her some clothes for an extended stay in Connecticut.

On the drive down to Connecticut, the Greenwich Police Department reached him on his cell phone and asked him to come in for an interview. Carlos agreed to come in the next morning after spending the night in Bridgeport. "That," Carlos said, "was my first mistake."

Carlos had never had problems with the police— anywhere. He was particularly careful, because he hadn't had a green card until just February. Even a minor traffic violation could spell deportation. Carlos called his brother George and asked the long-time resident of America what he should do. George advised him to "just go in and tell the police the truth," assuring his brother he had nothing to worry about, since he had done nothing wrong.

On Tuesday, in a hastily arranged press conference at police headquarters in downtown Greenwich, Police Chief James Walters stood at a podium. The media was there in force.

Walters announced that Andrew Kissel ". . . was the intended target of the assault. This wasn't the act of somebody out there finding random residences to break into."

Dispelling the rumor that Kissel had been shot, Walters announced that the victim had died from "multiple stab wounds."

Walters said there were no signs of forced entry, suggesting the victim may have known the assailant(s). To many present, the first words out of the police chief's mouth were an obvious attempt to calm the jittery nerves of the "back country" Greenwich residents. The one thing the chief wanted to make clear was that there was no homicidal maniac running around the wealthy town.

Walters said the victim had last been seen alive late on Sunday afternoon by an unnamed acquaintance. The police concluded that there was a seventeen-hour time window for when the murder had been committed. The Connecticut State Police had supplied three criminal forensic scientists who'd worked the crime scene, and the FBI had been notified, since the victim was under investigation by the Department of Justice.

Reporters asked the police chief if Kissel's estranged wife was a suspect. Walters answered by saying that Hayley Wolff Kissel "has been interviewed . . . has cooperated

with us . . . and we feel confident that if we need to speak
with her again that she'll be available."

On the day after Andrew's body had been found and removed, there still were media—some would say circling
like vultures—outside number 10 Dairy Road. Still cam-
eramen and four video camera crews with on-air talents
nervously eyeing about for someone to interview stood outside the yellow police crime-scene tape and took background shots for fill. One by one they all approached an
elderly gentleman who stood quietly watching the whole cir-
cus from across Dairy Road. He shook his head and said no
to all requests. Had the assembled media known they were
addressing William Kissel, father of the victim, they certainly would have been more aggressive in their entreaties.

    Mr. Kissel did make a statement to the press later, ad-
mitting that his son rarely contacted him, but they'd still
spoken to one another, adding: "Andrew was a very sweet
boy, and he was our first child, and we adored him. I have
pictures of him on the television set as a two-year old. I
was his father, what can I say but I loved him?"

    That same morning Carlos Trujillo showed up at the
police station and willingly answered—without a lawyer
present—all the questions about his movements over the
past week. The police seemed to be satisfied with his answers. That, Carlos thought, was the end of it. On Friday
morning the detective called and asked if he would come
in again for some more questioning. Carlos agreed to
come in, again without legal representation. The tone of
questioning by Detective Lieutenant Mark Marino and
Detective Sergeant Timothy Duff had changed. They went
over the same questions as the last time, but they seemed
to be more aggressive. When they were done, Lieutenant
Marino asked if Carlos would return soon to be fingerprinted, since there were a lot of prints found in the house
and they wanted to eliminate him as a suspect. Carlos said
he would.

◆ ◆ ◆

On April 4, Hayley Kissel and her lawyer had a "no comment" for the media. The New York *Daily News* reached the victim's father. Mr. Kissel expressed his frustration: "Job never lost faith in God, and I never had any faith," the bereaved 77-year-old grandfather said, "but what can you do? What can I do? Nothing."

As agreed, Carlos Trujillo showed up at the Greenwich Police Department in the center of town on Wednesday. After they fingerprinted him, they took a DNA swab. They surprised the nervous immigrant when they next ordered him to remove all his clothes. Photos were taken of his nude body. The detectives were looking for defensive wounds. Carlos winced each time the flash fired. Naked, he felt scared and vulnerable. They also sat him in a chair and hooked him up to a polygraph machine and administered the notoriously unreliable—and inadmissible in court—lie detector test. Then the accusations began.

Detectives Marino and Duff took turns saying they knew he'd gone down to Colombia to hire a hitman to kill Andrew Kissel at his behest. Carlos was dumbfounded. He denied it vehemently, but it didn't seem to convince the two detectives. They were particularly interested in Trujillo's nephew, who'd come to the States just in the past week. The two cops claimed that the $18,000 worth of checks for the watches Carlos had cashed was payment to him from Andrew to find and pay an assassin. Carlos told them no, he had given the cash to Andrew, saying it was crazy to suggest he was hiring a killer from Colombia. After spending all day at the police station, Carlos Trujillo was finally told he could go. He was not under arrest.

By now Carlos knew he needed a lawyer. The only lawyers he knew were the ones that Andrew retained. He called Philip Russell's law office in Greenwich. Carlos knew Russell, since he had made numerous shuttle runs to his office to drop off and pick up paperwork for his boss. Russell's office gave him three names. Stamford criminal attorney Lindy Urso was the only one who didn't demand a hefty up-front sum for a retainer.

On Friday, April 7, after a morning of steady rain, a handful of Kissel family and friends assembled graveside at the Riverside Cemetery in Saddle Brook, New Jersey. It was a familiar scene to many of them. It was just two and a half years before when they'd witnessed the interment of Andrew's brother Rob, who had joined his mother in the family plot.

Hayley and the couple's two children were not present. For fear of creating a scene with her estranged father-in-law, she had opted to stay away.

After consulting with William Kissel, Rabbi Joseph Herman decided on recalling Andrew's happy youth in his graveside homily. There was no mention of Andrew's fall from grace, the tragic murder of his brother or his own mysterious death.

Andrew Kissel was buried the day after he'd been scheduled to be heard by the Southern District of New York Federal Court for real estate fraud. His criminal defense attorney Philip Russell had been hopeful about the outcome. Andrew was prepared to plead guilty and agree to a forfeiture of all his remaining assets. The sentencing would probably have waited until the summer of 2006. From studying the known sentencing guidelines, Russell had determined that Andrew was looking at a total of 5 to 10 years in a minimum security federal penitentiary. With any luck, he would have been out of prison not long after his 50th birthday.

The Kissel family tragedy was best summed up by family friend Jill Endres, a 41-year-old California surgeon, who'd dated Robert Kissel for two years when they both attended the University of Rochester and had remained a friend of the Kissels ever since.

"This was a blessed, model family. They had everything," Endres said. "It was not supposed to turn out this way."

CHAPTER TWENTY

On Tuesday, April 18, the Greenwich PD obtained a search warrant for a storage room Carlos Trujillo had rented in Bridgeport three days before Andrew Kissel was killed. They were looking for the murder weapon, Andrew's personal property and his cell phone. It was clear that Trujillo was still their prime suspect.

In a statement to the press, attorney Lindy Urso said, "I don't believe there was anything of evidentiary value in there. If they [GPD] had asked, Carlos certainly would have let them in."

Trujillo said he had rented the storage bin so he could store some of the furniture that the Kissels had given him. GPD did remove some of the items, but Urso and his client were not informed what was taken. Urso also said he was alarmed at the GPD's latest move, since it indicated to him they were still focusing on his client and not pursuing leads on other suspects. Urso was not, as he said, "shying away from the press," claiming that the extensive publicity the murder of Andrew Kissel was getting helped assure that the GPD, under the glare of the media light, would do a thorough job. His client would have nothing to fear then, since the attention, said Urso, "can serve to counterbalance the danger of a quick and wrongful arrest."

According to Trujillo the police also searched his house and harassed his extended family. Soon thereafter, his nephew was deported by the Immigration and Naturalization Services (INS). Trujillo said the police, once they saw he had a 2004 minivan and a plasma TV—and because he was a Colombian—accused him of being a drug dealer. "They wouldn't believe me," said Trujillo, "that I paid for them from my salaries."

There is some evidence that would seem to exonerate Trujillo himself from having been at 10 Dairy Road when Andrew Kissel was murdered. Trujillo claims to have gone home to Queens after he saw Andrew early Sunday evening. His E-ZPass record substantiates that claim. E-ZPass is a computer-aided automatic toll collector popular in the tri-state region of New York, New Jersey and Connecticut. It would have recorded when his car, equipped with the transponder, passed through the toll gate on the Whitestone, Throgs Neck or Triborough Bridges—all span the Long Island Sound and connect New England to Queens. If the transponder is transferred to another vehicle, a security camera would catch the switch. Trujillo, of course, may have had someone else drive his car, but his alibi of being in Queens that night did check out.

The fact that he has yet to be arrested bodes well for Trujillo, especially since he'd most likely passed the polygraph he was administered. Although a polygraph test result is inadmissible in court, it is a huge tool in the police's arsenal. It narrows down the field of suspects whether they take the test or refuse to. Armed with the results, "sources close to the investigation" have been known to leak test failures or refusals to the media to increase pressure on a targeted suspect—playing "mind games" as one detective called it. As of this writing, such information has not surfaced.

Bill Kissel believes his son's right-hand man had nothing to do with the death. "Carlos was a close friend of Andrew's. Why would he do it?" Bill Kissel said. "What would be the motive? And why in such an angry and bloodthirsty way?"

◆ ◆ ◆

Presently Carlos Trujillo is still the Greenwich Police Department's primary suspect. According to Trujillo, he, his family and friends are still being harassed by the police. He told the author in November 2006 that he suspected his phone was being tapped and he was being watched by the police. Carlos Trujillo has never been charged or arrested for any involvement in the murder of Andrew Kissel or for any other crime. Today he makes a living as a limo driver. He still has faith in American justice and expects to be fully vindicated.

Alison Statler was questioned by the GPD in their investigation of the Kissel murder. The 48-year-old businesswoman allegedly was having an affair with Andrew and was discovered to be at his side during the infamous party weekend in Florida that Andrew was a part of back in May 2005. That information had been given to the GPD by Hayley Kissel, who had obtained it from a private investigator under her hire.

The attractive brunette had done some promotional and marketing work for Hanrock and Epona Stables, a horse boarding and riding facility that Andrew had a financial interest in. Her lawyer, Stephan Seeger, denied that Statler had been having an affair with Andrew, claiming she was simply a business associate, and for that reason, and that reason alone, she was naturally questioned by police. Seeger claims that his client has fully cooperated with the investigation.

Statler's ex-husband gave credence to the rumor of an affair between Alison and Andrew in the *New York Post* article in which he was quoted. Greenwich resident Craig Statler, 53, had divorced his wife and the mother of his three children five months after Alison began working for Kissel in August 2000. The retired stockbroker blamed the break-up of his marriage on Andrew Kissel.

• • •

Andrew Kissel's toxicology report, done from blood taken at the autopsy, has not been leaked. It is known, however, that the state medical examiner's office tested for Rohypnol—the date rape drug—the same drug that had rendered Rob Kissel unconscious prior to his being bludgeoned to death.

It is not known if lawyered-up Hayley Kissel has ever agreed to a polygraph test. On April 25, 2006, according to the GPD, she had gone from being a cooperative witness to becoming an "uncooperative" one. Chief Walters refused to say if she was a suspect or not, saying only that they wished she would be "more cooperative."

Her attorney Joseph Martini disputed the description of his client, saying that Mrs. Kissel had answered all the police questions and would continue to do so.

Eugene Riccio, a Greenwich attorney, was contacted by the *Greenwich Time* and asked for his assessment of this latest development. He said Hayley's alleged lack of cooperation might have been rooted in "personal factors besides avoiding incriminating statements or police scrutiny." He added:

"Police investigators and defense attorneys might be unable to agree on some requests for information. A parent such as Mrs. Kissel might balk at allowing police to interview her children. You could certainly see in a case like this someone may have reasons to not want to provide information that has absolutely nothing to do with incriminating themselves."

Riccio believed that Andrew Kissel was killed because he might divulge compromising information to federal authorities. Killing him eliminated a potential problem.

On April 19, another sensational news story broke about the continuing investigation into Andrew Kissel's murder. E-mails written by the victim's estranged wife appeared in the *Greenwich Time* and the New York newspapers. The

exchange was between Hayley and her sister-in-law and
long-time friend Jane Clayton. Hayley and Jane knew each
other from their teenage years as ski bums in Vermont. It
was Jane who'd introduced champion skier Hayley Wolff
to her brother Andrew.

On May 22, Hayley wrote:

God I hate your brother!!!!!!!!! Sorry, just had to vent.

On May 23, she wrote:

I am ok. He is just such an awful, awful pathetic person. I
just fucking hate him, his I am the king attitude, his value
system (or lack thereof), his anger, his meanness. I JUST
HATE HIM!!!!!!! HE WILL NEVER BE A GOOD,
RESPONSIBLE PERSON. . . . . HE IS HORRI-
BLE, JUST HORRIBLE AND I HATE HIS FUCKING
GUTS. Do you know last night in bed I could actually see
myself pummeling him to death and just enjoying the sen-
sation of each and every shot and then this morning as I
pulled out of the garage to go to spin class all I wanted to
do was crash into his two Ferraris. . . . . It is like
haha I am going to bump into that stupid thing you put in
the garage as a little fuck you. I [hate the] fucker.

Hayley's New York lawyer downplayed the e-mails, which
had somehow been obtained by the Associated Press (AP)
wire service. Her lawyer, Nathaniel Dershowitz, would not
comment on the details of them. Dershowitz did claim that
they did not show intent by a frustrated spouse to actually
kill her husband, but simply a frustrated woman who had
learned that her husband was involved in legal irregularities. Dershowitz said, "She had nothing to do with his
death. If she had any thought, you don't do an e-mail to
your sister-in-law. I don't think anyone views these e-mails
as anything but venting."

William Kissel was quoted as saying that Hayley's

e-mails "concerned him," and that, "People don't verbalize things like this. The e-mail speaks for itself."

What wasn't known by many was that Hayley had a pretty good reason for spouting off. The e-mails had been sent after she'd found out about Andrew's debauched weekend in Florida, when one of his girlfriends mistakenly intercepted Hayley's phone call.

On April 20, suspicious conversations between Hayley to Jane Clayton surfaced in a report in *New York* magazine. It seems that Mrs. Clayton had turned her notes of the conversations over to the reporter. The conversations spanned a year's period in 2004–2005.

On June 16, 2004, Hayley vented to Jane that while she "was busting her ass" raising five kids—her two and Robert's three—Andrew was carrying on with another woman, taking her to expensive restaurants and calling her all the time. Hayley also spoke of his mysterious business deals, which she thought may be a "Ponzi scheme," and that she did not want to be the one who will have to tell the kids "why dad is in jail."

On July 2, 2004, Jane noted that Hayley had decided to leave Andrew, having discovered that he was still having an affair. Hayley had said "it was the last straw" and that "he has embarrassed me enough."

New York magazine reported that when Hayley had asked her husband about his business deals, he'd warned her that "It's none of your fucking business." He went on to rant, "I don't tell you how to analyze stocks. Don't tell me how to run my business."

Jane also revealed a voice mail she had received from Andrew. He had been irate that she had spoken to a reporter about his legal troubles: "Jane, it's your ex-brother. You've managed to do what Dad has tried to do for seventy-five years: tear this family apart. You've done that. And we're going to bury you, Jane."

The Kissel patriarch did not escape Hayley's wrath. In a voice mail to her father-in-law, she said: "You're an evil man, and I would say that you'll get what you deserve. . . . Well, you already got what you deserve."

Both alpha personalities, William Kissel and Hayley had never liked each other. Reportedly the elder Kissel had once referred to the former champion skier as a "money-grubbing bitch." Mr. Kissel held Hayley at least partly to blame for Andrew's misdeeds when he was quoted as saying that his financially savvy daughter-in-law had to have known about then—"How could a wife not know?"

Hayley made a phone call to the 78-year-old Mr. Kissel on Saturday evening, April 1, 2006, the night before Andrew was killed. The story of the message content that went to voice mail was leaked to the *Hartford Courant* on May 22.

When Bill Kissel goes out, he is not accustomed to taking his cell phone with him, being of a generation who were not very dependent on that technology. The next day was Sunday and the only one who called him on the cell phone that day was his daughter, Jane, Mr. Kissel told the author. Hayley never called. Kissel did not access his cell phone until late Monday evening, after he had been told of Andrew's death by authorities.

"Hi, Bill. Hayley—Ah, I just wanted you to know," Hayley said, "that I moved out of the house last night, and Andrew stayed behind. Ah, I moved out of the house last night, and there is reason to be concerned he does something stupid with his life. Ah, I just thought I would let you know that. Goodbye."

Was Hayley truly concerned about her philandering, criminal husband, whom she was acrimoniously divorcing? Or was it a vindictive woman getting in one last lick at her despised father-in-law with a warning of what was to come?

Mr. Kissel retrieved the message after he learned of Andrew's death. Had he received it earlier, he would have immediately flown up from Florida to look in on his troubled son. Then he would have been the one, and not the movers, who would have discovered Andrew's tortured, bound and bloodied body.

Attorney for Hayley, Nathaniel Dershowitz, downplayed the importance of the taped message. He claimed his client had already informed the GPD about it, and that she was simply expressing her concern for his son. Bill Kissel's motive for making an issue of the phone message was questioned publicly by Dershowitz:

"For him to now try to use Hayley's trying to get support for his son against her is a sense of guilt that he must feel for not helping his own son in the first place. All Hayley was doing was letting them know the guy's alone, he is having trouble, help him—and no one from his family ever did."

When Hayley lost the custody battle for Robert's children and the income from the estate in December 2005, could she have taken a different tack in securing an income? Four months later her husband was dead and she was making a claim on his $10 million life insurance policy. Her good fortune, or a well-conceived plan? Only Hayley Wolff Kissel can say.

As early as Wednesday, April 5, rumors were swirling among the print and TV news corps that Andrew Kissel was suspected by police to have hired an assassin to kill him. According to the unsubstantiated report, an unidentified friend of Andrew had notified the police that the victim had said just weeks before the murder that he wanted to kill himself, "but couldn't bring himself to do it." The friend claimed that Kissel told him he had hired someone to do it.

Speculation had it that since he was looking at a long incarceration in a federal prison, leaving his wife and kids penniless, he had opted for an expedient way out. His life insurance policies would have to pay out $10 million in death benefits. The theory had credence (and was not denied by the GPD), because of Andrew's past shady business dealings, which were becoming well documented.

There were other demons that Andrew Kissel had been looking to escape from. According to federal court documents, Andrew had been grappling with numerous physical and mental disorders that included alcohol and drug abuse, bi-polar disorder, impulse-control disorder, post-traumatic stress from his brother's murder and an anti-social personality. Could Andrew have made a pact with an underworld hitman to end his wretchedness?

Lending more substance to the theory of "suicide by hitman" were statements by the GPD. Chief Walters said that Kissel had probably known the killer, since there were no signs of forced entry or burglary.

The killing had all the earmarks of a professional hit. Kissel's hands and feet had been bound by Flex-Cufs, plastic handcuffs used by police in mass arrests, and not available to the public.

William Kissel was quoted by a newspaper reporter about the "suicide by hitman" theory, which the father of the victim called "preposterous." He added, "If you were going to kill yourself, would you have somebody tie you up and stab you to death and pull your shirt over your head?"

Mr. Kissel also said that any insurance payoff would be "gobbled up" by debt and lawsuits, and Andrew would have known that.

Not necessarily so, says Howard Weitz, the lawyer who'd drawn up murdered sibling Robert Kissel's will. "If the policy is structured that a trust is the beneficiary," said Weitz, "that money may not be available to creditors."

Former homicide detective Vernon J. Geberth believes that the "suicide by hitman" is bunk. Geberth retired as the NYPD Commanding Officer of the Bronx Homicide Task Force, which handled over 400 murder investigations a year, and is author of what many consider to be the bible of homicide investigation, *Practical Homicide Investigation: Tactics, Procedures, and Forensic Techniques*. Geberth didn't buy into the theory in April 2006 and likes it even less now, saying "that there were too many better options."

"My gut feeling as a homicide cop," Geberth told the author, "is that I don't believe someone would hire someone to tie him up and stab him to death. It's a torturous way to die. It just doesn't make any sense. If you have to die for some reason, there are better methods. If it were me, I'd opt for a bullet to the back of the head. It would appear to be an execution. It's also quick and painless."

Andrew's lawyer Philip Russell also scoffed at the theory of suicide. Russell, who was in daily communication with his client, said that Andrew was reconciled to a jail term of at least 5 years. The Greenwich attorney said that Andrew ". . . had a lot to live for and, in the short term, he had problems, but he was not despairing."

The criminal defense attorney has his own theory. Admitting that he is just speculating, Russell thinks that Andrew may have been involved in some transaction—either borrowing or placing some money—with some "unsavory people" who believed they were best off by killing him. Rumor has it that the "unsavory people" may have come across the ocean looking for Andrew.

One of the many ventures Andrew dabbled in was the import business. He brought olive oil, vinaigrettes and jams into the United States from Sicily. Anybody who has ever seen the movie or read the book *The Godfather* knows what that can mean.

Vito Colucci Jr., a former Stamford, Connecticut, detective and investigator for the defense of Michael Skakel in the high-profile Martha Moxley murder case, concurred with Russell's motive assessment, but thought police should look closer to home.

"There are literally dozens of people screwed by him [Andrew Kissel]. There is a laundry list of people who didn't lose millions, but lost $10,000, $15,000, or $20,000."

Lindy Urso thought that a lot of things he was reading in the papers were "bullshit." A Greenwich resident himself, he knew that the fact that the house showed no signs of a break-in did not mean anything. Residents, especially in the wealthier north end of town, habitually left doors unlocked and alarm systems unarmed. The gate and wall around the Kissel house could be vaulted easily without getting attention in the private wooded neighborhood.

Urso believed the murder could easily have been a "crime of opportunity," a possibility that was never broached in the media or spoken about in GPD press releases. Urso said his client, Carlos Trujillo, told the police that Kissel had mentioned to him that he was using the services of call girls. Trujillo was sure that Andrew had done some entertaining of the fairer sex as late as his last Saturday night.

Assuming that was true, said Urso, "Those girls don't fend for themselves." They always work with protection, usually an intimidating thug who assures the girl's services get paid for.

Urso had also learned from his client that Hayley and her husband had had a fight on Saturday. Trujillo was told by Andrew that it was over the cash that had come from the sales of Andrew's watches, which Hayley had found in the house.

If indeed prostitutes had made service calls to 10 Dairy Road it would be logical, since they don't take checks or credit cards, that once done, Andrew would have retreated to a room where the cash was located, counted some out and paid the girl. It's no stretch of the imagination to consider that the hooker and her pimp might have thought there had to be a lot more where that came from. Also, Kissel's always-handy BlackBerry, police discovered, was missing. Could the device with all the information Kissel wanted at the touch of a key been taken to conceal his private contact list? Certainly it was a piece of evidence the murderer(s) would not want found.

Andrew Kissel, according to Trujillo, had been using cocaine fairly regularly. Carlos routinely found empty plastic zip bags under Andrew's bed when he cleaned his boss's room. If Trujillo was being truthful about his employer's use of the illegal drug, that meant that someone, perhaps a dealer, was bringing it to Kissel while he was under house arrest. Once again, crime of opportunity was a distinct possibility.

Another possible motive was that someone wanted to silence Andrew Kissel before he appeared in front of the federal bench and pleaded out. Lawyer Lindy Urso didn't believe that someone who'd been defrauded out of some money by Andrew would risk life in prison just for vengeance's sake, but "for someone facing future jeopardy, to save their ass—absolutely!"

It was a well-publicized fact that Andrew would be standing in front of a judge in the federal courthouse in White Plains, New York, to plead out on the federal charges on Thursday, April 6. It was conceivable, some in the media mused, that Andrew might have been planning to trade information on others for a lighter sentence. The fact is, Russell told the author, Kissel hadn't been planning to cut a deal. All of the legal work he'd done for Andrew Kissel was aimed at minimizing the gravity of his misdeeds by trying to make financial amends to the people and companies— over fifty—he'd victimized. Andrew Kissel was planning on entering a plea of guilty when he was to stand in front of the bench on April 6. He had no other option.

"He wasn't going to burn anybody. It wasn't that kind of a case. He was a lone shooter, with no second shooter."

Could one or more of the pimps or drug dealers returned to the house Sunday night? It would explain why the murderer(s) had been let into the home by the victim. Andrew Kissel could have been overpowered and bound to the chair in the basement and tortured until he revealed where the money stash was. Once they had the money in hand, Andrew had been killed. The GPD has never revealed if any cash was found—or was missing from—the house at 10 Dairy Road.

Dr. Lawrence Kobilinsky, PhD, a professor of Forensic

Science at John Jay College of Criminal Justice in New York City, was intrigued with the information about Kissel's drug and prostitute use prior to his murder. The often-quoted expert had not put much credence in the speculation about a "suicide-for-hire" plot that was being splashed across the tabloids after the victim's body had been found.

If a person had paid a hit man to kill him, common sense and case studies would tell us that the intended would be dispatched quickly and painlessly to the hereafter. Andrew Kissel did not go that way.

Kobilinsky does not think the murder looked like a random crime, but it does appear to be a targeted crime: "They were after him."

The use of "they" was no slip of the tongue by the professor. Because Kissel was bound, Kobilinsky believes there must have been two murderers: one to restrain and tie him up and the other to wield the threatening weapon.

Before learning of the cocaine and prostitute use, he believed Kissel's murder was "assigned to professionals" where information could be elicited by torture, hence the non-lethal stab wounds.

"Superficial stabbing," says Kobilinsky, "is a very effective way to get information from a victim. It's extremely painful and bloody."

On May 10, 2006, there appeared to be a break in the case when a murder victim was found in the bedroom of a house not far from Hayley and Andrew's Stratton, Vermont, home. The victim, 27-year-old Renato Wieser, was sprawled across a bed, bound and stabbed multiple times. The Andrew Kissel connection fell apart two weeks later when two known associates of the victim, Joshua Gould, 26, of Rutland, Vermont, and Christopher Kosmalski, 27, of East Dorset, Vermont, were captured by the Vermont State Police and charged with the murder. Their case is pending.

At the same time GPD was looking into the possible Vermont connection, the case got a high-profile personality to help with the investigation. Henry Lee, the former state public safety commissioner, was asked by the state crime lab technicians for his help in the blood spatter analysis. Lee is a world-renowned criminal forensic scientist who has testified as an expert witness in numerous high-profile cases, including the O. J. Simpson trial. Although GPD Chief Walters admitted he had no knowledge of Lee's involvement, he did say that his department sent all blood found at crime scenes to the state labs for typing and DNA analysis. As of this writing, Lee's analysis of the blood spatter pattern from the Dairy Street crime scene has not been divulged.

As far as Philip Russell is concerned, all the theories on Andrew Kissel's murder are plausible, but as he told the author, "There is not enough proof for the theories that are being bandied about so that they could be called a real living, breathing possibility. Insurance-motivated suicide by murder, and all the rest of them are just pure speculation. It's a murder mystery that I don't think will ever be solved."

CHAPTER
TWENTY-ONE

The Andrew Kissel case is presently in the hands of the Greenwich Police Department, a fact that doesn't bode well for a timely resolution of this murder mystery. At the time of this writing, six months later, no one has yet been arrested for any crime connected to the death of Andrew Kissel.

Unfortunately the GPD has a history of homicide investigations that eventually end up in the cold case file. There are two glaring examples. The first one is the infamous Martha Moxley case.

Moxley was a popular and attractive 15-year-old who lived in Belle Haven, one of the more exclusive neighborhoods in the wealthy town of Greenwich. On the night before Halloween, 1975, she was bludgeoned to death with a golf club on the grounds of her stately home. Despite intense scrutiny from the media, pressure from the community, help from the state police, a wealth of leads and a likely suspect, the GPD never got an indictment or made an arrest of a suspect.

The homicide detectives assigned to the case had never investigated a murder before, the last one in Greenwich having occurred in 1949. To the GPD's credit they did enlist the help of the Detroit Police Department, who at the time had the biggest case load of homicides in the country. Why they didn't ask the NYPD—only 30 miles away—for help is open to speculation. Some said the GPD didn't want to go asking a neighboring police department with such a high profile. The two departments did compete for personnel and were often publicly critical of each other.

Former cop turned crime writer Mark Fuhrman took an interest in the Moxley case, and his book *Murder in Greenwich* came out in 1998.

Fuhrman named Michael Skakel, a once-troubled youth and a neighbor of the Moxley girl, as the prime suspect. Skakel, the nephew of Ethel Kennedy, wife of Bobby Kennedy, was now in his late 40s. For parochial reasons the GPD had never pressed their case against him.

With the uproar the book caused nationally and the bad press that judicial authorities in the state of Connecticut were getting, the state police officially took over the case and re-investigated it. Its findings were presented to a special grand jury of one, and Skakel was later indicted, tried and found guilty of the murder on June 7, 2002. He was sentenced to 20 years to life in prison. In November 2006 the U.S. Supreme Court refused to hear his appeal.

The GPD was vilified in the media for their lack of success in the Moxley case, and was often lumped with the Boulder, Colorado, police, with their role in the JonBenet Ramsey case, as departments full of incompetents. Whether deserved or not, the lampooning continues in light of the Andrew Kissel murder.

Another Greenwich homicide was quietly relegated to the cold case files much to the dismay of the victim's relatives. The victim's name was Matthew Margolies.

Arising the morning of August 31, 1984, the soon-to-be 8th grader at Western Junior High grabbed one of his favorite fishing rods and set out as he had so many times before to idle away the waning days of summer casting for trout in the Byram River.

At around 5 PM, Matthew's mother Maryann drove over

to her mother's house to pick up her son to bring him home for dinner. Matthew was not there, and that worried her. At around 7 PM, with no word or sign of Matthew, Maryann knew that something was drastically wrong. She called the police.

A Greenwich youth division officer, along with a few neighbors, fanned out across the area of Byram River. Concerned phone calls were made to the homes of Matthew's friends inquiring if they knew his whereabouts. No one had seen or heard from the boy.

On Saturday the search intensified. More police were assigned to the dragnet and the volunteer firemen pitched in. The boy's father, who was now living in the Dallas area, was called. He had not been contacted by his son. On Sunday the FBI was notified.

On Sunday, September 2, Maryann and her boyfriend Jim decided to look in the area around Hawthorne Street. She remembered that just days before, her son had asked her about what was up there. His interest in the area had mystified her. She asked him why he wanted to know about the terrain that rose sharply to a secluded neighborhood of Glenville. He had replied that he was just curious. She asked him if anyone had approached him about going up there. Matthew said no. If he wanted to see it, Maryann had told him, she would happily take him. Otherwise, he was not to go there. He'd shrugged it off and the subject was dropped.

Near the dead end of Hawthorne Street in a rock-strewn dump area, Maryann and Jim detected a foul, overpowering odor. They did not investigate any further. She notified the police of the suspicious smell. The police did not search the area for two more days.

Fred Lambert had just returned from a trip to Virginia when he heard of the search for the lost boy. A life-long resident of Greenwich and a volunteer fire policeman who had experience in searches, he took it upon himself to look in the area across the street from where he worked. Lambert walked through the deserted dump area, then followed the densely forested path. Almost immediately he saw a single sneaker, a black-and-white–checkered one. He knew from reports that the missing boy had been described as wearing just such footwear when he was last seen. Lambert immediately marked the spot and dashed off to call the police.

At 4 PM, September 5, five days after the initial report, two youth division officers appeared on the scene and Lambert took them up to the area where he had discovered the sneaker. The two officers commenced searching. Lambert remembers leaning against a tree when he spotted a small foot poking up through the leaves. His heart sank and a wave of nausea swept over him. He managed to call out in a shaken voice to the two officers, "Guys, he's over here."

Matthew Margolies had been dead for some time. There were multiple stab wounds on his torso. An autopsy determined that Matthew had died of the stab wounds and traumatic asphyxiation. There were no signs that the boy had been sexually molested. Several days later, a ten-inch kitchen boning knife was found near the area where the body had been discovered. Other than declaring it the weapon used to inflict Margolies' wounds, the Greenwich police claimed to know nothing more about it, having spent hundreds of hours trying to track it down. Matthew's fishing rod was nowhere to be found.

It had been nine years since they'd investigated the last homicide—the notorious Martha Moxley murder. The results would be the same. No arrests, no indictments, no convictions.

As in the Moxley case, there were some crucial mistakes made by the GPD. In 1986, Police Chief Thomas Keegan, over the protests of his detective division, commissioned outside consultant Vernon J. Geberth, a former lieutenant commander in the New York City Police Department, to evaluate how the GPD had handled the investigation. The report was kept secret until a Freedom of Information suit brought by the *Greenwich Time* forced the town to release it in 1992. There were significant sections that had been blacked out on the order of Superior Court

Judge Harold Dean, who allowed the police to withhold that information, since the GPD claimed making it public would "harm the Margolies investigation."

It was revealed, however, that there was a "clear lack of effective coordination in the early stages of the investigation." No detective had been assigned to check into the missing persons report. If not for that oversight, the department might have had a chance of cracking the case early. Geberth added that by the time the body was found, "the investigative arm of the Greenwich Police Department had, in effect, lost six days of crucial informational interviews and neighborhood canvasses, which would later prove to be significant to the homicide investigation."

This fact is even harder to reconcile after then Police Chief Peter Robbins admitted in a 1999 interview that the GPD had suspected "foul play" twenty-four to forty-eight hours after the initial missing persons report. Still, no detective was assigned to the case early on. It has also been learned that after the body was found, only one detective assigned to the case actually viewed the crime scene.

Geberth also criticized then Captain William Andersen, head of the investigation, for not delegating more authority to subordinates. The department was praised, nonetheless, for conducting a "diligent, professional investigation." But recently discovered facts concerning the case would seem to challenge that ultimate pat on the back for a job well done.

Twenty-two years later the Matthew Margolies case is still unsolved, and many unanswered questions remain. Many familiar with the GPD, or those who have been peripherally touched by their investigations, are not too surprised.

Maryann Margolies has been continually stonewalled by the police. She never hears from the GPD, and her phone calls to the detectives assigned her son's cold case are rarely returned. The Connecticut State Police announced to the shocked Margolies family in October 2006 that they would not take the investigation.

Kissel family members report the same intransigence from the GPD in regard to Andrew's murder. One relative reported that a detective hung up the phone on them when they had called with a potentially valuable piece of information.

The Greenwich Police Department has had its share of problems; a lot of them were internal. One disturbing revelation about how fractious things were in the department surfaced on December 23, 1998, when the present police chief James Walters was Captain of Criminal Investigations.

According to the complaint lodged by Walters with GPD's Internal Affairs, Walters had been sexually harassed and threatened by a fellow officer, Capt. Frank Branca. In his one-page complaint, Walters had accused Branca of creating "a hostile and offensive work environment which has deprived me of my right to work in a safe and professional environment free of such intimidation."

Then Chief Peter Robbins suspended Branca with pay pending a complete investigation of the charges. Branca had to surrender his gun, badge and his town-owned car. The 28-year veteran of the force did not comment on the charges but denied any wrongdoing. The local police union, the Silver Shield Association, came to Branca's defense, claiming the GPD was violating Branca's freedom of speech.

In May of 1999, the GPD dropped all charges when Branca (and another captain charged on an unrelated offense) agreed to take retirement after a 5% pay raise. In the agreement both men were to receive 75 percent of their final base pay ($81,984) for their yearly pension. The terms were generous and hard for the two accused police captains to refuse in light of the charges they were facing, which could have resulted in their firing and subsequent loss of their pensions. Their departures, claimed First Selectman (the town's version of a mayor), Tom Ragland would allow the GPD "to fully implement a planned reorganization." The underlying implication was that the town was purging its police department of dead wood and dinosaurs with large salaries. The "dinosaurs" that had handled the department's most notorious failures, the Moxley and Margolies homicide investigations, were all finally gone, and when Peter Robbins retired in 2002, James Walters, strangely the anointed, ascended to the post with high expectations. The Andrew Kissel murder investigation, one would expect, would yield different results than the department's past failures. On the one-year anniversary of Andrew's death, the GPD would be no closer to solving it then they were on day one.

On April 26, 2006, Chief Walters announced his retirement after twenty-six years as a Greenwich cop and just four as chief. In his announcement, he said he was leaving public service for a job in private security. He said his only regret was not being able to crack the now twenty-three-year-old Matthew Margolies kidnap/murder case. He made no mention of the Andrew Kissel homicide.

GPD Police Chief James Walters has refused to discuss the Andrew Kissel case with the media, considering it is still open. That, of course, is standard procedure for any police department involved in an ongoing criminal investigation. The lack, however, of systematic leaks from the GPD and scuttlebutt among the local legal community as to the progress of the investigation is unusual. What that usually means is that there *is* no progress. Time is not a friend of a homicide detective, even a very good one.

CHAPTER
TWENTY-TWO

With Andrew Kissel dead and buried, divorce proceedings brought by Hayley continued without him on May 26. Hayley was able to get $7.1 million as a "prejudgment remedy" in 2005, but that was before Andrew's real estate empire had collapsed under the weight of a criminal probe of his sleazy business practices. That, of course, threw the settlement into doubt.

There was a light moment at the beginning of the proceedings when Judge Kevin Tierney noted there was no death certificate for Andrew Kissel in the case file, prompting him to ask Andrew Kissel's attorney Howard Graber if he was in fact dead. Graber confirmed that he was.

Graber then expressed his frustration and dismay when he said, "I'm at loss to understand how I can continue to represent a deceased client in a divorce matter."

"The mere fact that there is a death of a party," Judge Tierney fired back, "does not necessarily mean the marriage has been dissolved."

Tierney went on to order that the $7.1 million still stood "for the time being."

Hayley's lawyers had filed a fraud amendment to her divorce suit citing Andrew's mortgaging her house in

Vermont—which Andrew had signed over to her for protection against creditors—without her knowledge. Her claim, however, had been improperly filed by her lawyers.

Judge Tierney encouraged Hayley to re-file, but this time in civil court where undoubtedly she would "have to take a number" behind other litigants looking to recoup investments in Hanrock Group LLC.

Erich Gaston, Hayley's lawyer, said he would do as advised and then requested that they drop the divorce suit, but keep the present docket number for the civil action with the $7.1 million prejudgment attached.

The court agreed to consider the request. If denied, Hayley would have to stand in line with everyone else and wait for her money.

Stripped of an income from her late brother-in-law's estate for the custody of Robert's children, who were taken away from her, with her husband murdered and creditors coming out of the woodwork, Hayley Kissel suffered the ultimate indignity: she was fired from her job. The large stock brokerage firm in New York where she was a stock analyst decided the baggage she came with was not offset by her prodigious financial analytical skills. On October 19, 2006, the widow stood in front of the probate court judge in Greenwich to ask for a $9,000-a-month survivors' benefit.

Hayley acknowledged that she was receiving $3,640 a month, which represented a stipend from Social Security and unemployment benefits, but the sum couldn't even cover the tuition for her two daughters at a private school in town. Presently she was relying on her father to see her through these difficult financial times. Defending the choice of sending her two girls to an expensive private school when the Greenwich public school system was considered to be one of the very best in the nation, she said tearfully, "They've been through so much with their cousins moving in and out. They are in a really stable environment in school and I don't want to take them out of that environment."

Among the debts she was obligated to pay were $8,000 a month for legal bills, $6,000 a month to her father, who had loaned her the $1.7 million to buy her Greenwich home and $1,366 a month for car expenses. The money would come from the sale of some Greenwich property that was owned by the Wolff family. The sale of the property generated $235,000. Two title companies swindled by her murdered husband contested her claim, having already slapped liens on the property.

The legal battle over expensive pieces of Connecticut and Vermont properties had begun.

"Suffice it to say," said estate attorney Patrick Gil, "that everyone is trying to lay claim to every asset or piece of property that I find."

It was to be one of Andrew Kissel's unfortunate legacies.